A Mill on the Point:

One Hundred and Twenty-Five Years of Steelmaking at Sparrows Point, Maryland

"When all is said and done
and we sit down to count
our blessings, all you may
have is a handful of memories
and a pocketful of dreams."
Elmer Hall

To George Beard

Elmer Hall
2014

1

Table of Contents

Table of Contents

Table of Contents

In Memory of Charles "C.H." Echols

I first met C.H. Echols while researching my first book at the Dundalk Patpsco Neck Historical Society. Our friendship was instant and he took me under his wing and became a long-time mentor. I spent countless hours in C.H.'s basement darkroom while he developed photographs for me. He reproduced nearly all of the photographs in my first three books. An article entitled, "Tin Mill Memories" written by C.H. is included in this publication. C.H.'s passion for local history was unparalleled and his contributions to its preservation were priceless. C.H. passed on July 12, 2013 at the age of 96. I will deeply miss this wonderful man and the time we spent together.
~Elmer J. Hall

PURPOSE

This publication is not intended to be a manual on how to make steel, although some aspects of the steelmaking process are included. Nor does it cover every facet of the physical plant at Sparrows Point. Its purpose is twofold. One is to preserve the memory of what was, at one time, the largest tidewater steel mill in the world. The second purpose is to pay tribute to the tens of thousands of men and women who plied their trade in the mill over a period of 125 years. Nothing more, nothing less.

Acknowledgements

Without the help, assistance and cooperation of several organizations and the personal interest and contributions of many individuals, this project could not have been completed. Their guidance, support, and encouragement were a constant source of inspiration that has been greatly appreciated.

The following organizations were invaluable resources. As with my other three publications, I began my research at the Dundalk Patapsco-Neck Historical Society and the material that I found there laid the foundation for all that followed. I would also like to thank the following historical institutions for assisting me in researching their archives: the Sparrows Point High School Alumni Heritage Center, the Enoch Pratt Free Library, the Baltimore Museum of Industry, the Hagley Museum in Delaware, and the University of Maryland Hornbake Library.

One group that deserves special recognition for their contributions to this publication are the retired steelworkers who met at the Union Hall on Dundalk Avenue on the third Wednesday of each month. These men and women were extremely proud of their steelmaking history and heritage. Many of the photographs and stories contained in this publication came from them. I am grateful for their enthusiasm and contributions.

Putting a project like this together starts with an idea. As you gather pieces of information – a story here, a photograph there – you sometimes wonder whether you will be able to gather enough material to tell the whole story. That's where luck comes in. Out of the blue, you find a wealth of information, data or photographs from a single individual. I call these people "gold mines" because of the wealth of information that they provided. I was fortunate enough during my research to find several of these gold mines. I am especially grateful to the following: Pete Wolfkill, for providing me with decades of volumes of the Sparrows Point *Spirit*, and the *Bethlehem Review*. They were an invaluable resource. Hillard "Digger" O'Day, Jr., for providing numerous photographs, books, and articles related to the mill at Sparrows Point. Mike "Hydraulic Man" Stilwell, for providing me with so much information and photographs that it would require several pages to document. Rich (1117 "H" Street) Glenn, who sent me a book entitled *From Ore to Ships*. This book, along with photographs, provided the proverbial "missing links" of the 1930s and 1940s in the evolution of the history of Bethlehem Steel's Sparrows Point plant. John Lovis, author of *The Blast Furnaces of Sparrows Point*, who provided much appreciated knowledge of the technical aspects as well as the historical records of blast furnaces at the Point. Al Hastings, who provided photographs, diagrams, and a wealth of personal knowledge related to refractories. Last but not least, I would like to extend my sincere appreciation to Bill Goodman for all of his contributions to this publication. Not only did Bill provide many of the color photographs contained in this publication, he was also the photographer. Nearly all of the black and white photographs in the book were reproduced by Bill, many from his own extensive collection. I am so thankful that our paths crossed when they did because I could not have done this without him.

A tremendous debt of gratitude is also extended to the following individuals: my daughter, Andrea Jamison, for typing every word of this publication, cover to cover; my wife, Clara, for once again (the fourth and final time) allowing the clutter of photographs, newspaper articles, books, and boxes of stuff to accumulate; Andrew and Matthew Jamison, for allowing Poppy to work on his book; Joe and Sue Pollio, for having the unenviable task of proofreading the manuscript from cover to cover.

I would also like to extend my sincere appreciation and gratitude to the following individuals for their contributions. In alphabetical order: Craig Adams, Bill "Junior" Ambrosewicz, Bill Barry, John Belas, Norma Belas, Frank Cantalupo, Shirley Cantalupo, Sue Clarke, Dick Delahay, Lettie DeWit, Tom Donet, Phyllis Dryden, C.H. Echols, Gladys Echols, Bob Falk, Betzy Falk, Elnora Fenlock, Larry Fenlock, Milton Fenlock, Ken Fowler, Jean Frazer, Teri Furst, John Glabb, Lisa Greenhouse, John Henry Hahn, Lloyd Hauser, George Hellems, Mike Homa, Toms Jacob, Gary "Hon Bun" James, Butch Johnson, Don Kellner, Dale Kelly, James Kidd, Amber Kohl, Ray Kollner, Bill "Coke" Kotroco, Ed Kraemer, Rick Krause, Sue Krause, Clarence "Chuck" Kuser, Jerry Lauterbach, Carol Fondella Ledley, Celia Lesser, Debbie Guice Lutz, Denis Marron, John Mason, Don Mason, Jack McCardell, Doug McElrath, Jim Narutowicz, Jr., Steve Painter, Joe Papa, Al Paul, Dave Paul, Sr., Ben Pritchett, Mike Punko, Les Rabuck, Joe Rogers, Regina Ewing Rosenberger, Deborah Rudacille, Tony Saladino, Catherine Scott, Roy Shepherd, Doug Skeen, Pete Sorrentino, Don Spittle, Ruth Stilwell, Charlie Swaytek, Bob Swinski, Lil Tirschman, Bill Trentzch, Mary Ellen Underwood, Henry Harvey Underwood, Jim Vadas, Jean Walker, Don Walters, Ernie Walters, Huyette Walton, Reba Walton, Don Waters, Bill Wilhelm, Ralph Wilson, Marian Wilson, Jack Yard, Dan Yeager, Bill Zablocki.

Sparrows Point Timeline

1652   Thomas Sparrow purchased 600 acres on the east side of the Patapsco River and named it Sparrows Rest. The peninsula of land was owned by the Sparrow family for the next 160 years, eventually becoming known as Sparrows Point.

1886   Craighill Channel Upper Range Rear Light built at Sparrows Point.

1887   Pennsylvania Steel Company acquired several farms at Sparrows Point for the purpose of building a steel mill. Construction of "A" and "B" Blast Furnaces was started. Construction of a company town at Sparrows Point started.

1888   Construction began on a Blooming Mill.

1889   February 11th – Service began on the Baltimore & Sparrows Point Railroad. October 23rd – first pig iron cast. October 31st - "A" Furnace blown in.

1890   March 11th – "B" Furnace blown in.

1891   June 27th – The Maryland Steel Company of Baltimore County was formed as a subsidiary of the Pennsylvania Steel Company. August 1st – Two 18-ton Bessemers started up; the first heat was tapped. On August 7th the rail mill was completed and first rail rolled. October 3rd – "C" Furnace blown in. Shipyard started. First ingots rolled on the 36-inch Bloomer.

1892   Shipyard launched its first vessel. January 23rd - the tug boat Pennwood (Hull #3) was delivered. The first kindergarten south of the Mason Dixon line was established at 5th and E Streets in Sparrows Point.

1893   April 15th – "D" Furnace blown in. The steel mill produced 167,495 tons of Bessemer steel, rolled 120,000 tons of rail, and 20,000 tons of billets.

1894-1897   The Maryland Steel Company went into receivership due to a nationwide business depression. The plant closed its doors until the recession ended in 1897.

1896   November – "A" Furnace restarted.

1902   A third 18-ton Bessemer converter was installed.

1903   March 24th – Coke ovens with four batteries of 50 ovens each came on line. Streetcar service from Baltimore City to Sparrows Point commenced.

1904   After resigning from US Steel in 1903, Charles Schwab acquired the Bethlehem Steel Company from the United States Shipbuilding Company, which had run into serious financial difficulty. On December 10th, the Bethlehem Steel Corporation (Bethlehem, PA) was formed.

1906   Bay Shore Amusement Park opened for business.

1907   Blast furnaces produced a record 410,000 tons.

1909   Five 50-ton tilting Open Hearth furnaces erected.

1910   No. 1 Open Hearth built with 12 furnaces. (Operated until 1966 when the BOF was built in its place.) Five open hearths were installed, 50 tons each.

1911-1915   "A", "B", "C", and "D" furnaces rebuilt with skips. "A" – 1911; "B" – 1913; "C" – 1914; "D" – 1915. New Ore Dock with unloaders for ships was installed. Bethlehem Steel initiated its First Aid Training sessions.

1913   Sinter plant built for processing flue dust. Two new Koppers 60-oven coke batteries authorized.

1914   July 28th – World War I began. First coke produced.

1916 February 16th – the Bethlehem Steel Corporation acquired the Maryland Steel Company. Dundalk boasted 62 homes, one church, and two stores. The same year, Bethlehem Steel bought the Sparrows Point plant from the Maryland Steel Company. As a result, Dundalk became one of the country's first planned communities. The steel giant created the Dundalk Company, which purchased 1,000 acres of land near McShane's railroad stop. The company hired E.H. Bouton, designer of Roland Park, to create a working man's Roland Park. The community was designed to be close enough to the Point to commute to work, but far enough away for workers to escape the noise of the mills. With the United States entry into World War I in April 1917, there was an immediate housing need for Bethlehem Steel defense workers and shipbuilders. The government took over the Dundalk Company project and sold houses to workers for as much as 50% below construction costs. One report said the houses, 531 in Dundalk and 284 in St. Helena, were raised as quickly as one every three hours. Bethlehem Steel offered assistance to its employees by offering the cash needed for down payments on the stucco homes. April 1st – Bethlehem Steel Corporation acquired the Baltimore Sheet and Tin Plate Company and transferred the entire facility to Sparrows Point. Fourth Bessemer 18-ton converter installed.

1917 The Sparrows Point landscape is transformed by the new owners. Steel pilings were placed 2,367 feet from the south shore and filled in with slag, stone, earth, and gravel. The net result was 100 additional acres of land. Also, a 30-foot deep channel was dug to the high pier and a turn-around basin was created for ore steamers. July – Black Plate production began. July 26th – first hot dip tin mills began operation. An additional set of 12 hot dip mills was added in 1920 and a third set of 12 came on in 1925 for a total of 36. Two years later in 1927, the addition of 12 more mills brought the total to 48 and a capacity of 210,000 tons annually. September 10th – 110 inch plate mill started up. Also in 1917, a Coal Handling plant was under construction. No. 5 and No. 6 blast furnaces under construction. (No. 5 and No. 6 also known as "E" & "F".)

1918 Patapsco and Back Rivers Railroad (PBR) founded. Frederick Wood resigns.

1919 Sewage disposal plant built behind the Bungalows. Water treatment plant built for town water. Six stand 24-inch inline continuous billet mill online. Six stand 18-inch inline continuous billet mill online. May 21st – 40-inch blooming mill started up. No. 2 Open Hearth built with three furnaces (BOF later occupied this site). A nine-hole golf course was planned on Sparrows Point property which was the former home of Dr. John Trotten. The Trotten family cemetery is located just west of the intersection of 9th and "H" Street.

1920 March – the fourth furnace was added to No. 2 Open Hearth. E & F blast furnaces blown in. The Ore Dock was increased to 1200 feet, dredged to 35 feet deep, for 20,000 DWT ships. April – the 60-inch Universal Plate Mill started up. Sheet and jobbing mills with 8 hot mills, pickling, cold rolling, annealing, and galvanizing facilities start up.

1921 Toll bridge across Bear Creek completed.

1922 The Bungalows housing project completed. A rebuild of all five furnaces of the No. 1 Open Hearth authorized.

1923 February 4th – the first heat was poured on the fifth furnace for the No. 2 Open Hearth.

1925 Construction started on a new Rod and Wire Mill. May 16th – Sparrows Point Golf Course opened. It was located across the street from the 68-inch Hot Strip Mill.

1926 Tin plate production rose to four million boxes per year and accounted for $20 million in annual sales. No. 1 Rod Mill under construction. This was to be the first of three rod mills. The 40-inch Blooming Mill was installed. The 44-inch Blooming Mill was authorized. The 46-inch electrically driven Blooming Mill received its first ingot on June 12th. The town of Sparrows Point had grown to 1,200 homes and 8,000 residents.

1928 Coke Plant under construction. Major rebuilds of blast furnaces: "A" (1928), "B" (1929), "C" (1930).

1929 U.S. stock market crashes and the Great Depression begins. Work begins on the construction of No. 3 Open Hearth on the site of the West End housing development. Operation was delayed on No. 3 Open Hearth due to the Depression.

1931 Bethlehem Steel Corporation dismantled the Flange Mill and the 152-inch Plate Mill at the Coatesville facility and transferred them to Sparrows Point. The 152-inch mill was enlarged and became the three high 160-inch Plate Mill.

1932 3,500 employed at Sparrows Point, down from a one-time high of 18,000 due to the economic depression.

1936 John L. Lewis establishes the Steel Workers Organizing Committee (SWOC). The first of two 42-inch Tandem Mills and the No. 2 Rod Mill were built. The Hot Dip Tin Mills were dismantled. 40-inch Slabbing Mill installed. The 40-inch by 80-inch Blooming Mill was constructed.

1937   Major rebuild of "D" furnace. The second 42-inch Tandem reduction mill built. The 56-inch continuous Hot Strip Mill was constructed to replace all of the other 66 Hot Dipped Mills combined. No. 2 Rod Mill comes online. No. 3 Open Hearth started up (it was shut down in 1971).

1939   October 18th - Chairman of the Board Charles Schwab dies.

1940   The Pipe Mill was modernized with the installation of two continuous butt weld Pipe Mills. Nos. 79-81 furnaces were added to No. 3 Open Hearth.

1941   North Point Boulevard completed. Bethlehem Steel Company continued to be the only principle holdout in the steel industry to resist union representation. Main Office on North Point Boulevard completed. September 25th – Steelworkers vote in SWOC. September 30th – Sparrows Point shipyard workers join the Industrial Union of Marine and Shipbuilding Workers. December 7th – Japanese bomb Pearl Harbor which rapidly ended the Great Depression. "G" furnace blown in.

1942   Nos. 77 and 78 furnaces added to the No. 3 Open Hearth. The last of the Hand Dipped Tin Mills disappeared. Coke oven battery No. 7 comes online (it was shut down in March 1977). The first of three Alkaline lines were installed.

1943   February 5th – the first electrolytic tinning and fusion lines installed. Two additional lines were installed in April and October.

1945   The fourth slab heating furnace was installed on the 56-inch Hot Strip Mill. May 25th – Sparrows Point received the fourth Army Navy E Award for its outstanding wartime production.

1946   The 56-inch cold sheet mill anneal under construction.

1947   January – the 56-inch cold sheet Tandem Mill started up (Originally built as a four stand mill. A fifth stand was added in 1951.) December - The 68-inch Hot Strip Mill started up. Bay Shore Amusement Park closed. The property was purchased by the Bethlehem Steel Company.

1948   "H" furnace blown in. October – "H" furnace would set a world record of 51,231 tons in one month. The oxygen plant was completed. The Pennwood Power Plant begins operation. Nos. 7 and 8 coke batteries were added, each with 62 ovens (it was shut down in March 1977).

1950   Sparrows Point was still using open top ladle cars. They had 52 of them in operation. At this time, they were converting to hot metal sub cars. At the time, they had six of them. 4,700 employees were hired at Sparrows Point, raising the level to 24,000.

1951   The 66-inch four stand Tandem Mill came online. Continuous galvanizing lines under construction. August – "H" furnace breaks old record with 55,835 tons. The annual payroll at Sparrows Point is $90 million dollars. Fourteen direct fired annealing furnaces were added. Annual steel making capacity is over 5 million tons. Approximately 11,200 tons of coal are used daily. 550 million gallons of water are used daily. No. 2 slitter came online. No. 1 galvanizing line came online (No 2. galvanizing line – 1955; No. 3 galvanizing line – 1956).

1952   Basic Oxygen Furnace invented in Austria. Facilities put into operation at Sparrows Point during 1952 included a sintering plant, a continuous galvanizing unit for sheet and strip, equipment for the distribution of coke oven gas and for conditioning it for use as Open Hearth fuel, a battery of coke ovens and auxiliaries. Bethlehem Steel Company erects the Chesapeake Bay Bridge. PBR begins plans for the East Belt line, which would run through the Sparrows Point Golf Course site. "H" Furnace sets new world production record of 56,569 net tons of pig iron in one month.

1953   The Ore Dock basin was extended from 1,000 feet to 2,200 feet. A 15-ton unloader and a 20-ton unloader were also added. Sparrows Point now employs 26,000 workers. "J" furnace blown in. A 30-inch inline continuous billet mill is constructed. May – "J" furnace became the world's largest monthly iron producer with 61,424 tons. Third steam boiler and electric generator came online at Pennwood Power.

1954   40-inch Blooming Mill rebuilt from the original 1919 mill. 46-inch Blooming Mill rebuilt to 54-inch Blooming Mill. Clubhouse and first nine-hole golf course of the Sparrows Point Country Club on Wise Avenue completed. Reconstruction of two coke oven batteries. Enlargement of nine soaking pits. Facilities to increase the capacity of five Open Hearth furnaces and three Blooming Mills. Authorized additional water supply, sintering facilities, a continuous sheet galvanizing line, and additional electrolytic tin plating facilities.

1955 Nos. 1 and 2 lap weld Pipe Mills dismantled and replaced with electric weld Pipe Mill. A battery of 14 new high speed nail makers installed. The following facilities were added: a new four high, 160-inch sheared plate mill, a five stand, 48-inch high speed cold reducing mill with a two stand, four high skin pass mill, two continuous annealing lines, additional electrolytic tin plating facilities with necessary shearing and warehousing facilities, two additional continuous sheet galvanizing lines, an electric-weld Pipe Mill for the production of pipe in the range of 4 ½ to 16 inches in diameter, additional facilities for the production of flanged and dished heads, improvements to the 24-inch billet mill, additional water supply facilities, and additional iron ore screening and sintering facilities. New ore handling conveyer system placed in service at the Ore Dock.

1956 Major additions and improvements to the facilities included: enlarging a blast furnace, three continuous annealing lines, a continuous sheet galvanizing line, an auxiliary ore yard, and Nos. 3 and 4 sintering lines put into production. No. 7 electrolytic tin plate line went into production. No. 8 was under construction. No. 1 continuous anneal line installed. 200 houses razed and 1,250 residents displaced to make way for the No. 4 Open Hearth. Construction began on a new wing for the main office. $200 million dollars to be spent to enlarge ingot capacity.

1957 Improvements included Nos. 5 and 6 sintering lines, additional electric and steam generating equipment, No. 12 coke oven battery starts up, additional scrap preparation facilities, enlargement of a blast furnace, construction of "K" furnace (blown in in March), No. 4 Open Hearth shop to include seven 350-ton Open Hearth furnaces and auxiliary equipment, eight blocks of soaking pits, a 45 x 90-inch universal slabbing mill and related facilities, a four high 160-inch sheared plate mill, a five stand 48-inch high speed cold reducing mill, two four high skin pass mills, two additional electrolytic tin plating lines with necessary shearing and warehouse facilities, Nos. 3 and 4 continuous annealing lines, a new coil handling and storage facility, No. 1 Electric Resistance Weld pipe (ERW) mill, No. 3 pickling line (modernized in 1989). Sparrows Point plant sets new production record of 6,158,256 net tons and now employs approximately 30,000.

1958 Sparrows Point plant with a rated steelmaking capacity of 8,200,000 ingot tons as of January 1958 became the country's "biggest" steelmaking plant. Between January and June 1958, foreign steel imports doubled. Plant access road system completed (Route 151 and 158). February 9th - Last heat tapped from the Bessemer at 9:02 p.m. No. 10 electrolytic tinning line completed (first installed in 1943). This makes Sparrows Point the largest single Tin Mill in the world.

1959 The average steelworker wage is $3.10 an hour. Peak employment at Sparrows Point reaches 30,920. Facilities to increase production at Sparrows Point include: a 56-inch four stand cold reducing mill and additional skin passing capacity and auxiliary equipment, a program to increase the production of hot-rolled sheets and the necessary steel producing facilities to support the increase. Facilities included a battery of coke ovens, two new Open Hearth furnaces, soaking pits and auxiliary equipment. Additional facilities for cold reducing sheets, galvanizing sheets, and electrolytic tin plating consisted of a 66-inch cold reducing mill, an additional stand for the 56-inch cold reducing mill, a continuous galvanizing line, an electrolytic tin plating line, complete with buildings, annealing furnaces, cranes, and other auxiliaries. Improvements to the 56-inch Hot Strip Mill included a new downcoiler. The ingot expansion program included extension to the Ore Dock, an ore bridge, a new sintering plant, a new coke oven battery, a new blast furnace, additions to the Pennwood Power Station, rebuilding of a battery of coke ovens, and other facilities necessary to support this program. A July 15th walkout resulted in a 116 day labor strike. It was the largest strike in steel industry history.

1960 Former Chairman of the Board Eugene Gifford Grace dies. Sparrows Point's capacity is now 12 times as large as when the Bethlehem Steel Company acquired the plant in 1916. The "tin can" celebrates its 150th birthday. January - Reynolds Aluminum introduces aluminum cans to the citrus market. A plan to increase capacity of ingot tons 10% by adding oxygen to the No. 4 Open Hearth. Electrostatic precipitators installed on the No. 4 Open Hearth. Proposal to construct Pennwood Wharf, No. 5 Continuous Anneal, and No. 6 Coil Prep line. Construction begins on No. 2 Duo mill. Bear Creek drawbridge Peninsula Highway completed.

1961 Bethlehem Steel Corporation opened the Homer Research Laboratories. Modernization of the 56-inch Hot Strip Mill. No. 3 trimmer installed.

1962 No. 2 Duo mill started up. Pennwood Wharf began operation of an 870 foot dock with 50,000 square foot warehouse facilities (climate controlled).

1963 July – No. 1 Halogen line started up. No. 2 Electric Resistance Weld (ERW) mill built.

1964 68-inch Hot Strip Mill modernized.

1965 Plastics rapidly replacing steel in automobiles, etc. Two Basic Oxygen Furnaces built inside of No. 1 and No. 2 Open Hearths.

1966   April – first BOF tapped. No. 1. Open Hearth ceased production (two months after startup of BOF). No. 2 Halogen line begins operation. "J" furnace altered with two tap holes. Blown in in November.

1967   May – No. 3 Rod Mill completed (replaced No. 1). Upgraded finishing stands in the 68-inch Hot Strip Mill.

1968   Peninsula Highway Bridge completed. May 3rd – explosion at No. 7 Steam Generator plant kills 2, injures 22.

1969   Best year of Sparrows Point shipments at 5,796,974 tons. Yoder Universal Gauge System installed at the 16-inch Pipe Mill.

1970   No. 3 Duo mill online.

1971   New ore pier constructed south of the auxiliary ore field. The length of the pier was 1,020 feet and the channel was dredged to a depth of 42 feet. Three unloaders were installed on the pier. A new shipbuilding basin was constructed. It was large enough to handle 300,000 DWT tankers. No. 3 Open Hearth shuts down.

1972   Demolition begins on the town of Sparrows Point to make way for the "L" furnace. "Mini mills" emerging as a competitive alternative to giant steel mills. Galvalume – a new aluminum zinc sheet invented by Bethlehem Steel and to be produced only at Sparrows Point.

1973   Tension Leveler added to No. 3 Skin Pass Mill in the Sheet Mill. New electric furnace added to the Iron and Brass Foundry.

1974   Ground broken for the "L" furnace. "E" and "F" furnaces banked. Webb Coil Compactors in No. 3 Rod Mill to replace the OEM Morgan compactors.

1975   "G" and "D" furnaces banked. E.C.P.P.P. (Experimental Coke Pellet Pilot Plant) was an unsuccessful experimental project to make coke in an environmentally better and continuous process, to replace coke ovens. Bedding Plant added to the Ore Dock to layer the raw materials for blast furnaces.

1976   March – sintering plants 1 through 6 shut down. A new Dravo-Lurgi single strand sintering plant started up and is referred to as #7 Strand.

1977   Francis Scott Key Bridge opens. Sparrows Point fined $500,000 for missing pollution control deadlines.

1978   November 8th – "L" furnace blown in and casts its first iron. November 10th – "A" furnace completed its last cast. "A" furnace, "B" furnace, and "C" furnace banked.

1979   Bethlehem Steel Corporation celebrates its 75th anniversary. August 4th – "J" furnace banked. "K" furnace banked.

1981   "A", "B", "C", "D", "E", "F", "G" furnaces razed (this occurred over a two-year period). 56-inch Hot Strip Mill permanently shut down (dismantled in 1990). Installed facilities for Galvalume-coated wire.

1982   Bethlehem Steel Company reports a quarterly deficit of $67 million. $160 million "A" coke oven battery starts up. April 23rd – "A" battery coke oven's first push at 1:30 p.m. U.S. falls into recession. Bethlehem Steel Corporation loses $1.47 billion. May 7th - Plant layoffs increase to 5,030, the highest level since 1933. September 30th – USA Today newspaper headline: "Steelworkers: Look for a New Job." Billet grinder and auxiliaries to prepare billets for No. 3 Rod Mill.

1983   Dismantling work began on No. 3 Open Hearth, Ladle Houses, Nos. 1 – 6, and 9 & 10 coke oven batteries, one ore bridge at the Ore Dock, and the gas engine buildings. Removal of blast furnaces on Blast Furnace Row, the old sinter strand facility, the former Gas Training School, the Bragg School, the Real Estate Shop, the North Side Restaurant, No. 1 Electrical Repair Shop, the Iron Foundry and Pattern Shop, the 40x80-inch slabber soaking pits, some of the Blooming Mill soaking pits, the old ore screening building, associated conveyers, and the No. 1 Open Hearth. Pipe Mill shuts down. Rod and Wire Mill shuts down.

1984 $60 million modernization of the BOF to prepare for the new Continuous Caster. Two idle furnaces at No. 4 Open Hearth taken off the books. No. 6 Washer came online. President Ronald Reagan places quotas on imports of semi-finished slabs. Bethlehem Steel Corporation's employment shrinks by 50%, many due to lump sum retirement packages, layoffs, buyouts, and including cost cutting measures of eliminating top executives.

1985   December 19th - $300 million Continuous Caster started up (first slab cast heat #432 EO34 Slab Caster #2).

1986   Bethlehem Steel abandoned ship construction at the Sparrows Point Yard. $30 million modernization of the 160-inch plate mill. Addition of AGC (Automatic Gage Control) to the 160-inch four high Plate Mill.

1987	January 23rd – improvements made to the Plate Mill. May – Tin Mill Box Anneal ceased to operate. The Maryland Department of Nature Conservancy acquires 1,310 acres of Black Marsh from the Bethlehem Steel Company. This property would later become North Point State Park.
1988	Bethlehem Steel authorizes $200 million for the modernization of the 68-inch Hot Strip Mill. The North Point State Park opened.
1989	"J" furnace started up after being idle for 10 years. 48-inch Tandem Mill modernized (December 29th – rolled its first coil). Tin Mill Pickler modernized. Bethlehem Steel Company announces plans to invest $100 million for construction of a new sheet coating line. No. 1 Skin Pass rolls 901 tons on a turn. $92 million to be invested in an environmental improvement program for the coke ovens and other facilities. No. 3 Pickler modernization. Two hundred new "saturn doors" installed on the coke ovens.
1990	Interiors removed or sold: 40x80-inch slabber, the Wire Mill, the Pipe Mills, Nos. 4, 6, 9, and 10 Coating Lines in the Tin Mill, No. 4 Skin Pass, two box annealing rooms, Nos. 1 and 2 Annealing Lines, batch pickling, shearing, and skin pass lines in the 68-inch Hot Strip Mill, most of the interior of the 56-inch Hot Strip Mill, and the dismantling of 60-inch Plate Mill. A $60 million 100-day reconstruction of the "L" furnace took place between March 16th and July 1st. "L" furnace relined and covered by "H" and "J" furnaces. After the reline, "H" and "J" were banked and "K" was razed. New slab carrier transport system in place. $200 million modernization of the 68-inch Hot Strip Mill included two walking beam-type furnaces, a new de-scaler, a reversing rougher, a coilbox and coilers, and their controls. The 48-inch Tandem Mill was upgraded.
1991	Severe U.S. economic recession. December - Sparrows Point coke works shut down, reportedly due to battery failures and the high cost of installing controls to meet environmental regulations. Trimming unit on No. 2 Halogen Line installed. No. 3 Rod Mill shut down. No. 1 Skin Pass and No. 5 Slitter modernized.
1992	September 12th – Sparrows Point celebrates the 75th anniversary of the Tin Mill. December 12th – No. 4, 49-inch Hot Dip Coating Line starts up (galvanized and Galvalume). No. 2 Skin Pass modernized. Slab Cut-Up Line at the Plate Mill.
1993	New galvanizing lines begin production. Sparrows Point plant becomes the first integrated steel producer in the U.S. to be certified to ISO 9002. December 10th – No. 1 Halogen Line rebuilt after being knocked out of service by a fire.
1994	No. 4 Galvalume Line starts up.
1995	May – "L" Furnace established a North American monthly production record of 305,904 tons of iron (an average of 9,868 tons per day).
1996	Ladle Slag Skimmer at the BOF Shop.
1997	October 3rd – Sparrows Point Shipyard sold to Veritas Capital; the yard was named Baltimore Marine Industries. Between December 1997 and August 2001, 26 steel companies filed for bankruptcy.
1998	Plate Mills shut down. Bethlehem Steel merges with Lukens Inc. The Bear Creek Bridge extension of 695 completed.
1999	The "L" Furnace was relined and equipped for coal injection. "H" and "J" blast furnaces razed. Construction of scrap yard processing. Construction of new roll grinding facility. Conversion to improve and widen #1 strand of the Continuous Caster. BOF rehabilitation.
2000	Air Products installed new $160 million pulverized coal injection system (PCI). The facility increased gaseous oxygen supply to the "L" Furnace. Start up of the $200 million new Cold Mill.
2001	October – Bethlehem Steel Corporation files for Chapter 11 and later in the year filed for bankruptcy.
2003	April 30th - International Steel Group (ISG) buys Bethlehem Steel Corporation's assets. ISG did not acquire any of the retirement and health benefit responsibilities.
2004	Improved Humphrey's Creek Water Treatment Plant. Modernization of the Tin Mill No. 3 Pickler.
2005	April 13th – ISG sold the steel plant to Mittal Steel Company.

2007   February – the Department of Justice ordered Mittal Steel to sell their interest in the Sparrows Point plant.

2008   May 7th – Mittal Steel Company was sold to the Russian company Severstal for $810 million.

2010   Severstal fined $2.5 million by the State of Maryland for repeatedly discharging high levels of hazardous gases and soot from the blast furnace. July 25th – the "L" furnace was shut down "until market conditions improve." August 11th – Severstal announces that the steel mill at Sparrows Point is up for sale. 90% of the mill was idle.

2011   March 1st – Severstal agrees to sell the facilities at Sparrows Point to R.G. Steel, a unit of the New York based investment company Renco Group for $1.25 billion. December 29th – headline in the Dundalk Eagle "Point: Plant Shuttered Until at Least First Part of Year." Most of the plant's 1,250 union employees were temporarily laid off until further notice. "It's going to be a blue Christmas at Sparrows Point."

2012   January 5th – layoffs at the plant were projected to last until March 2012. Concerns grew about shutting the "L" Furnace down: "If they let the iron cool, it's lights out."

January 6th – Executives from G.E. Capital, the corporate finance arm of General Electric, toured the facility of Sparrows Point. R.G. Steel was hoping to secure a loan to keep the mill going.

January 12th – sources inside R.G. Steel told the Dundalk Eagle that the 68-inch Hot Strip Mill was shut down and all hot mill employees were laid off indefinitely. The "L" Furnace was currently in a state of "hot idle."

January 26th – headline in the Dundalk Eagle: "Capital Gain: R.G. Steel Gets Money to Reopen." Employees who received layoff notices were scheduled to return to work by the end of the month. "With this new capital in place, and improving market conditions, R.G. Steel is well positioned to service its customers now and in the future."

February 24th – headline in the Dundalk Eagle: "R.G. Steel Considering Sale of Assets at Sparrows Point."

May 26th – Baltimore Sun headline "Steel Mills Idling Shadows Its Future." R.G. Steel announced it will lay off 1,975 workers and shut down operations beginning June 4th.

June 7th – Dundalk Eagle headline: "Steel Mill Owner Files for Bankruptcy, Looks to Sell." R.G. Steel was ordered to sell all assets by July 27, 2012.

June 15th – the last slab (bar) to go through the 68-inch Hot Strip Mill occurred on June 15, 2012 at 7:19 a.m.

August 7th – R.G. Steel sold the Sparrows Point plant at auction. Liquidator Hilco Trading Incorporated purchased the mill for $72.5 million – well below the $810 million it sold for in 2008 to Severstal.

August 16th – headline in the Dundalk Eagle: "End of the Road."

October 4th – Hilco Trading Incorporated and Environmental Liability Transfer (ELT) announced that they were putting the mill back up for sale. Bids were to be accepted until Friday, November 21st. If necessary, an auction would be held on Thursday, January 3, 2013.

December 20th – headline in the Dundalk Eagle: "Cold Mill Sold." North Carolina steelmaker Nucor purchased the Cold Mill complex for use in its own mill. Bethlehem Steel built the Cold Mill in 2000 for $300 million. Nucor paid $35 million.

The sale of the Cold Mill complex was the final blow that ended all hopes that a new owner would be found to restart the plant. Shortly thereafter, Hilco began a 40-month program to systematically dismantle the steel complex at Sparrows Point and take it to the ground.

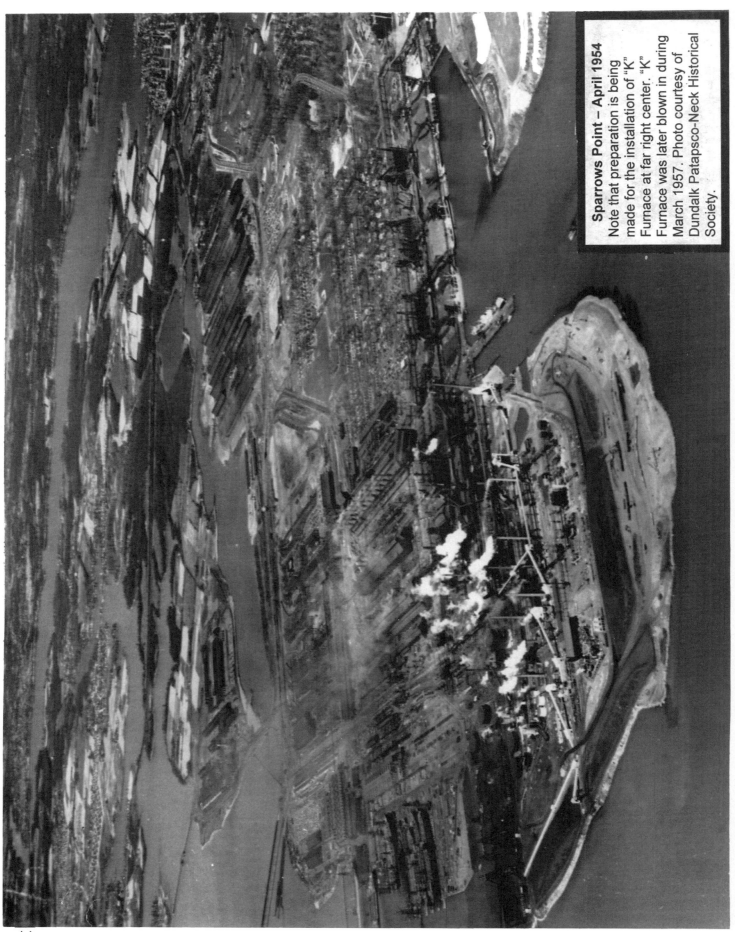

Sparrows Point – April 1954

Note that preparation is being made for the installation of "K" Furnace at far right center. "K" Furnace was later blown in during March 1957. Photo courtesy of Dundalk Patapsco-Neck Historical Society.

History of the Steel Works at Sparrows Point, Maryland
Part 1: 1887 - 1916

In 1652, Lord Baltimore granted Thomas Sparrow, an English colonist, a parcel of land on the east side of the Patapsco River. The peninsula of land became known as Sparrows Point. The land remained in the Sparrow family's possession for over 160 years. After the War of 1812, the property changed hands several times and was eventually sub-divided into several farms. It remained that way until 1887, when it was purchased by the Pennsylvania Steel Company.

In 1886, the Pennsylvania Steel Company began to explore options for a tidewater plant to produce pig iron. Luther Bent, General Manager, of the Pennsylvania Steel Company, saw that costs were moving against inland manufacturers. Depending on railroads and their freight rates for raw materials seemed illogical. Bent believed that a steel producer who could get his ore by water would gain a significant advantage over his competitors. Bent had heard rumors about significant ore deposits around Santiago, Chile and sent Frederick Wood, his top engineer, to investigate. Wood found an area honeycombed with veins of ore. The Pennsylvania Steel Company then formed Juragua Iron Company, Ltd. to mine the ore.

With vast amounts of ore available, the company then sought a tidewater location where the ore could be converted directly to pig iron rather than shipped via rail at a penalty to their Steelton facility. Frederick Wood was again commissioned to find a suitable tidewater state. After scouting several locations, Wood decided that Sparrows Point, Maryland was the best location because of its proximity to Cuba, the bituminous coal fields of Western Pennsylvania, and the access to deep water channels around Sparrows Point. In 1887, the Pennsylvania Steel Company purchased the Sparrows Point peninsula from five local landowners for a total of $57,900.

On March 1, 1887, surveyors for the Pennsylvania Steel Company landed on Sparrows Point. The first summer was challenging as crews battled the heat and swarms of mosquitoes. They struggled to drain the marshland using sump pumps powered by windmills. Despite the challenges, progress was made and by July 18th, the first locomotive arrived and was delivered on a new pier 900 feet long and 100 feet wide. The first building completed on Sparrows Point was the brickyard. It was soon producing 30,000 bricks daily. The fledgling steel company had about 100 employees at this time. Rufus Wood, brother of Frederick, had been appointed General Agent for the town and recognized that the growing mill and town would soon need some kind of law enforcement. He wrote the County Commissioner to request the appointment of one John Campbell as Commission Officer of the Law. Rufus also sought to ban the sale of liquor on Sparrows Point property and was also successful. Sparrows Point remained a dry town until it was demolished in 1972 and 1973. In August, the Sparrows Point Company Store was started, and in October, ground was broken for "A" and "B" Blast Furnaces.

In the second summer, conditions were greatly improved. Sickness was reduced due to the successful drainage of the bogs and careful attention to sanitation. During the second year, over 100 houses were completed and the streets were graded. Work had also begun on the Sparrows Point Railroad. An elementary school was completed on the northeast corner of 4th and "D" Streets and two blocks away, the Catholic Church was nearing completion.

Because of Sparrows Point's relative isolation, transportation to and from the area was a problem that needed to be solved. In the very beginning, a "bugeye" was used to bring passengers into Humphrey's Creek at a location near where the Chesapeake Lumber Company was located. Later, the company purchased the steam launch "Viola" but because of her size, she was undependable. Arrangements were later made for the steamer "Olive" to ferry passengers between Sparrows Point and Baltimore City. In the meantime, work had progressed on the railroad line to Colgate Creek. When completed on February 11, 1889, the Baltimore and Sparrows Point Railroad connected with the Pennsylvania and B&O Railroads. Later, in 1903, the No. 26 "Red Rocket" streetcar services began to operate between Sparrows Point and Baltimore City and the transportation problem to Sparrows Point was solved. Keep in mind, all of this occurred before the advent of the automobile.

Between 1889 and 1893, a great deal of progress had been made on the steel works at Sparrows Point. "A", "B", "C", and "D" furnaces were completed and blown in. "A" Furnace tapped its first iron on October 23, 1889, followed by "B" Furnace on March 11, 1890, "C" Furnace on October 3, 1891, and "D" Furnace on April 14, 1893. The company also began to construct a shipyard during this year and the first ingots were rolled on the 36-Inch Blooming Mill.

In 1891, the Pennsylvania Steel Company and its "Maryland Extension" underwent a serious change. It was no longer profitable to ship cold pig iron to Steelton for conversion to steel. Sparrows Point was an ideal location for assembling raw materials and the subsequent distribution of its steel to eastern railroads, coastal and foreign ports. With this in mind, it was decided to build a Bessemer Department and a Rail Mill at Sparrows Point with the necessary shops and foundries for their maintenance. Once this plan was in place, it was determined that the steel making operation could best be conducted by incorporating the works at Sparrows Point. Accordingly, on June 27, 1891, the Sparrows Point plant ceased to be the Maryland Extension of the Pennsylvania Steel Company, and became the Maryland Steel Company of Baltimore County. On August 1, 1891, the first Bessemer steel ever made in Maryland was produced at Sparrows Point and a week later, the Rail Mill produced its first rail.

Just as the plant was beginning to find its identity as a Rail Mill, the great panic of 1894 occurred. This economic downturn progressed into a full-blown depression that lasted until 1897. The recently organized Maryland Steel Company was forced into receivership and closed its doors for three years. Eventually, the depression ended and the company resumed its production of rails.

Over the next several years, the mill and town continued to grow and prosper. In 1901, a By-product Coke Plant was built. In 1902, a third Bessemer converter was added. By 1903, the town had added a new two-story 12 room elementary school in the 700 block of "D" Street and a new town hall (later the Lyceum Theater). The town had grown to 1,200 houses with a population of 8,000.

To meet the growing demand for rails, the construction of an open hearth furnace was started in 1909. The first steel was tapped on March 28, 1910. By this time, the steel works at Sparrows Point was approaching its 25th birthday. The plant embarked on a major reconstruction program. A concrete bulkhead was built at right angles to High Pier and the basin immediately in front of the bulkhead was dredged to 30 feet. A new Hoover and Mason bridge equipped with a 15-ton grab bucket was added to serve the ore storage yard. Between 1911 and 1915, all four blast furnaces were completely rebuilt and enlarged. Skip hoists were added, giving each furnace a rated capacity of 400 tons per day. Two new coke batteries of 60 ovens each were added, the first push occurring on July 16, 1914. In addition, a new gas blowing unit consisting of five blowers was built to coincide with the rebuild of "A", "B", "C", and "D" furnaces. Also during this time period, a new sintering plant was constructed. By the close of 1915, the steel works of the Maryland Steel Company had been overhauled and modernized. The iron producing unit was on a par with the best in the country. Despite the fact that the plant was in excellent physical shape, the Maryland Steel Company was on the brink of financial disaster. Overseas rail sales had plummeted and the company was posting losses in revenue. The Rail Mill was put in part-time and two of the furnaces were banked. Layoffs followed. Two thousand of the plant's 4,000 workers found themselves out of work.

With the company floundering, it was ripe for a takeover. On February 16, 1916, Charles M. Schwab, President and Chairman of the Board of the Bethlehem Steel Company, consummated a deal to acquire all of the assets of the Pennsylvania Steel Company and its subsidiaries, which included the Sparrows Point plant. Schwab also appointed Frederick Wood as the overseer of the new plant. What lay ahead was a major transformation of the peninsula at Sparrows Point.

Part 2: 1916 – 2012

Realizing the potential of the Maryland Steel Company site, Bethlehem Steel Company began at once to plan for numerous extensions at Sparrows Point. They immediately began to secure more land. By the end of 1917, the company owned 2,097 acres. The shoreline around the peninsula was also reshaped. Steel pilings were installed 2,367 feet beyond the south shore and filled in, adding another 100 acres of property.

The transformation from a single product rail mill to a diversified steel mill was swift. A 30-foot deep channel was dug to High Pier and a turn-around basin was constructed for ore steamers. A coal handling plant was installed on a pier extending westward into the harbor and preparations were made for a 240-battery coke oven facility to be built next to the coal handling plant. On April 1, 1916, Bethlehem Steel acquired the property and rights of the Baltimore Sheet and Tin Plate Company and moved the site of the proposed plant to Sparrows Point. The first unit of 12 hot mills with facilities for pickling, annealing, cold rolling and tinning began operating on July 26, 1917. When completed in 1925, there would be a total of 36 hot mills installed. It was the only fully integrated tin plant east of Pittsburgh. On September 10, 1917, the 110-Inch Plate Mill was placed in service. The purpose of the mill was to provide large plates to be used in the nearby shipyard. As part of Bethlehem's massive expansion program, the following were authorized in 1916: four additional blast furnaces ("E" and "F" Furnaces would come on-line in 1920); a 60-Inch Universal Plate Mill; a 40-Inch Blooming Mill combined with a 24-Inch Billet Mill and an 18-Inch Continuous Bar Mill; three 25-ton Bessemer Converters; three 200-ton tilting Open Hearth Furnaces; six Gas & Electric Generators; and eight gas-driven blowing engines.

Maryland Steel had built the No. 1 Open Hearth in 1910, but it was totally inadequate for supplying steel to the new finishing units being installed by Bethlehem. With the completion of four furnaces, No. 2 Open Hearth was operational by March 1920. With the completion of these new mills and the introduction of other products, the Rail Mill, which had once been the main product at the mill, lost its prestige and was subsequently shut down. In 1918, Frederick Wood, the man who designed and built the steel works at Sparrows Point, resigned. He had been at the helm for nearly three decades, but times had changed and so had the direction of his creation at Sparrows Point. Frederick Wood died in 1943 at the age of 86.

With the completion of its original construction program, Bethlehem turned its attention to further capitalize on the tidewater location of Sparrows Point. In 1924, it pursued an even greater diversification of its products, which included a Rod and Wire Mill and four Pipe Mills. The first wire was drawn on April 15th, the first rods were rolled on March 20th, and the first nails were made on May 13, 1926. Also in 1926, a fourth battery of 60 coke ovens was authorized to complement the ones completed in 1918, 1920, and 1922. This battery was completed in December 1926, making a total of 360 ovens.

Between 1928 and 1930, furnaces "A", "B", and "C" were rebuilt again. "D" Furnace would follow in 1937. This construction program replaced the older furnaces built between 1911 and 1915. Each new furnace had an increased hearth diameter, new stacks, new casthouses, larger stoves, larger skips, and a new top design. When the Great Depression began in 1929, some projects were delayed. No. 3 Open Hearth was one of them. The original authorization for the furnace was in July 1925, but the furnace did not begin operating until 1937. The Depression also had an effect on employment at the Point. In 1932, there were 3,500 employees compared to a one-time high of 18,000. Despite the harsh economic conditions, Bethlehem dismantled the Flange Mill and the 152-Inch Plate Mill in Coatesville, PA in 1931 and transferred them to Sparrows Point. The 152-Inch Mill was enlarged and became the three-high 160-Inch Plate Mill. In 1936, the first of two 42-Inch Tandem Mills and the No. 2 Rod Mill were built. A second 42-Inch Tandem Mill was built in 1937. This new technology brought an end to the old Hot Dip Tin Mills and they were subsequently dismantled. Coinciding with this new technology was the construction of the 56-Inch Hot Strip Mill.

As World War II approached, it brought with it some unsettling times. In August 1939, President Roosevelt created the War Reserves Board, followed in 1941 by the Office of Production Management, and later in 1942, the War Production Board. All of these were designed to mobilize the nation's industrial base and provide critical supplies. Sparrows Point would play a major role in this effort. The government recognized this role and subsidized an expansion at the plant that would include a new blast furnace, additional furnaces for the No. 3 Open Hearth, and a new coke oven battery.

In 1941, there was also a movement to organize unions on a national level. The movement was initiated by John L. Lewis in 1936, with the formation of the Steel Workers Organizing Committee (SWOC). All of the other major steel manufacturers in the United States had joined the movement. Bethlehem Steel Company was the only holdout in the steel industry to resist union representation. On September 25, 1941, steelworkers across the nation voted in favor of SWOC and the union movement was born. The Shipyard workers followed on September 30th by joining the Industrial Union of Marine and Shipyard Workers. Shortly thereafter, the Japanese bombed Pearl Harbor and the nation was plunged into war. With increased production to support the war, the Great Depression went into decline and prosperity loomed in the future.

Progress and growth continued in the 1940s at Sparrows Point. "G" Furnace, the seventh furnace along Blast Furnace Row, was blown in during 1941. Also in 1941, the Main Office Building on North Point Boulevard was completed. In 1943, the first electrolytic tinning lines were installed. In 1947, the 56-Inch Cold Sheet Tandem Mill was started followed by the 68-Inch Hot Strip Mill. In October 1948, "H" Furnace was blown in and the Pennwood Power Plant began operations.

Expansion and growth continued into the 1950s and 1960s. In 1951, the 66-Inch Tandem Mill came on-line and "H" Furnace continued to break old tonnage records. In 1952 to 1953, the Point employed 26,000 workers and had an annual payroll in excess of $90 million dollars. During this same time frame, Bethlehem Steel erected the Chesapeake Bay Bridge. Also in 1953, the ore dock basin was extended from 1,000 feet to 2,200 feet and "J" Furnace was blown in. Shortly thereafter, it would become the world's largest monthly iron producer with 61,424 tons.

Between 1955 and 1960, the steel works at Sparrows Point experienced unparalleled growth. It was approaching its zenith. In 1955, major improvements included: a new four-high 160-Inch Sheared Plate Mill; a five-stand 48-Inch Cold Reduction Mill; a two-stand four-high Skin Pass Mill; two Continuous Annealing Lines; additional Electrolytic Tin Plating Lines; and a new ore handling conveyor system at the ore dock.

1956 marked a sad time for residents of Sparrows Point. It was a foreshadow of things to come. Residents of the 200, 300, and 400 blocks of "D", "E", and "F" Streets were forced to move from their homes. This section of town would be demolished to make room for the No. 4 Open Hearth, which came online in 1957. In 1958, the plant was rated with a steelmaking capacity of 8,200,000 ingot tons and would be proclaimed the country's largest steelmaking plant. The average steelworker was making $3.10 an hour. Employment at the plant had reached 30,920. The good news was brief, however. Between January and June 1958, foreign steel imports had doubled. What occurred next is what many historians refer to as a critical pivot point in the steelmaking industry. On July 15, 1959, steelworkers across the nation went on strike. The strike lasted 116 days. During this strike, many customers had no recourse but to turn to foreign steel to keep their companies afloat. When the strike ended nearly four months later, it was difficult to get a lot of those customers back. Foreign steel now had its big foot in the door and it was there to stay. To further complicate matters, Reynolds Aluminum introduced the aluminum can and plastics were rapidly replacing steel in automobiles. To improve competitiveness and increase their steelmaking capacity, Sparrows Point built a Basic Oxygen Furnace (BOF) in 1966.

Despite some of the setbacks, Sparrows Point had its best year for shipments at 5,796,974 tons. In 1970, it introduced the No. 3 Duo Mill to compete with the aluminum business. In 1971, the plant built a new 1,020 foot ore pier south of the auxiliary ore field. The Shipyard added a new shipbuilding basin as its ways were becoming too small to accommodate the new super tankers.

In 1972, the residents of Sparrows Point received some earth-shattering news. As was the case in 1956, the residents were ordered to vacate their homes. The town was to be demolished to make way for the colossal "L" Furnace. By 1974, the town was completely gone and work had begun on the foundation for the new furnace. On November 8, 1978, the "L" Furnace would cast its first iron. The new furnace exceeded all expectations. As a result, most of Blast Furnace Row would become obsolete. By 1983, "A", "B", "C", "D", "E", "F", and "G" Furnaces were razed. Other facilities would follow with the wrecking ball. That same year, the No. 1 Open Hearth and the No. 3 Open Hearth, No. 1-6 and 9 and 10 Coke Batteries, the Gas Engine Buildings, and the Iron Foundry and Pattern Shop were all demolished. Other facilities that closed included the Pipe Mills and the Rod and Wire Mills.

During this time frame, Bethlehem Steel Corporation lost $1.47 million dollars and plant layoffs increased to 5,030, the highest since 1933. Despite this gloomy report, the plant at Sparrows Point embarked on a $60 million modernization of the BOF to prepare for the new Continuous Caster. Employment at the Bethlehem Steel Corporation had shrunk by 50%, much of this attributed to lump sum retirement packages, layoffs, buyouts, and cost-cutting measures of eliminating top executives. On December 19, 1985, the $300 million Continuous Caster started up. The following year, Bethlehem Steel abandoned shipbuilding at the Sparrows Point Yard.

As Sparrows Point moved into the 1990s, it was still striving to compete. In 1990, the 68-Inch Hot Strip Mill received a $200 million modernization. The "L" Furnace had a $60 million 100 day reconstruction and a new slab carrier transport system was put in place. 1991 saw the US economy slide into a severe recession. That same year, the coke ovens shut down. The "A" Battery was built in 1982 for $160 million. Its short life was attributed to battery failures and the high cost of installing controls to meet environmental regulations. On September 12, 1992, Sparrows Point celebrated the 75th anniversary of the Tin Mill. That same year, the No. 4 – 49-Inch Hot Dip Coating Line started up and No. 2 Skin Pass was modernized. In 1994, the No. 4 Galvalume line started up. In 1995, the "L" Furnace established a North American monthly record of 305,904 tons of iron. In 1999, the furnace would be relined and equipped for coal injection. In 2000, the Sparrows Point plant started up its $300 million state-of-the-art Cold Mill. A year later, the Bethlehem Steel Corporation filed for Chapter 11 and soon after declared bankruptcy.

The saga of the next decade is one of many owners and false hope. On April 30, 2003, International Steel Group (ISG) purchased the Bethlehem Steel Corporation's assets. ISG did not acquire any of the health and retirement benefit responsibilities. On April 13, 2005, ISG sold the steel plant to Mittal Steel Company. In February 2007, the Department of Justice ordered Mittal Steel to sell their interest in the Sparrows Point plant. On May 7, 2008, Mittal Steel sold the plant to the Russian Company Severstal for $810 million. In 2010, Severstal announced that the mill was up for sale. At that time, 90% of the plant was idle. On March 1, 2011, Severstal agreed to sell the facilities at Sparrows Point to RG Steel for $1.25 billion. RG Steel experienced problems from the very beginning. In January 2012, they announced that layoffs at the plant would last until March of that year. Shortly thereafter, RG Steel announced that the 68-Inch Hot Strip Mill would be shut down and its employees laid off indefinitely. On May 26, 2012, RG Steel announced that it would lay off 1,975 workers and shut down all operations at Sparrows Point beginning June 4th. On June 7, 2012, RG Steel filed for bankruptcy. On August 7, 2012, the Sparrows Point plant was sold at auction. Liquidator Hilco Trading, Incorporated purchased the mill for $72.5 million.

On October 4, 2012, Hilco Trading, Incorporated and Environmental Liability Transfer announced that they were putting the mill back up for sale. On December 20, 2012, it was announced that North Carolina steel maker Nucor purchased the Cold Mill complex for its own use. They paid $35 million for the mill. The sale of the Cold Mill was a final blow that ended all hopes that a new owner would be found to restart the plant. Shortly thereafter, Hilco began a 40 month program to systematically dismantle the steel mill at Sparrows Point and take it to the ground. A truly sad ending to a great era.

The North Point Peninsula – 1870

Entrance to Baltimore Harbor North Pt. Lower Light, bearing N.W. by W. distant 5 miles

Frederick W. Wood and Rufus K. Wood

Frederick W. Wood
President, Maryland Steel Company

Frederick Wood was born in Lowell, MA on March 16, 1857. He gradated from MIT and joined the Pennsylvania Steel Company. Frederick was given the task of finding a site for a steel mill and he chose Sparrows Point. Frederick oversaw the development of the Sparrows Point peninsula as President of the Maryland Steel Company. He shaped the landscape and the structure of the mill, its furnaces, and the rail mill at Sparrows Point.

Rufus Kidder Wood
General Agent, Maryland Steel Company

Rufus Wood was born in Lowell, MA on November 8, 1848. His brother, Frederick, appointed him General Agent for the Maryland Steel Company. Rufus was responsible for the design and layout of the town. He was a fanatical believer in education. He built the first kindergarten south of the Mason Dixon Line in 1892. Rufus also established the Sparrows Point High School in 1908. A teetotaler, Rufus was also responsible for the liquor ban in the town of Sparrows Point.

A Town and A Mill Emerge from the Swamp

Top photograph: The first houses built, which appear to be the 200 block of "E" Street, can be seen in the upper left hand corner. Humphrey's Creek is visible as is the bridge to the North Side. The elementary school at 4th and "D" Streets and the Company Store on 3rd and "C" Streets can be seen. The photograph dates to circa 1890, and was taken atop one of the new blast furnaces.

Bottom photograph: This photograph, taken from approximately the same location, is dated 1905. The town has grown considerable in 15 years. At far right are the homes on "B" Street. Visible from right to left are the "B" Street Clubhouse, the Methodist Church Steeple at 8th and "C" Streets, the elementary school at 7th and "D" Streets, the Company Store, and the train depot.

Both photographs courtesy of Dundalk Patapsco-Neck Historical Society.

The Sparrows Point Company Store

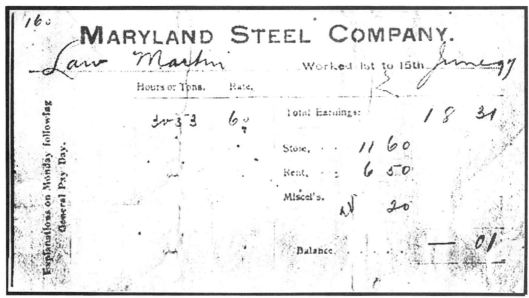

The coupons in this book are good only for Merchandise and will not be replaced if lost. They are Not Transferable and will not be honored if detached from this book.

This book must be handed to the Store Clerk who will detach coupons for the amount of the purchase.

SERVICE STORES CORPORATION

The Sparrows Point Company Store began in business in July 1887 in a room in one of the original brickyard shanties located near the pump house. In 1888, a new store and office building was erected. It would eventually occupy the entire north side of the 300 block of "C" Street. On the west side of the store was the new train depot. Passengers could step off the platform and immediately enter the clothing department on the ground floor. Traveling west to east, they would enter the men's shoe department, the dry goods department, ladies shoes, confectionary, book stalls, and the grocery department. Continuing on, they would encounter the hardware and house furnishing goods, displaying carpets, dining room, parlor, and bedroom furniture before reaching the refrigerated meat market on the corner of 4th and "C" Streets. On the second floor were the offices of the Maryland Steel Company. The Company Store closed in 1944.

Note that the paycheck is dated June 15, 1897. Note that the balance after deductions is one cent.

Photo courtesy of Dundalk Patapsco-Neck Historical Society, dated 1904.

24

"A" and "B" Furnaces Begin to Emerge – 1888

Between the time the surveyors landed at Sparrows Point on March 1, 1887 and the date that this photograph was taken on July 2, 1888, a lot had happened. A receiving wharf was built 900 feet out into the water and railroad tracks were laid on this pier. On July 18, 1887, five months after the surveyors arrived, the first locomotive landed on the shores of Sparrows Point. Tracks were extended to all parts of the fledgling steel mill. In October 1887, ground was broken for the first blast furnaces. This photograph illustrates the progress that had been made nine months later. Four of the **70-foot high by 22-foot diameter stove shells for "B" Furnace** have been erected and two stove shells for "A" Furnace are visible. The **245-foot high stack for the stoves of "A" and "B" Furnaces** had been erected. The scaffolding structure at right center was the Babcock and Wilcox steam boilers. The skeletal structure behind the stove shells was the framing for the Stockhouse, which ran the length of all four furnaces to be completed. The 1,180-foot long building was used to store ore, coke, and limestone. Photo courtesy of Dundalk Patpsco-Neck Historical Society. Photograph dated July 7, 1888 by Massey. **Footnote 1**

Blast Furnaces "A", "B", "C", and "D" – 1893

At the time this photograph was taken in 1893, the steel mill at Sparrows Point was only six years old. The view is looking southeast and is of the original four furnaces built at the plant. These furnaces were designated as "A", "B", "C" and "D". You can actually see the letters A and B on the north end of the casthouses. The tall tower at right is the **blast furnace stove stack** for "A" and "B" furnaces. The tower at left is the furnace stove stack for "C" and "D" furnaces. The building at far right and running behind all of the furnaces is the old **stockhouse** where raw materials were kept. The tower-like structures behind each **casthouse** are the **vertical hoist platforms** used to raise materials such as ore and coke to the top of the furnaces. Between 1911 and 1915, all four of these furnaces were rebuilt with inclined skips. The large overhead line at left carried compressed air from the engine house to the Bessemer Converter shop. Photo courtesy of Dundalk Patapsco-Neck Historical Society.

Creation of the Maryland Steel Company of Baltimore County

State of Maryland
Baltimore County, Sct;
I William P. Cole, Clerk of
the Circuit Court for Baltimore
County, do hereby certify that it
appears of record in my office,
that the Maryland Steel Co.
of Baltimore County as a duly
incorporated body, having been
incorporated in Baltimore County
State of Maryland on June
27" 1891, and recorded in
Liber W. M. I. no 2 folio
530 &c

Test
Wm. P. Cole
Clerk

On June 27, 1891, Luther S. Bent, President of the
Pennsylvania Steel Company turned over the Sparrows Point
complex to his protégé, Frederick Wood. On this day, Bent
signed the incorporation papers creating the Maryland Steel
Company of Baltimore County, a wholly owned subsidiary of the
Pennsylvania Steel Company. He appointed Wood President of
the enterprise. **Footnote 2**

Williamsport and Chesapeake Co.

INCORPORATED JULY 23, 1889.—CAPITAL $100,000.00.

Manufacturers of Lumber.

Post Office and Mills, Sparrow's Point, Baltimore County, Md.
Telegraph Office, Chesapeake Mills, Baltimore County, Md.

Sparrow's Point, Md., June 3, 1891.

The Williamsport and Chesapeake Mills were established soon after the flood of the Susquehanna River in 1889, when large numbers of logs were carried away from Williamsport, PA and recovered in the Chesapeake Bay. The plant was one of the largest and completely equipped in this section of the country and produced 250,000 feet of lumber per day. The supply of drift logs lasted more than three years. The saw mill was located on the northwest side of the Sparrows Point Peninsula where Humphrey's Creek and Bear Creek meet.

"The Williamsport and Chesapeake Company will begin on next Monday at Sparrows Point to saw up the logs which came down the Susquehanna River in the great frishet of June. The mills at Sparrows Point have been closed since May 27, 1893, when the last of the logs which floated down in the disastrous flood of 1889 had been sawed. There are about 40,000,000 feet to be disposed of now and it's estimated that it will take a year and a half to complete the work. One hundred and twenty five men being employed in the saw mill and one hundred and fifty in collecting logs on the carious shores of the bay. The employees will be mainly from Baltimore, although a number of out of town lumbermen are being employed. Every day logs are being brought in and salvage of twenty five cents per log is paid for those logs that have been washed on private shores. The flood of 1889 sent down a much larger number of logs, four years being employed in transferring them into lumber."
Source: From an undated and unidentified news article found in the files at the Dundalk Patapsco-Neck Historical Society.

Blast Furnace Filling Equipment in the 1880s and the 1890s

In the 1890s at Sparrows Point, there was a lot of manual labor involved in filling a blast furnace. In the photograph above, workers at the **Stock House** behind the furnaces prepare to shovel ore into the **charging cars** on the rails. Note that the **transporter** at right is at a right angle to the set of tracks. It would line up its transport receiver and once the men had filled one car they would push the charging car onto it. Then, the transporter would move to another set of tracks to receive the second car filled with ore. If you look closely, you can see the separation between the Stock House tracks and the receiving car. Photo courtesy of the Dundalk Patapsco-Neck Historical Society. Photo circa 1895.

The diagram at right demonstrates how most blast furnaces were filled in the 1880s using two wheelbarrows similar to the one shown in the diagram. The furnaces at Sparrows Point were designed to use **charging cars** that were supported by rail. (See photo above.) The top platform was fitted with tracks running across the **hopper** on either side of the **bell rod**. The two cars were raised on the same hoist and run behind the other on one of these tracks. "After the bottom of the car has been dropped and the load discharged, a **special air cylinder** lifts the far end of the track and the cars return to the hoist by gravity. In order to secure better distribution of the stock than dropping only at four places...the tracks spanning the hopper are placed on a turntable which can be revolved through an angle of 45 degrees." Between 1911 and 1915, **inclined skip hoists** were installed on A, B, C, and D furnaces and the charging car system described above was discontinued.

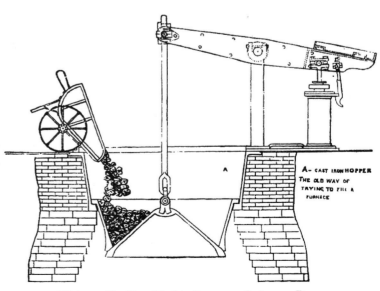

A- CAST IRON HOPPER
THE OLD WAY OF TRYING TO FILL A FURNACE

Weimer Machine Works Company, Lebanon, Penna.

Diagram courtesy of John B. Lovis
Footnote 3

29

First By-Product Coke Plant – 1903

In the latter part of 1901, the Maryland Steel Company built a **by-product coke plant**. Four batteries of 50 ovens each of the **Otto Hoffman type** were contracted for and the first battery was put into service on March 24, 1903. The other three batteries were in operation by August of that same year. These ovens were capable of producing approximately 30,000 net tons of coke, 325 gross tons of sulfate of ammonia, and 287,900 gallons of cold tar per month. This tonnage of coke did not quite meet the requirements and additional quantity was brought from the Connellsville, Pennsylvania region. The only by-products recovered were tar and ammoniacal liquor from which ammonia sulfate was produced.

A contract had been made with the consolidated gas company of Baltimore to take the surplus gas. A 12-inch pipeline was constructed from Sparrows Point to the Spring Gardens Works of the gas company through which between three million and four million cubic feet were pumped each day. A 16-inch and a 20-inch line were later added.

To further fortify its resources of raw materials, the Pennsylvania Steel Company (parent of the Maryland Steel Company) acquired approximately 16,000 acres of coal lands in Cambria and Indiana counties in 1905 and 1906. **Footnote 4**

Photo courtesy of Dundalk Patapsco-Neck Historical Society.

West End Houses

3092. 33 W. G St. 8-29-12

▲ The above view is of the **West End housing development** looking east in 1904. The buildings at right are the foundry and machine shop. The West End houses were comprised of three streets: **West "E", West "F" and West "G".** It was the only time in Sparrows Point history that a "G" Street existed. The buildings ran from the unit block to the 100 block. The West End housing was torn down in the late 1920s to make room for the No. 3 Open Hearth, which was completed in 1931. Note: many maps of Sparrows Point will show the town starting with a 200 block and running eastward to the 1100 block. The streets were lettered south to north from "B" Street to "K" Street. However, **there was no "G" Street**. The reason that it was omitted was because when the town was laid out, Humphrey's Creek nearly bisected the town. The street letters stopped at "F" Street at the south shore of Humphrey's Creek and picked back up on the north shore with "H" Street. In the late 1910s, the creek was filled in and the area became used for recreation. "G" Street was never developed.

◄— At left is a view of the houses on West "G" Street. Note the address in the lower left corner of the photograph.

31

No. 1 Open Hearth – 1910

Open Hearth, Sparrow's Point, Md.

3-16-10

↑ Above is a view of the No. 1 Open Hearth shortly after it began operation. To meet the growing demand for open hearth rails, the Maryland Steel Company began construction of an open hearth in 1909. When completed, it had five 50-ton tilting furnaces with the necessary gas producers. The first steel was tapped on March 28, 1910. A trestle was built between the Bessemer and the Open Hearth for the transfer of the recarvurizer from the former to the latter. By transferring blown metal from the Bessemer to the Open Hearth, steel could be made by the duplex as well as the straight basic method. No. 1 Open Hearth ceased production in 1966 when it had 12 furnaces with a 120-ton capacity.

←—— At left is a view of the interior of the No. 1 Open Hearth. The photograph is dated March 16, 1910. This was 12 days before the first steel was tapped. Both photographs courtesy of Dundalk Patapsco-Neck Historical Society.

Maryland Steel Company Ore Handling Facilities - 1910

↑ The Maryland Steel Company Ore Dock Unloading Facility in operation on July 22, 1910. Photo courtesy of Dundalk Patapsco-Neck Historical Society.

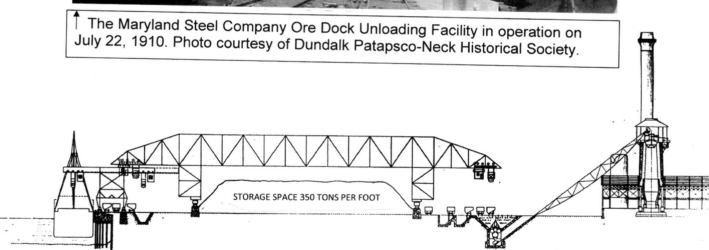

STORAGE SPACE 350 TONS PER FOOT

PROPOSED ORE HANDLING PLANT FOR BLAST FURNACES
MARYLAND STEEL CO. SPARROWS POINT, MARYLAND   SCALE=1 inch = 30 feet

NOVEMBER 2, 1906

Around 1906, the Maryland Steel Company built a concrete bulkhead at right angles to the "High Pier" and mounted two electrically operated Brown hoists for unloading ore. The basin directly in front of the bulkhead was dredged to a depth of 30 feet. The Brown hoist had a combined unloading capacity of 600 gross tons per hour. Later, a Flower and Mason Bridge with a 15-ton grab bucket was added. **Footnote 5**

"A" Furnace Modernization – 1911

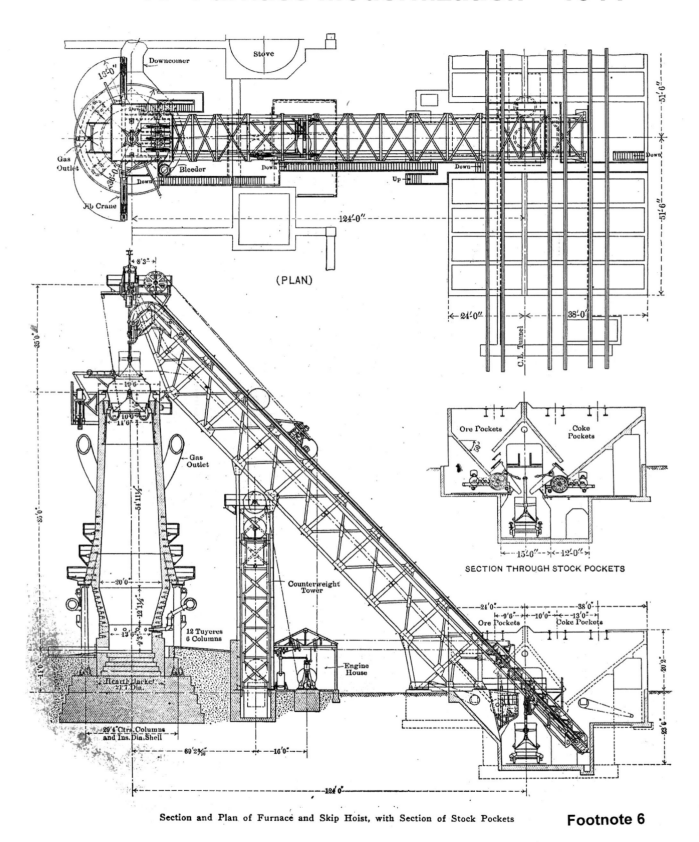

(PLAN)

SECTION THROUGH STOCK POCKETS

Section and Plan of Furnace and Skip Hoist, with Section of Stock Pockets

Footnote 6

"A" Furnace Modernization – 1911

"A" FURNACE TOP – 1911 MODERNIZATION

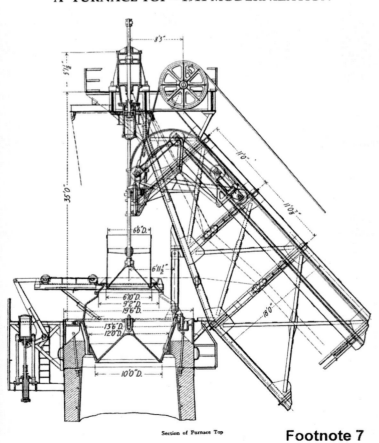

Section of Furnace Top

Footnote 7

↑ A view of "A", "B", "C" and "D" furnaces looking west. The modernization of the four furnaces took place between 1911 and 1915. You can see that "A" furnace has already been converted with a **new mechanical top** and an **inclined skip** and "B", "C" and "D" furnaces still have the **old elevator system**. The building at left center with the tower is the **ship's chandlery**. Visible at right is the No. 1 Open Hearth, which was built in 1910.

"A" Furnace Modernization – 1911

Between 1911 and 1915, blast furnaces "A", "B", "C" and "D" were enlarged and rebuilt with inclined hoists and mechanical tops which increased capacity of each furnace to 400 tons per day. Shown above is "A" furnace looking northeast on August 10, 1911. It had been converted to an inclined skip hoist configuration from the old elevator system. This elevator system can be seen on "B" furnace just east of the stove. Note the M. S. Co. (Maryland Steel Company) on the rail car. Photo courtesy of Dundalk Patapsco-Neck Historical Society.

"A" Furnace Reline – 1914

"A" Furnace was rebuilt with an inclined skip in 1911. The photograph above shows the furnace during a **reline** three years later. The **bosh** has been opened and you can see some of the coke, ash and old brick to the right of the furnace on the **casthouse floor**. Also visible are stacks of brick to be used in the relining process. In the foreground are a pile of **blowpipes**. This furnace had 12 **tuyeres**. Once this reline was completed, the furnace was capable of producing 400 tons of iron a day, which was significant for the time period. Photo courtesy of the Dundalk Patapsco-Neck Historical Society.

Maryland Steel Company
SPARROWS POINT – 1915

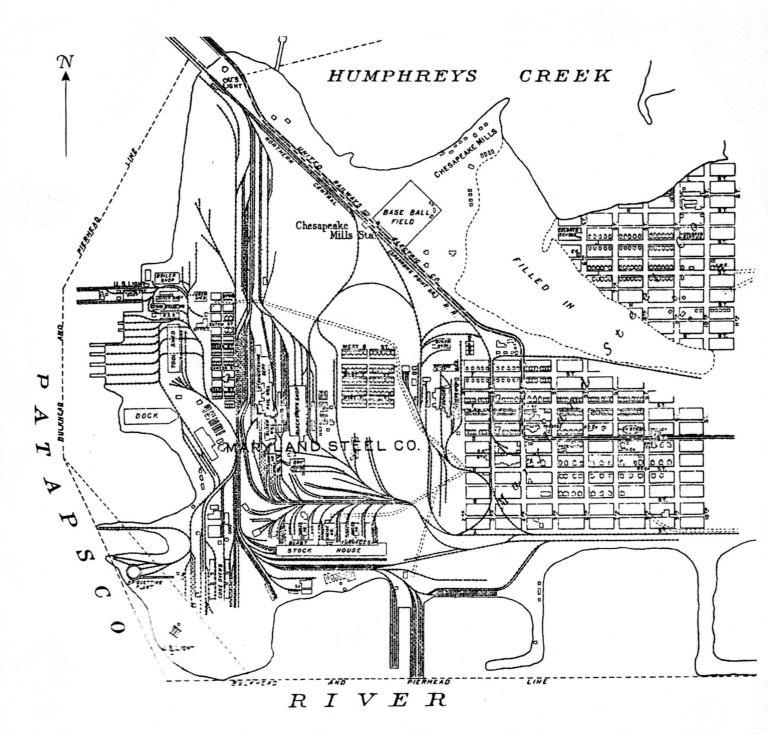

SPARROWS POINT
Scale 600 ft. to the Inch.

Rail Mill

Sparrows Point was an ideal location for the economical assembling of raw materials and for the distribution of steel to the Eastern railroads as well as by water along the eastern coast and to foreign ports. With this in mind, it was decided to build a **Bessemer Department** and a **Rail Mill** at the site with the necessary shops and foundries for their maintenance. Work on the Bessemer and Rail Mill was started before "C" and "D" blast furnaces were completed.

On August 7, 1891, the first rail was rolled, weighing 60 pounds per yard and was made for the Pennsylvania Railroad Company. In February 1893, the first export order for rails was taken from the Western Railways of Havana, Cuba. The plant at Sparrows Point continued to be primarily a rail producer until the **Maryland Steel Company was acquired by Bethlehem Steel Company in 1916**. At that juncture, major diversification of steel products occurred.

Rail Mill of the Maryland Steel Company - 1910

Above: The ingots from the Bessemer Department were reduced to blooms in a steam-driven **36-Inch Blooming Mill**, located in what became known as the **Rail Mill Building**. The product passed directly to a 3-high train of 28-inch diameter steam-powered rollers, which converted it to rails. In 1911, the Rail Mill produced 35,000 tons of rails per month. It was the only finished product then made at the Sparrows Point plant. Photograph courtesy of Dundalk Patpasco-Neck Historical Society, dated February 28, 1910.

Below: **The diagonal or angular method** of rolling is represented by the roughing stand, shown in the diagram below. The shaping of the rail is begun with the first pass in the roughers, and instead of first compressing the bloom to a smaller size and then forming the section partly through compression and partly by spreading, the process is one of compression from beginning to end. Note: Compare the similarities between the diagram below and the set of 3-high rolls in the photograph above.

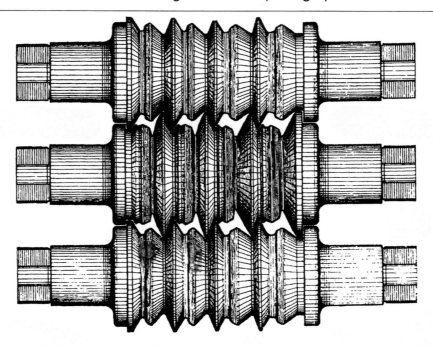

The Rail Straightener
Maryland Steel, Circa 1910

Above, the gentleman seated is applying pressure to straighten rails fresh from the **26-Inch Rail Mill**. Maryland Steel had only one rail mill. It was a three-stand mill that had a monthly capacity of 39,000 tons. The mill could also roll 4 x 4 billets. Blooms for the Rail Mill were produced in the steam driven 36-Inch Blooming Mill. Photo courtesy of Dundalk Patapsco-Neck Historical Society.

Cross-sections of rails showing the evolution of modern railroad rail design between 1865 and 1947.

Work Hours of the Rail Straightening Department in 1892

DAY TURN (one week)

Sunday	Off	
Monday	7 a.m. to 6 p.m.	11 hours
Tuesday	7 a.m. to 6 p.m.	11 "
Wednesday	7 a.m. to 6 p.m.	11 "
Thursday	7 a.m. to 5 p.m.	10 "
Friday	7 a.m. to 6 p.m. (Pay day)	11 "
Saturday	7 a.m. to 5 p.m.	10 "
	Total	64 hours

NIGHT TURN (one week)

Sunday	7 a.m. to 7 a.m. (Mon.)	24 hours
Monday	6 p.m. to 7 a.m. (Tues.)	13 "
Tuesday	6 p.m. to 7 a.m. (Wed.)	13 "
Wednesday	6 p.m. to 7 a.m. (Thur.)	13 "
Thursday	5 p.m. to 7 a.m. (Fri.)	14 "
Friday	6 p.m. to 7 a.m. (Sat.)	13 "
Saturday	5 p.m. to 7 a.m. (Sun.)	14 "
	Total	104 hours

In 1892, there were only two shifts: the day shift and the night shift, and the employees would swing between the two. Operating only two shifts allowed the plant to operate around the clock. On the day shift, the men worked 11 hours a day for a week. On Thursdays and Saturdays, they worked 10 hours.

The night shift worked 13 hours a day for a week. On Thursday and Saturday, they worked 14 hours. When the shift changed on Sunday, the night shift worked 24 hours straight through. The following Sunday, the night crew had the day off while the day shift worked from 7 a.m. on Sunday to 7 a.m. on Monday.

There were no vacations for these men and only two holidays a year. The holidays were July 4th and Christmas Day, and on these days the employees were not paid.   **Footnote 8**

The Bessemer at Maryland Steel – 1895

The first Bessemer steel ever made in Maryland was produced on August 1, 1891 at Sparrows Point. The Bessemer started with two 18-ton converters with an estimated capacity of 20,000 to 25,000 tons of ingots per month. A third converter was added in 1902 and in 1916, a fourth one was installed. This brought the total Bessemer steelmaking capacity at that time up to approximately 45,000 tons per month. Photo courtesy of Baltimore Museum of Industry.

Bessemer

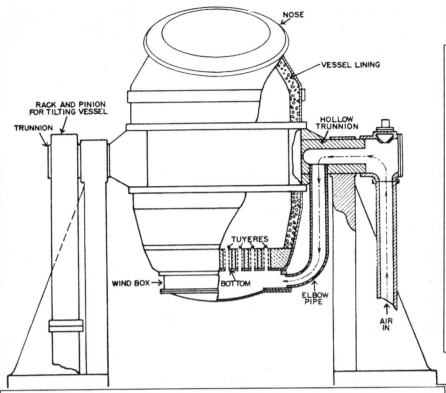

The cylindrically shaped **vessel**, at left, consisted of a steel shell of riveted or welded construction, and was supported on two **trunnions** which allowed it to be rotated. One of these trunnions was hollow, through which the blast is passed by a pipe called the **gooseneck** or **elbow pipe**, to the **wind-box** at the bottom of the vessel. A **pinion** was fastened to the other trunnion and engaged an electrically operated **rack** to tip the converter. The **bottom,** which was detachable, was pierced with 28 **tuyeres** through which the air blast passed from the wind-box into the metal bath.

The diagram above illustrates the details of construction that permit air to enter the converter through a hollow **trunnion**, so that the vessel can be turned down without interrupting the flow of air.

Footnote 9

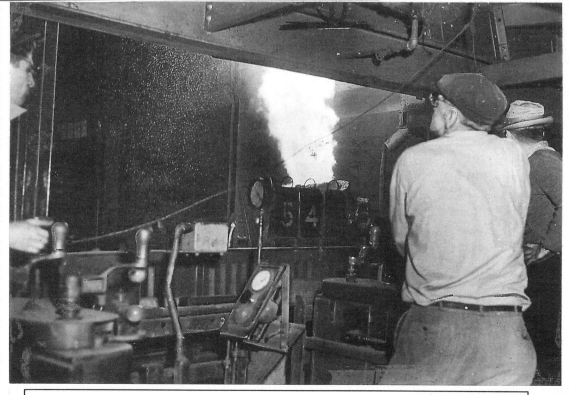

A Bessemer Converter blows at Sparrows Point on February 15, 1953.

Bessemer - 1917

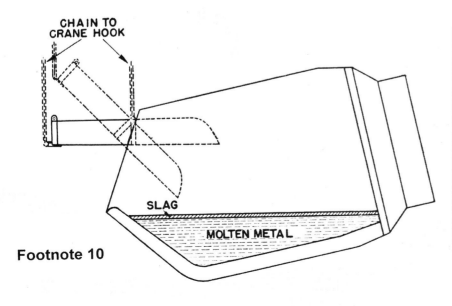

CHAIN TO
CRANE HOOK

SLAG

MOLTEN METAL

Footnote 10

The diagram at left illustrates the use of a crane operated chute for making additions of solid materials to a Bessemer Converter. The photo above shows the Bessemer Converters approximately one year after Bethlehem Steel acquired the Mill at Sparrows Point. Photo dated February 7, 1917, courtesy of Dundalk Patapsco-Neck Historical Society.

Bessemer Blow

A **Bessemer Converter** blows on December 11, 1951. These blows were always spectacular to witness. As technology improved, the Bessemer process was surpassed. **No. 4 Open Hearth** began operation in 1957. Shortly thereafter, **on February 9, 1958, the last heat was tapped** from the Bessemer at 9:02 p.m.

In 1917, work began on two new blast furnaces. When completed, **"E" and "F" furnaces** would sit due east and in line with the other four furnaces built by Maryland Steel. These furnaces were larger, having a 22-foot **bosh** and 17-foot **hearth**. Note in the far center distance, the "B" Street Clubhouse located between 4th and 5th Streets.

BETHLEHEM STEEL CO.
MARYLAND STEEL PLANT
SPARROWS POINT, MD.

8134. 8-23-17   BLAST FURNACE NO. 5

Prior to Bethlehem Steel purchasing the steelworks at Sparrows Point, the **Maryland Steel Company's primary product was rails. Bethlehem's plan was an immediate diversification of products.** By September 1916, appropriations were authorized for the following: four additional blast furnaces, four batteries of Koppers ovens, extension and additions to the ore unloading dock and discharge yard, thirteen gas-driven blowing engines, eight gas and electric generators, three 200-ton tilting open hearth furnaces, three 25-ton Bessemer converters, a 40-inch Blooming Mill combined with a 24-inch Billet and an 18-inch Continuous Bar Mill, one 110-inch Sheared Plate Mill, one 60-inch Universal Plate Mill, one 166-inch Sheared Plate Mill (never completed), one 36-inch Slabbing Mill (never completed). By the end of 1917, 4,000 workmen had been added to the payroll and another 3,500 were added early in 1918 due to this rapid expansion program. **Footnote 11**

BETHLEHEM STEEL CO.
MARYLAND STEEL PLANT
SPARROWS POINT, MD.

8026. 8-8-17   UNIVERSAL PLATE MILL

Shown at left is the excavation for the foundation of the **60-inch Plate Mill.** It would not be ready for operation until April 1920. It was located on the east side, and immediately adjacent to the Sheared Mill. Both mills were served with hot slabs and with the same transfer system from the **40-inch Blooming Mill.** Both photos courtesy of Dundalk Patapsco-Neck Historical Society.

At left: the ore dock is under construction on June 13, 1917. A 30 foot channel was dug to high pier and a turnaround basin was built for ore steamers.

Shortly after Bethlehem Steel **purchased the steelworks at Sparrows Point on February 16, 1916**, the landscape underwent a tremendous transformation. Steel pilings were rammed 2,367 feet beyond the southern shoreline and completely filled in with earth, stone, slag, and gravel. The Sparrows Point peninsula had grown 100 acres larger. Both photos on this page are courtesy of the Dundalk Patapsco-Neck Historical Society.

On the farthest tip of the peninsula, a coal handling plant was installed on a pier extending westward into the harbor. Adjacent to the coal handling plant was a 240 battery coke oven works, built by Koppers Company. All of the coal for the coke ovens was hauled by barge from the B&O and Western Maryland Railway wharves in Baltimore as well as from Norfolk, Virginia.

Footnote 12

The Ore Basin – 1925

At left is the **ore basin** built by Bethlehem Steel in 1917 as part of the massive plant expansion program. The channel to the basin was dug to 30 feet and extended to high pier. In the distance, you can see "E" and "F" blast furnaces, which were completed in 1920.

Below, the S.S. Cubore is docked at the ore basin at Sparrows Point, circa 1925. The **S.S. Cubore (Hull #160) was the first ship delivered by the Bethlehem Steel Shipyard** after they purchased the steelworks from the Maryland Steel Company. The ore carrier was christened by Mrs. Rana Schwab, wife of Charles M. Schwab, Chairman of the Board of Bethlehem Steel.

Blast Furnaces "E" and "F" - 1920

When Bethlehem Steel acquired the Maryland Steel Company on February 16, 1916, they immediately **embarked on a program of development and expansion**. One of these projects was to add two new blast furnaces. They were located due east and in line with the other four existing furnaces. These two new additions would become **"E" and "F" Blast Furnaces**. They were larger than the other four, having a 22-foot bosh and a 17-foot hearth. The first iron from **"E" Furnace was tapped on March 22, 1920 and "F" Furnace had its first cast on July 7th of the same year.** The addition of these two furnaces brought the total pig iron capacity up to 75,000 gross tons per month. Shown above are "E" and "F" Blast Furnaces looking south in 1921 shortly after they were blown in. The two-story brick building in the right foreground (in front of the water tower and gas holder) was the Blast Furnace Office. It was still used in that capacity into the late 1950s. The top floor was used as a locker room for salaried foreman. Blast furnace mechanical and blast furnace superintendent offices were on the ground floor. Photograph courtesy of Dundalk Patapsco-Neck Historical Society.   **Footnote 13**

Blast Furnace Row, Circa 1925

On the left side of this photograph are Blast Furnaces "A", "B", "C", and "D". The view is looking east from the coke works. All four furnaces had been rebuilt with inclined skips between 1911 and 1915. Changes had been made to the stoves on "A" and "B" Furnace **in anticipation of the modernization planned for 1928 and 1929**. Three of the stoves for "A" Furnace have been enlarged and one had been upgraded for "B" Furnace. The two tall structures in the center photograph are coke oven stacks. Barely visible to the right of these stacks is the stack for "E" and "F" Blast Furnace stoves. The large structure on the right is a coal bin with a conveyor. In the right foreground are the coke oven works. Photo courtesy of Dundalk Patapsco Neck Historical Society.   **Footnote 14**

Rebuild of "A" Furnace – February 21, 1928

All of the rebuilds on "A", "B", "C", and "D" furnaces took place on the original sites of the furnaces constructed between 1889 and 1893. All four furnaces were also rebuilt between 1911 and 1915. At left, the framing for the new **casthouse** has begun to take shape. At the base of the furnace stack is the **bustle pipe**, which was used to distribute hot blast around the base of the furnace. The holes visible near the top of the furnace stack are for **cooling plates**. At right is the **new hoist incline**. The shed-like structure at lower right is the **hoist house**. The new furnace had a **hearth diameter** of 25 feet, 6 inches and it was 11 feet, 11 inches high. The **bosh** had a diameter of 28 feet, 9 inches. The height from the tap hole to the furnace ring was 99 feet, 8 inches. The furnace had 16 **tuyeres**. Photo dated February 1, 1928, courtesy of Dundalk Patapsco-Neck Historical Society.

Rebuild of "A" Furnace Nears Completion
March 6, 1928

A view of "A" Furnace looking east. The new furnace was built from the hearth up, including a new stack, filling equipment, top, and enlarged stoves. **The rebuild of "A" Furnace was completed in March 1928**. "B" Furnace would follow with a complete rebuild in March 1929. The photo is dated March 6, 1928 and was very near the completion of the rebuild of "A" Furnace. Note "C" and "D" Furnace stack is visible at far right. Photo courtesy of Dundalk Patapsco-Neck Historical Society.

New Tin Mill Begins To Take Shape - 1916

Above: The foundation for the new Tin Mill began to take shape during the summer of 1916.

Below: **The original 12 Hot Mills** began to take shape in June 1917. A single shaft, with a power wheel at its center, drove six mills shown just to the left of the truck. **Reheating furnaces** are at far left. These mills were marked "National Roll & Foundry Co., Avonmere, PA." Photos courtesy of Dundalk Patapsco-Neck Historical Society.

BETHLEHEM STEEL CO.
SHEET & TIN PLATE PLANT
SPARROWS POINT, MD.

Bethlehem Steel Acquires the Baltimore
Sheet and Tin Plate Company – April 1, 1916

On April 1, 1916, Bethlehem Steel acquired the property, rights and goodwill of the **Baltimore Sheet and Tin Plate Company**. This company had been financed locally and was headed by J.E. Aldred of New York. The company had been organized for the manufacture of tin plate and sheets to serve the Baltimore area. They had acquired a tract of land in the southeastern section of Baltimore City and had contracted for buildings and equipment to be erected. Bethlehem at once moved the site of the proposed plant to Sparrows Point. It would be near a source of sheet bar from their own mills and they would also have the maximum advantage of the tidewater location for coastwise and export shipments. The Baltimore area was home to large packing and manufacturing interests in the city, and canning operations throughout Maryland. It annually consumed approximately 4 million base boxes of tin plate. The Sparrows Point site for a tin mill was a prime location to be a supplier of this canning industry.

The first unit authorized was for 12 Hot Mills accompanied by Pickling, Annealing, Cold Rolling, and Tinning facilities. This unit began operating on July 26, 1917 and had an annual capacity of one million base boxes. As the Bar Mills had not yet been completed, sheet bar was purchased from Corrigan, McKinney & Company, Cambria Steel Company, and from Bethlehem. **An additional unit of 12 hot mills was authorized in 1919** and by September 1920, they were in operation, bringing the total output up to 2 million base boxes annually. **A third unit of 12 mills was authorized in June 1924** and six of these mills were ready by January 1925. The other six mills with the necessary finishing facilities were in operation by April 1, 1925. That gave the operation a total annual capacity of 3 million base boxes. Photo courtesy of Dundalk Patapsco-Neck Historical Society. **Footnote 15**

Hot and Cold Tin Mills
Circa 1920

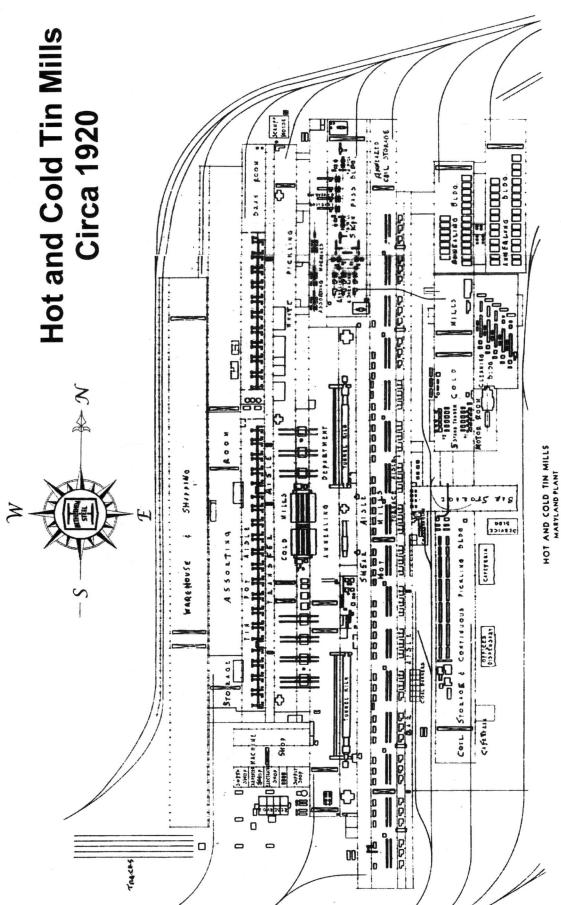

HOT AND COLD TIN MILLS
MARYLAND PLANT

"My grandfather and his twin brother started their steel working career at Monongahela Steel in Morgantown, West Virginia, then going to Wheeling Steel in Wheeling, West Virginia. They then went to US Steel in Pittsburgh, PA. As they followed the then-booming steel industry, they came to Bethlehem Steel in Sparrows Point in the early 1920's. My grandfather, Roy White, contacted his brother, Ray, about the prospects of a job at the Bethlehem Steel Sparrows Point plant. He was informed that if he could bring a crew, he had a job. He brought a crew and he was the **Roller-Operator**. Both men stayed in the Hot Mill until it was shut down due to automation in the mid- to late-1930's. This brought job changes for both men. My grandfather became a **Battery Repairman** in the 42-Inch Mill. My uncle Ray became a **Battery Changer** in the 42-Inch Warehouse. These batteries were used in the tractors transporting plated coils and sheared-to-size packages of tin plate to load trucks and rail cars." ~ Roy E. Shepherd, 56-Inch Cold Mill Crane Operator, 1956 - 1995

Old Hot Mill Operation 1934

At left is a view of an **old Hot Mill** in operation. The man in front is the **catcher**. He is shown using **tongs** to grasp the sheet of hot metal and pass it back over the rolls to the **roller**. The sheet would be passed back and forth through the rolls until thin enough to be used to make **tin plate**.

At right is shown the **finishing end** of the Cold Sheet Rolling Mills. Note the stacked squares of finished sheets behind the workers. Photo courtesy of Dundalk Patapsco-Neck Historical Society. Photo dated circa 1934.

Tin Mill Memories

"On April 6, 1917, the United States declared war on Germany. The **Tin Mill plant at Sparrows Point was started on July 26, 1917**, no doubt due to the increased demand for canned food products created by World War I.

"**Tin plate** is made by producing a sheet of steel 14 inches by 20 inches in size and about 10 thousandths of an inch thick – suitable to be covered with a thin coating of pure tin. It required the effort of a number of individual rolling mills using large steel rolls with an adjacent furnace to heat the steel.

"**Each mill required a crew of six men** under the responsibility of a **master Roller**, who trained his group for their specialized duties. There were **48 mills in use** at the Sparrows Point plant. The crew members were designated as follows: a **Roller**, who was in charge of the group; **a Heater; a Rougher; a Catcher; a Screw Boy; and a Doubler.**

"The process was physically demanding for the workers. Operations began with a sheet bar of low carbon steel, 8 inches wide, 30 inches long, and about 3/8ths to 5/8ths inches thick. After being heated to a cherry-red rolling temperature and placed on the rolling stand by the Heater, a Rougher would grab the bar with his tongs and inserts it in between the turning rolls. As the bar emerged on the other side, it is grasped by a Catcher with tongs. The Rougher then passes a second bar into the mill and gives the first bar a second pass. In the meantime, a Screw Boy twists a screw mechanism on the mill to bring the rolls closer together. The steel bars are reheated again and again as they are passed through the rolls over and over getting wider and wider, and a little thinner each pass as the Screw Boy brings the rolls closer and closer together. The Doubler, using a special device, folds the pack of thinning sheets and starts passing them back and forth through the rolls again and again until they reach the desired measurement determined by the Roller in charge of the mill. After cooling, the sheets were placed on the floor and pried apart for further processing, such as trimming, annealing, and repassing them through a separate set of cold mills to flatten each sheet." ~C.H. Echols, worked at Sparrows Point in the 1930s and early 1940s.

BETHLEHEM STEEL COMPANY

Tin Mill Plant

Operating Rules & Regulations for Hot Mill Department .

January 10, 1936.

1. Safety: This is a most vital problem in connection with our
    rolling operations. An employee must observe and practice
    Safety along with his line of duties. Also, caution his
    fellow workman, should said workman be guilty of any
    infraction of SAFETY FIRST.

    Employees must not cross spindles; use bridges for
    this crossing. Do not grease gloved hands on spindle bearings
    Also, all "horse play" must cease, such as wrestling, throwing
    of articles, etc. Also, keep out of grease pits when mill is
    in operation, and do not tamp grease on spindle bearings with
    foot. Be on the look-out when overhead cranes travel with
    loads.

    A safe workman is an asset to himself, family and the
    corporation for which he works. An unsafe workman is a
    liability to everyone. Therefore, be one of the SAFETY
    FIRST EMPLOYEES.

    In case of accident, employee must notify foreman.

2. Quality: This item is the Keystone for a continuous operation,
    in this age of unparalleled competition for business.
    Satisfied customers mean repeat business and work for our
    employees. Dissatisfied customers mean loss of their
    business and idle mills.

    Therefore, to produce quality, Cleanliness is most
    essential. See that mill standings, both rollers and
    catchers sides of mill, are clean and free of all dirt,
    grease, etc. Each roller should be a leader of his
    respective crew to attain this Cleanliness requisite;
    because dirt and grease strewn over the product, or the
    product dragged over grease and dirt, means Second Quality
    Plate, which customers do not care to take.

3. Sanitation: Employees have, in the past, complained about foul
    smells, due to decomposed waste food matter. The mills are
    equipped with "Garbage Cans", and it is up to each individual
    employee to use same for the deposit of all waste food, paper,
    etc. By adopting this practice of depositing all waste food,
    paper, etc., our mill will be free of foul odors, and will be
    orderly and clean. The mill is your home while working;
    then, let us make it home-like.

4. Limit: On warm up turns, number of pairs to roll are limited,
    and shall be as follows:

Turn No.	Small Mills	Big Mills
First Turn	250 Pairs	240 Pairs
Second "	260 "	250 "
Third "	280 "	260 "

5. Heating: A "Flame" must be visible on both Sheet and Pair
    Furnaces at all times to eliminate oxidization and scaling
    of product. Sheet Furnace Heaters positively must not
    edge packs.

6. Steam on Rolls: Rollers must see to it that the steam blower is
    functioning at all times. Also the scale blower. Steam
    should always be blowing on the rolls, as long as they are
    revolving. Steam is most essential for the producing of
    quality product.

7. Screw Pressure: Application of screw pressure is a vital part
    of the rolling product. Results of excessive pressure are:
    Broken Rolls, Rough Rolls, and Strains in packs. Maximum
    draft must not exceed 30% reduction.

(Operating Rules, continued)

8. <u>Rough Rolls:</u> If roughness has developed on rolls, immediate steps must be taken by the roller to correct same; by immediately polishing the rolls, using preferably the rotating method instead of the straight method; adjusting the running water on the roll necks, and working the mill at a retarded or longer time on parts; thereby giving the rolls a chance to go back to their normal condition.

9. <u>Brushing of Bars:</u> The Pairs must be clean of scale or oxide. Both bars must be brushed clean, and to be assured of clean pairs, bottom bar should be turned over by the Rougher.

10. <u>Pair Heaters:</u> Should use only one door of furnace when pulling pairs; keeping the other door shut at all times, thereby reducing oxidizing of furnace and pairs materially.

11. <u>Rollers and Pair Heaters:</u> Must keep accurate account of the number of pairs to a heat; and all pairs must be reported that have gone through the rolls, regardless of spoilage between the Break Downs, or Roughs, and Finishing Part.

12. <u>Order Records:</u> It shall be the duty of each Roller to keep a permanent record of the orders he has rolled on his respective mill for future reference. The Foreman will call on him some time, perhaps in reference to off quality or off gauge, and Roller should possess records for verification, as orders of large quantities are rolled on numerous mills.

13. <u>Packs on Standing:</u> Rollers, when finishing, must not allow accumulations of packs on standing. A pack on standing must be picked up and finished immediately after the pack he is working with is finished.
    This rule must be rigidly observed and carried out.

14. <u>Aligning Mills:</u> Rollers, under no consideration, are allowed to place <u>Liners</u> in their respective mills. We have mill-wrights for this work.

15. <u>Fore Plate:</u> Rollers must quit the practice of raising cross bar under the fore-plate.
    This rule must be observed.

16. <u>Tongs:</u> On the last turn of each week's operations, Rollers must see to it that four (4) pairs of Tongs are deposited in the Hot Mill Foremen's office.

17. <u>Pairs per Heat:</u> When packs are finished in Eights, the following limit of pairs per heat shall be, and must be the practice:

32 1/2" and wider	- 18 pairs per heat	
28" to 32 1/4"	- 22 " " "	
Under 28"	- 24 " " "	
Tagger Iron	- 24 " " "	
Matched Iron:		
35" and wider	- 24 " " "	
Under 35"	- 27 " " "	

    18 Pairs shall constitute a heat for Big Mills on 1st, 2nd, and 3rd turns of the week, or warming up turns, and 20 Pairs for Small Mills.

18. <u>Finish Length of Packs:</u> In order to obtain accurate gauge thickness and weight for our customers orders; Rollers must roll packs to the specified length, with the following allowances for Scrap and Curl Ends:-

Finished in Eights

Gauge		Lengths			Scrap & Curl
112# & lighter		Lengths 66" & shorter		5 Inches for Scrap &
" "		" 67" to 72" long		5 1/2" " " Curl.
" "		" 73" to 80" "		6 " " " "
118# to 123#		" 54" & shorter		5 " " " "
" "		" 55" to 66"		5 1/2" " " "
124# to 135#		" 44" & shorter		5 " " " "
" "		" 44" to 54"		5 1/2" " " "
" "		" 55" to 65"		5 3/4" " " "
136# to 155#		" 44" & shorter		5 1/4" " " "
" "		" 45" to 54"		5 1/2" " " "
" . "		." 55" to 65"		5 3/4" " " "

Finished in Sixes

26 Ga. to 28 Ga.	Lengths 70" & shorter	5 " " " "
" "	" 71" to 80"	5 1/2" " " "
" "	" 81" to 96"	6 " " " "

Finished in Fours

22 Ga. to 25 Ga.	Lengths 70" & shorter	4 1/2" " " "
" "	" 71" to 80"	5 " " " "
" "	" 81" to 96"	5 1/2" " " "

Finished in Twos

21 Ga. & heavier	Lengths 70" & shorter	4 " " " "
" "	" 71" to 80"	4 1/2" " " "
" "	" 81" to 96" .	5 " " " "

Above practices must be applied by the Rollers in order to assure proper Gauges and Base Weights; as steel ordered for specifications is figured by the Order Department to the above enumerated tolerances. Therefore, all packs must be measured.

19. Doublers: To assure proper Gauges for our customers doubling plays an important part. Therefore, you must avoid excessive cutting of packs, but should be sure to see that packs are sheared clean with minimum scrap loss to avoid Crescents.

20. Pinchers and Jumpers: Rollers must shear such packs, so that said packs may readily be identified by Shearmen; thereby helping to avoid such product from being processed and reaching our Cold Roll Department, and thereby eliminating the marking of Cold Roll Department rolls, and spoiling other Prime Product.

21. Furnace Temperatures: Sheet and Pair Furnaces should not be in excess of 1500 Deg. Fahrenheit. Maintenance of said mentioned temperature will give results that will be helpful to producing Quality Product.

22. Roughers: Must exercise extreme care in the entering of bars on Break Downs, as losses from scraps and off gauge materials are the results of crooked entering of bars. Five passes shall be given to Roughs, unless permission changing same shall have been authorized by Foreman.

23. Screw Boys: Must exercise extreme care in the manipulation of screws on Break Downs, thereby aiding the Rougher and Crew in the elimination of unnecessary scrap losses and off gauge products.

24. <u>Catchers and Screw Boys:</u> Must see that necks of hot mill rolls are, at all times, properly lubricated. Positively no pit grease must be placed in the necks or grease pots. Refined grease from the grease house, melted in your mill grease pots, is the only grease that is allowed to be used.
Use rod provided for, and not Curl Ends, for cleaning grease accumulations under rolls.

25. <u>Single Boys:</u> Must see to it that every sheet is opened all the way to the Curl End in the Fours, thereby eliminating the producing of Jumpers.

26. <u>Rolling of Fours:</u> Standard rule requires that all "Fours" shall have 3 passes. No deviation to said rule, unless authorized by Foreman.

PENALTIES

<u>Draft or Screw Pressure</u> in excess of 30%. Not less than one (1) day lay-off.

<u>Overcharging of Pairs</u> in excess of the maximum number of pairs per heat rule. 1st offense, one (1) day lay-off for Roller and Pair Heater.

Violations of any of the other rules enumerated in this set-up will be dealt with as the Supervision may see fit and just. Therefore, it is up to each employee to see that he does not violate any of these established rules.

CONCLUSION: The rules and regulations herein incorporated must be carried out; and it shall be the duty and responsibility of all Rollers to see that the members of their respective crews perform their individual portion of these said rules and regulations.

Should a member of the crew willfully and deliberately refuse to comply with these rules and regulations; then, the only recourse left will be the removal of such an employee from the service of the Company.

Co-operation and team work on the part of every employee will result in mutual benefits both to himself, as well as to the Company. High Quality standards of Products necessitates these Rules and Regulations.

Prior to the installation of the **56-Inch Hot Strip Mill in 1937**, sheet and tin products were rolled on single-stand sheet and tin plate hot mills, as shown in the photograph at left. Mills of this type were called **"jobbing mills"** and were used to roll heavy gauge sheets. **"Pack" or "finishing" mills** were used for light gauge sheets and tin plate. In the original manual process of hot rolling, sheet bars were used to produce sheets. Packs made up of multiple thicknesses of steel first were prepared by **"breaking down"** or cross-rolling sheet bars cut to the correct length to produce the width desired. The bars were then passed through the rolling mill repeatedly in pairs, one bar closely following the other through the rolls of a **2-high or 3-high Roughing Mill**. A number of final passes with the bars, placed one on top of the other, to form a pack for finish rolling. For light gauges, the pack was usually doubled or folded over to finish rolling.

Workers visually inspect galvanized sheets. Note the revolving mechanical device for distributing individual sheets to the two workers. Both photos courtesy of Rich Glenn, dated circa 1935.

Electrolytic Cleaning
Five electrolytic cleaning lines, designed for a maximum strip width of 42 inches, served to remove palm oil from the strip after cold rolling. Coils were brought to the cleaning lines by ram-type 12,000-lb. tractors, and placed on a feed reel. A strip welder served to tie the coils into a continuous feed, which passed first through a washer 10 feet long and 5 feet by 5 inches wide at speeds ranging from 300 to 1,000 feet per minute and onto an electrolytic cleaning tank 63 feet long and 5 feet wide and 2 feet 6 inches deep. The strip passed through a scrubbing unit and onto a rinse tank which was automatically held at 200 to 210 degrees Fahrenheit, followed by an air jet dryer. 63

The Assorting Room

Above: an early photograph showing women inspecting tin plate in the **Assorting Room**. These women were known as **Tin Floppers**. Management insisted that only women could perform this task because men were considered too "heavy handed." The only men permitted in the Assorting Room were the **Reckoners**, who counted out **112 sheets of inspected tin plate** and packaged them for shipment. Photo courtesy of Dundalk Patapsco-Neck Historical Society, circa 1920.

Old Hot Mill Box Anneal

After **the first 12 Tin Mills** were successfully operating in July 1917, the building of **Sheet and Jobbing Mills** was authorized. The sheet unit consisted of eight hot mills with the necessary cold rolling and annealing facilities. Shown above is an early version of the **Box Anneal process**. A furnace was placed over the stacked sheets of steel and put through a series of heating and cooling cycles to give the steel the desired temperature. Box annealing or **batch annealing**, was still utilized at Sparrows Point into the 1990s. This process was used for **softer tempers** and the continuous annealing lines were used for **harder tempers**. Photo courtesy of Rich Glenn, dated 1938.

56-INCH HOT STRIP MILL AND SHEET MILLS
MARYLAND PLANT
BETHLEHEM STEEL COMPANY
SPARROWS POINT, MARYLAND
1938

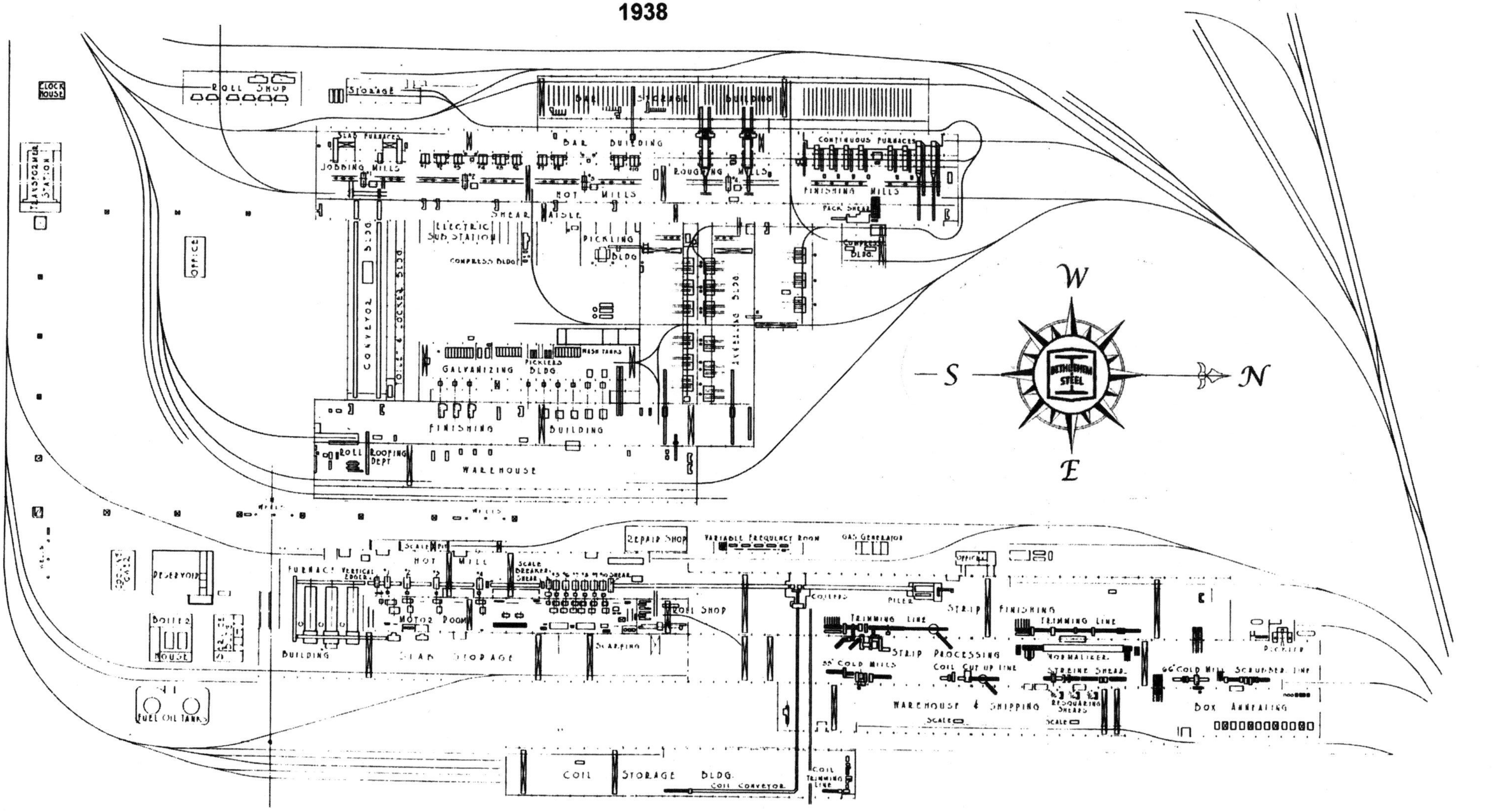

The above diagram shows the 56-Inch Hot Strip Mill layout shortly after it came on-line in 1937. The top portion of the diagram shows the old Hot Dip Mills that it replaced. Diagram courtesy of Rich Glenn.

ROD AND WIRE MILL DEPARTMENT

GENERAL   (Information compiled as of October 1960)

Operating personnel—1,800
Acreage—50
Annual rated capacity—600,000 tons

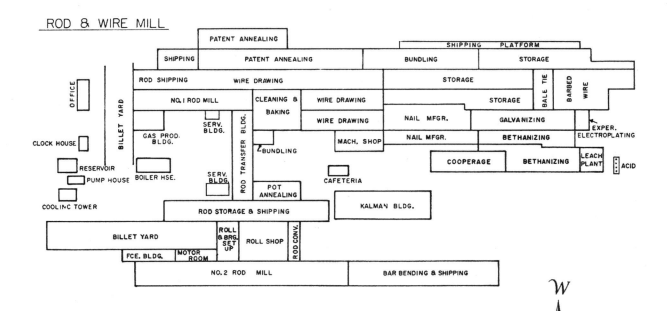

ROD & WIRE MILL

NO. 1 ROD MILL

First steel rolled in 1926
3 strand continuous mill
17 two high stands
Finishing speed—3,800 ft./min.
Capacity 25,000 tons per month (400 lb. coils)

Furnace

Size—25' x 30'
Capacity—75,000,000 BTU per hour
Heating rate—35 tons per hour

No. 1 Mill Data Chart

Stand No.	New Roll Dia.-IN.	Motor RPM	HP	Gear Ratio Motor:Roll	Pinion Dia.-IN.
0	$12\frac{7}{8}$	375	4,000	23:1	$12\frac{7}{8}$
1	$13\frac{3}{4}$			18:1	$13\frac{1}{4}$
2	$13\frac{1}{2}$			10:1	$13\frac{1}{4}$
3	$12\frac{1}{8}$			7:1	12
4	$12\frac{11}{16}$			5:1	12
5	$12\frac{7}{8}$			3.5:1	$13\frac{1}{4}$
6	$13\frac{1}{16}$			2.5:1	$12\frac{7}{8}$
7	$10\frac{3}{8}$	NOTE:		1.5:1	$10\frac{3}{8}$
8	$10\frac{5}{8}$	One motor		1:1	$10\frac{3}{8}$
9	$10\frac{13}{16}$	drives entire		0.7:1	$10\frac{3}{8}$
10	$10\frac{13}{16}$	mill.		0.6:1	$10\frac{3}{8}$
11	$11\frac{1}{4}$			0.5:1	$10\frac{3}{4}$
12	$11\frac{1}{4}$			0.4:1	$10\frac{3}{4}$
13	$11\frac{9}{16}$			0.3:1	$11\frac{1}{4}$
14	$11\frac{11}{16}$			0.3:1	$11\frac{1}{2}$
15	$11\frac{7}{8}$			0.3:1	12
16	$12\frac{1}{4}$			0.3:1	12

NO. 2 ROD MILL

First steel rolled in 1937
4 strand continuous mill
27 two high stands
Finishing speed—4,000 ft./min.
Capacity—32,000 tons per month

Furnace

Size—25′ x 30′
Capacity—125,000,000 BTU per hour
Heating rate—50 tons per hour

No. 2 Mill Data Chart

Stand No.	New Roll Dia.-IN.	Motor RPM	HP	Gear Ratio Motor:Roll	Pinion Dia.-IN.
0	16½	250-750	500	30:1	16
1	17	250-750	500	24:1	16
2	17½	250-750	300	18:1	16
3	16⅞	150-450	1,500	7:1	16
4	16⅝	150-450	1,500	5:1	16
5	16⅜	150-450	1,500	3:1	16
6	14⅝	150-450	1,500	2:1	14
7	14⅝	150-450	1,500	2:1	14
8	14⅝	150-450	1,500	1:1	14
9	12⅝	300-900	700	3:1	12½
10	13	300-900	700	2:1	12½
11	13¼	300-900	700	2:1	13
12	13⅝	300-900	700	1:1	13
13	12⅛	225-625	700	1:1	11¼
14	12⅛	300-625	700	1:1	11¼
2-15	10¹⁄₁₆	500-750	1,250	1:1	10
2-16	10⅛	500-750	1,250	0.8:1	10
2-17	10⁷⁄₁₆	500-750	1,250	0.7:1	10¼
2-18	10⁹⁄₁₆	500-750	1,250	0.6:1	10½
2-19	10⅞	500-750	1,250	0.5:1	10¾
2-20	10¹⁵⁄₁₆	500-700	1,250	0.4:1	10¾

COLD WORKING OPERATIONS

Bar Shop

8,000 tons per month capacity

Cleaning and Coating

35,000 tons per month capacity
3 acid cleaning units

Wire Drawing

33,000 tons per month capacity
64 single block and double deck machines
60 continuous machines

Nail Mill

5,000 tons per month capacity
131 nail machines
4 staple machines

Regular Galvanizing Wire

2,000 tons per month capacity

Double Galvanizing Wire

300 tons per month capacity

Bethanizing

4,500 tons per month capacity
10 electro-zinc-plating cells

Bale Ties

1,400 tons per month capacity
15 machines

Barbed Wire

600 tons per month capacity
6 machines

Straightened and Cut

3,000 tons per month capacity
21 machines

Recoiling

900 tons per month capacity
6 machines

Strand and Cable

1,800 tons per month capacity
5 tubular stranders
1 snake strander

HEAT TREATING OPERATIONS

Air Patenting

10,000 tons per month capacity
4 — 50′ furnaces

Double Lead Patenting

600 tons per month capacity

Pot Annealing and Spheroidizing

4,500 tons per month capacity
6 portable furnaces
16 bases

Lead Annealing

600 tons per month capacity

Above: The **No. 2 Rod Mill** was controlled from the **operating pulpit**, where there was a **desk board** with switches for controlling armature and field circuits of the generators, mill motors, and the DC driver motor of the variable frequency M.G. set. There were ammeters for the generators and mill motors, voltmeters for the generators, and tachometers for all mill motors and for the variable frequency set. The desk also included lever operated vernier field rheostats for the last five motors.

Below: The **discharge end** of the No. 2 Rod Mill shows the **heating furnace and the nine roughing stands**. The capacity of this mill, depending on the size of product, was from 20 to 50 tons per hour. No. 1 Stand in the mill was a control cabinet with meters and control switches for operating the motor-driven coarse and vernier field rheostat, to give individual speed control of the first three main motors. The pulpit operator controlled the speed of these three motors as a group, thereby controlling the loop formed between stands #8 and #9. Photos circa 1938, courtesy of Rich Glenn.   **Footnote 16**

Rod Mill

Billets were transported from power operated skids to the heating furnace charging conveyor. Both photographs circa 1938, courtesy of Rich Glenn.

Billets of 30-foot length were heated in a single continuous furnace, side charged, and discharged. Billets were moved through the furnace by a double crank-type pusher, and a pinch roll-type push-out discharged them into the mill. The furnace had a hearth 32 feet wide by 50 feet long and was rated at 50 gross tons of 2 ¼ inch square billets per hour. The roof had a suspended arch and the entire furnace was well-insulated and encased in steel. A 2-pass recuperator served to pre-heat air used for combustion to temperatures of 600 to 700 degrees Fahrenheit. Thirteen gas burners and 12 oil burners were spaced across the width of the furnace, which was entirely over-fired. The fuel oil was supplied through the roof with mechanical atomizers.

Footnote 17

Above: This **double cooling bed and run-out table** was auxiliary equipment in the **No. 2 Rod Mill**. In the background is shown the **Rod Coil Conveyor and hook carrier**. The run-out table and cooling bed was 360 feet in length. Below: Heat treating equipment for the No. 2 Rod Mill included four radiant tube-type wire annealing covers using re-circulating fans. Both photos circa 1938, courtesy of Rich Glenn.

Following the nine stands in the roughing train are four intermediate roughing stands and two looping stands. Following these are the six finishing stands.

Muffle conveyors in the Wire Mill. Photos circa 1938, courtesy of Rich Glenn.

THE DIFFERENCE BETWEEN **NIGHT** AND **DAY**

The Nail Mill

The Nail Mill was part of the Rod and Wire Department. Wire that was drawn at the Rod and Wire Mills was used to produce many varieties of nails on machines like the one shown above at the plant's Nail Mill. In 1960, the Nail Mill produced 5,000 tons of nails per month. It had three nail machines and four staple machines. Photo courtesy of Bill Goodman.

BE YOUR BROTHER'S KEEPER

Stop ACCIDENTS

PIPE MILL DEPARTMENT

GENERAL   (Information compiled as of October 1960)

Operating personnel—1,300
Acreage—57
Annual rated capacity—630,000 tons

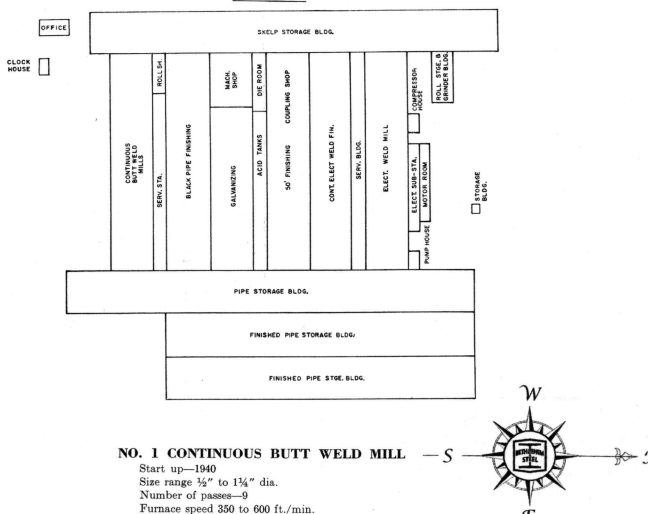

PIPE MILL

NO. 1 CONTINUOUS BUTT WELD MILL

Start up—1940
Size range ½″ to 1¼″ dia.
Number of passes—9
Furnace speed 350 to 600 ft./min.
Capacity 11,500 tons per month

Furnace

Size—2′-3″ x 163′
Maximum cu. ft. gas consumed per hour—200,000
Furnace temperature—entry 1800°F
                exit 2650°F
Number of burners—296
Total conveyor length—335′
Oil system—forced feed type

Butt Weld Mill Data

Passes	Motor RPM	HP	Gear Ratio	Roll Shaft Dia.—IN.	New Roll Dia.—IN.
1 Forming	400-1,200	125*	1.37:1	2½	8 1/16
1 Welding	400-1,200	125*	1:1	2½	8 7/16
4 Sizing	400-1,200	125*	1:1	2½	8 13/16 to 9¾
3 Descaler	400-1,600	50	11.40:1	5	16
*Forming, welding, sizing and hot saw share a common drive.					

NO. 2 CONTINUOUS BUTT WELD MILL

Start up—1941

Size range—1½" to 4" dia.

Number passes—9

Furnace speed 120 to 360 ft./min.

Capacity—21,500 tons per month

Furnace

Size—2'-4" x 170'

Maximum cu. ft. gas consumed per hour—265,000

Furnace temperature—entry 1800°F

exit 2650°F

Number burners—356

Total conveyor length—230'

Oil system—forced feed type

Butt Weld Mill Data

Passes	Motor RPM	HP	Gear Ratio	Roll Shaft Dia.—IN.	New Roll Dia.—IN.
1 Forming	400-1,600	10	14.4:1	4½	14
1 Welding	400-1,600	20	12.5:1	4½	14
4 Sizing	1,150-1,700	20	12.5:1	4½	14
3 Descaler	400-1,600	30	2.26:1	7¼	18
Hot Saw Carriage	600-1,500	20	7:1		

ELECTRIC WELD MILL

Start up—1957

Production size range 4½" to 16" dia.

Welder

4400 KVA

84 cycle

275,000 ampere peaks

Number of stands—17

Capacity—20,000 tons per month

Speeds—120 ft./min. for .152 gauge to 57.7 ft./min. for .500 gauge

Total conveyor length—580'

Oil system—forced feed type

Electric Weld Mill Data

Stands	Motor RPM	HP	Gear Ratio	Max. Roll Shaft Dia. IN.
Edge Trimmer	1,150-1,500	150	43.5:1	
* Shotblast	1,770	30		
**7 Forming	1,150-1,500	75	50.8:1	10
4 Fin Pass	1,150-1,500	75	50.8:1	10
3 Pull Out	1,150-1,500	75	50.8:1	10
3 Sizing	1,150-1,500	200	27.1:1	10
*** Flying Cut-off	900	30		

*4—30 HP motors in this unit driving 4 impellers

**4 driven stands plus 3 idler stands

***30 HP motor driven oil pump

FINISHING EQUIPMENT

Butt Weld Finishing Equipment

Black Floor

1 Large straightener	1½″ to 4″
3 Small straighteners	½″ to 1½″
*1 Large plain ending machine	1½″ to 4″
*1 Small plain ending machine	½″ to 1½″
1 Rotomatic beveler	½″ to 2″
6 Hydro-testers	½″ to 4″
1 Conduit cutting saw	½″ to 4″
2 Rotomatic threaders	½″ to 2″
*3 Stamets threaders	2″ to 4″
*2 Small mill type machines (see note)	½″ to 2″
*2 Large mill type machines (see note)	2″ to 4″
2 Small auto coupling machines	½″ to 2″
2 Large auto coupling screwers	2″ to 4″
1 Stripping machine	½″ to 4″
1 Small coating machine	½″ to 1½″
1 Large coating machine	1½″ to 4″

Galvanize Floor

2 Rotomatic threaders	½″ to 2″
2 Re-straightener presses	½″ to 3″
*2 Small mill type machines (see note)	½″ to 2″
1 Re-cut saw	½″ to 2½″
2 Small coupling machines	½″ to 2″
1 Large coupling screwer	2″ to 4″

Double Length Shop (50′ Line)

1 Straightener	1″ to 4″
*1 Cut-off machine	1″ to 4″
*2 Stamets threaders	2″ to 4″
1 Coupling screwer	2″ to 4″
1 Tester (double length)	1″ to 4″
1 Coating machine	1″ to 4″
*1 Mill type machine (see note)	2″ to 4″
Total conveyor length—765′	

NOTE: Used for threading, facing, cut-off, and grooving.

Electric Weld Finishing Equipment

*1 End facers (single length)	4½″ to 16″
1 Rotary cutoff machine	4½″ to 16″
2 Pipe coating gyromat machines	
*2 Cutoff machines	4½″ to 16″
1 Rotary pipe straightener	4½″ to 16″
*3 Threaders (single length)	2″ to 8″
*1 Threaders (single length)	5″ to 12″
*1 Threaders (double length)	5″ to 12″
*1 Threaders (double length)	6″ to 16″
1 60′ Hydrostatic pipe tester	4½″ to 16″
Total conveyor length—1590′	

*Indicates number of pairs of machines

GALVANIZING

Capacity—10,500 tons per month

Galvanizing Units

	No. 1	No. 2
Start up	1927	1940
Pot size	26′ x 4′-6″ x 5′-6″	26′ x 4′-6″ x 5′-6″
Firing	Side	Side
Size range	1½″ to 16″	½″ to 1¼″
Number of burners	36	36

Pipe Mill Circa 1934

Threading machine in the Pipe Mill.

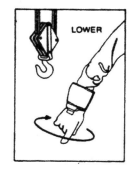

Loading pipe for shipment in the Pipe Mill. Photos courtesy of Bill Goodman.

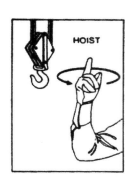

Wire and Pipe Mill Cafeteria Menu
September 18, 1929

Fresh Crabment Salad	30¢	Comb Sand Toasted Bread.	20¢
Fresh Shrimp Salad	30¢	Sliced Tom with Meals.	10¢
Red Pink Salmon Salad.	30¢	Sliced Cucum with Meals.	10¢
Lettuce & Tom Salad.	25¢	Potatoe Salad.	20¢
Hard Boiled Egg Salad.	25¢	Sardine Sandwich	10¢
Sardine Salad.	20¢	All Cold Sandwiches.	10¢

SOUPS

Beef Broth With Barley . . . . 10¢

ENTREES READY TO SERVE

Roast Beef Hash Home Style With Fried Egg. . . . . 30¢
Boiled Virginia Ham With Kale & Pot. . . . . 30¢
Baked Lamp With Spaghetti. . . . . 30¢
Pork Stew With Squash & Patatoes . . . . 30¢
Beef Stew Home Style . . . . 25¢
Baked Halibut With Spanish Sauce & Pot . . . . 30¢
Home Made Crab Cakes, Creole Sauce & Pot . . . . 30¢
Kidney Stew, Home Style With Vegetables. . . . . 25¢
Pot Roast With Spaghetti & Patatoes. . . . . 30¢
California Asparagus Tips on Toast & Bacon . . . . 30¢
Chipped Beef, Scrambles Eggs . . . . 30¢
New Spinach With Hard Boiled Egg . . . . 25¢
Baked Country Sausage, Mashed Patatoes . . . . 30¢
Ham & Eggs Country Style . . . . 30¢
Home Baked Beans . . . . 20¢
Pork & Beans . . . . 25¢
Spanish Omelette With Patatoes . . . . 30¢
Ham Omelette With Patatoes . . . . 30¢
Cheese Omelette With Patatoes. . . . . 25¢

ROASTS

Roast Lamb With Green Peas & Patatoes. . . . . 30¢
Roast Port, Baked Beans & Patatoes . . . . 30¢
Roast Beef, Green Peas & Patatoes. . . . . 30¢

COLD --------- MEATS

Cold Roast Lamb, Patatoe Salad . . . . 30¢
Cold Roast Pork, Patatoe Salad . . . . 30¢
Cold Roast Beef, Patatoe Salad . . . . 30¢
Cold Sliced Ham, Patatoe Salad . . . . 35¢

STEAKS & CHOPS TO ORDER

Small Sirolin Steak With Patatoes. . . . . 30¢
(2) Fried Pork Chops & Patatoes, ... 30¢
(2) Broiled Lamb Chops on Toast & Pot. . . . . 35¢
(2) Broiled Veal Chops & Patatoes. . . . . 30¢

The Coal Field

The Coal Field had three cranes in the 1950s. One 17-ton crane shown at left, and two 9-ton cranes. The structure under the crane at left is a **hopper**. Coal was blended in a 2 to 1 mixture and fed into the hopper and then transported by a **conveyor** to the coke ovens. Photo circa 1955, courtesy of Al Paul.

"I went to work at the Coke Ovens in 1948. I started out as a helper-learner working in the Belt Gang. We made repairs to the conveyor. In 1950, I transferred over to the Coal Field and worked as a millwright under Frank Turansky and Ernie Young. At that time, we were responsible for any maintenance that was required in the Coal Handling System. We did belt repair, table repair, and bucket repair. These coal handling buckets were huge and could weigh 15 tons. In 1972, I was promoted to assistant general foreman and in 1978, I became general foreman of the Coal Handling System. We had approximately 120 people working for us. The main objective of the Coal Handling System was to move coal from the Coal Field to the Coke Ovens where it would be converted to coke for use in the blast furnaces." ~Al Paul, General Foreman, Coal Handling System, 1948 to 1981.

The Coal Handling System

At left, the tug *Fells Point* assisted in the docking of the coal barge *Maryland*. Shortly after docking, two 9-ton capacity and one 17-ton capacity buckets began lifting and mixing the barge's West Virginia coal with an adjacent stockpiled Kentucky coal in predetermined quantities. Photo circa 1973.

Footnote 18

The coal brought in on the barge was moved away on a 1,600-foot long conveyer belt that took it to the Coke Ovens. Photo circa 1973.

Below are the Coal Fields, looking west. Photo dated February 16, 1956.

In 1938, it took approximately 3 ¼ tons of raw materials to produce one ton of iron ore. In the stock house, operators kept track of loadings on a board such as the one shown above. It was critical that they be at least 99% accurate by weight.

80

At right: Blaw Knox size G 6802 rated 17-ton net 4-rope geared hinge corner bar type Coal Rehandling Bucket. The bucket weighed 31,500 pounds and was built specifically for the Sparrows Point Coal Handling System. Photo courtesy of the Dundalk Patapsco-Neck Historical Society. Photo dated December 1949.

← Left to right: Frank Turansky, Millwright Foreman; Al Paul; Frankie Capp. The men are planning to repair this giant bucket. The job has been laid out in white chalk and will require cutting a 1-inch steel plate to be welded on the hinge pins. Photo courtesy of Al Paul, circa 1953.

"Hoppy the Welder" → prepares to attach the side plates to the hinge area of this massive bucket. Photo courtesy of Al Paul, circa 1953.

Before the new Ore Pier was completed in 1971, ore ships delivered their cargo in the Ore Basin, shown here. Note the close proximity of the blast furnaces to the Ore Fields. Shown left to right are blast furnaces "E" "F", "G", "H", and "J" and the future site of "K" furnace being cleared near the water tower. Photo dated 1954, courtesy of Dundalk Patapsco-Neck Historical Society.

New Ore Pier Under Construction

Shown above is the new Ore Pier under construction. When completed, shipments of ore were delivered to the Sparrows Point plant and unloaded by three rope trolley slewing unloaders on the 1,020 foot long Ore Pier. Each unloader had a reach of about 100 feet from the pier fendering system outward and had a free digging capacity of 2,000 tons per hour. The unloaders moved on a 925 foot long runway system and all three could rotate to service a ship on either side of the pier. Photo courtesy of Sue Clarke and James Kidd, General Foreman of the Ore Dock.

New Ore Pier

A new 1,020 foot long ore pier was built in 1971 to accommodate the super ore carriers that were emerging in trans-oceanic service. The channel into Baltimore had to be deepened to 50 feet from its former depth of 42 feet. The new pier would accommodate super carriers bringing in 160,000 gross tons of raw material. At the outboard end of the pier, shown here, was a mooring dolphin 83 feet in diameter. It was connected to the pier by a 50 foot long walkway. Three rope trolley slewing unloaders on the 83 foot wide pier each had a free digging capacity of 2,000 tons per hour. All three could rotate to unload vessels on either side of the pier. Note: blast furnaces "E" and "F", "G" and "H", "J" and "K" in the background. Photo courtesy of Sue Clarke and James Kidd, General Foreman of the Ore Dock.

New Ore Pier

Shown here, two ore carriers could be unloaded simultaneously at the new Ore Pier. The pier was equipped with three unloaders, each with a 26-ton capacity bucket. Photo courtesy of Sue Clarke and James Kidd, General Foreman of the Ore Dock.

"One time, I got called to the Ore Dock to do a job because another driver couldn't back out on the dock. It was very narrow. They had a 9 ½ wide lowboy to be repaired. I backed out on the dock and a crane lowered the huge bucket onto the flatbed. I took it out to the field where two Pettibones took it off. Pettibones are crane cars. They set it down and the welders fixed it. They loaded it back on my truck and I took it back out to the Ore Dock. Sometimes you had to volunteer to drive everything or do anything. It was job security. I drove everything from Yukes to 10-wheeled dump trucks. Sometimes the job was as easy as driving up to the Mack plant in New Jersey for parts." ~Bill Zablocki, Truck Driver, 1956 to 1998.

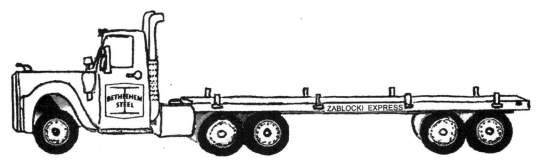

Stacker Reclaimer

One of the two new stacker reclaiming machines utilized in conjunction with the new Ore Pier. It was capable of passing ore directly from the pier to consumption or of stockpiling it at a rate of 6,000 tons per hour. The bucket-wheel, located at the end of the 220-foot boom, was 26 feet in diameter, and had nine buckets around the circumference. The operator's cab was located just to the right of the wheel. Each stacker reclaimer could be traversed on its own set of tracks a distance of 1,800 feet along its respective ore fields. Photo courtesy of Sue Clarke and James Kidd, General Foreman, Ore Dock.

Stacker Reclaimer

One of two bucket-wheel, stacker reclaiming machines that were used when the new Ore Pier complex started normal operations at Sparrows Point in 1972. Each could pass ore to the stockpiles or to the blast furnaces at the rate of 6,000 tons per hour. They could reclaim ore at the rate of 4,000 tons per hour. The bucket-wheel was located at the end of a 220-foot boom which could be moved vertically 90 feet. The stacker reclaimers and an additional new stacker, also with a 6,000 ton per hour capability, were normally operated from a control center, which could direct ore from origin to destination via 174 different routes on the mammoth complex of belts running from the pier to the blast furnaces. The pier and the attendant ore storage and ore handling facilities were the largest single port improvement in Baltimore Harbor's history at the time. Photo courtesy of Baltimore Museum of Industry.

New Ore Pier Control Center

The multi-million dollar Ore Pier and associated handling facilities at Sparrows Point were governed through a control center. The center directed ore from the pier to various destinations via 174 different routes, depending upon operation requirements. Master elements of the control center included a computerized route selection unit (RSU), computerized supervisory control unit, and a backup RSU. It also had a telemetering system to code and recode signals sent to remote stations and return. Photo courtesy of Sue Clarke and James Kidd, General Foreman, Ore Dock. Photo dated 1971.

The Distribution of Ore, Sinter, and Coke

A maze of covered conveyer belts and distribution points at the Sparrows Point plant moved thousands of tons of ore, sinter, and coke each day to blast furnaces that produced molten iron. The **Stockhouse**, the tallest of the buildings shown here, was one of the central distribution points from which raw materials were supplied to four blast furnaces, having a combined production capacity of about 17,000 tons per day of hot metal. Note the proximity of the new Ore Pier in the background. Photo courtesy of Sue Clarke and James Kidd, General Foreman; Ore Dock.

COKE OVEN DEPARTMENT

GENERAL

Operating personnel—1,010

Acreage—128

Annual rated coke production—4,174,000 net tons

(Information compiled as of October 1960)

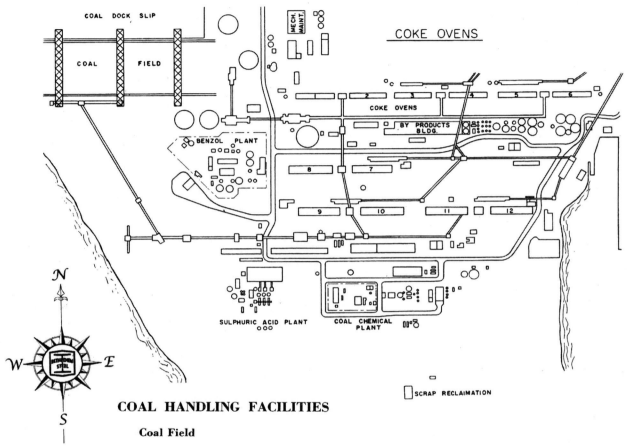

COAL HANDLING FACILITIES

Coal Field

300' x 1,000'

200,000 net tons high volatile coal capacity

100,000 net tons low volatile coal capacity

2 — Mead Morrison Coal Bridges—10 ton buckets

1 — Heyl and Patterson Coal Bridge—17 ton bucket

Auxiliary Coal Field

Storage as of July 1, 1960

125,000 net tons H-2 storage

220,000 net tons H-3 storage

60,000 net tons H-4 storage

100,000 net tons L-2 storage

Serviced by 17 ton Euclid trucks (outside contractor)

"A" Plant (1914)

1,000 tons/hr. rated capacity

Services batteries Nos. 1, 2, 3, 4, 5, 6, 7 and 8 (2 shifts/day)

4 — 400 ton breaker bins

6 — 500 ton mixing bins

2 — 500 tons/hr. breakers

4 — 250 tons/hr. hammer mills

1 — 350 tons/hr. hammer mill

Coke Oven, continued

Conveyor A

Coal Conveyor Belts

Qty.	Number	Capacity Tons/Hr.	Conveyor Length Ft. In.	Belt Length Ft.	Belt Width In.	Belt Speed Ft./Min.	Drive H P.
2	A	500 each	419-7	930	36	450	100
2	B	500 each	372	*760	36	450	100
2	C	500 each	*600	1,225	36	440	50
1	D	500	*620	1,270	36	455	50
1	E	500	*140	295	36	450	50
1	F	500	*140	295	36	450	50
1	G	500	*140	295	36	450	50
2	H,H1	750 each	*500	1,070	42	430	125
1	I	500	315-10	660	36	430	60
1	J	1,500	1130-3	2,212	54	556	125
2	1,2	250 each	11-9	32	48	30 or 60	7½
2	3,4	250 each	11-9	32	48	30 or 60	7½
2	6,7	500 each	25-8	64	42	315	7½
1	8	500	34-8	82	42	315	7½
1	8A	500	29-10	72	42	315	7½
1	9	500	34-8	80	42	315	4½
1	9A	500	29-10	70	42	315	7½
3	10,12,14	250 each	17-6	44	54	12 to 80	10
3	11,13,15	250 each	17-6	44	54	12 to 80	10
1	18A	700	256-6	425	42	430	20

*Approximate lengths.

60" feeder belts on Nos. 1, 2 and 3 bridges—800 tons/hr. each.

"B" Plant (May, 1954)

700 tons/hr. rated capacity

Services batteries Nos. 9, 10, 11 and 12 (1 shift/day)

2 — 500 ton breaker bins

4 — 500 ton/hr. mixing bins

2 — 465 ton/hr. screens, each screen has 15 HP motor

1 — 700 ton/hr. breaker, 150 HP motor

1 — 350 ton/hr. hammer mill, 500 HP motor

1 — 500 ton/hr. hammer mill, 700 HP motor

Conveyor B

Coal Conveyor Belts

Qty.	Number	Capacity Tons/Hr.	Conveyor Length Ft. In.	Belt Length Ft.	Belt Width In.	Belt Speed Ft./Min.	Drive H P.
2	1,1A	800 each	13-6	37	60	25 to 75	15
1	2	850	188-6	416	54	325	30
1	2A	850	241-6	522	54	325	30
1	3	850	994-9	2,038	48	400	100
1	4	850	212-5	436	48	400	100
2	4A,4B	850 each	76-5	168	48	400	40
1	5	1,000	642-10	1,370	54	360	200
2	5A,5B	500 each	11-0	30	48	60	10
1	6	1,000	30-0	71	54	375	15
2	7,8	700 each	15-0	42	54	35 or 70	20 or 10
1	9	700	500-1	1,075	42	450	150
1	10	700	35-2	81	54	360	15
2	11,12	700 each	29-2	67	54	360	15
2	13,15	350 each	17-5	42	54	30 to 119	10
2	14,16	730 each	17-5	42	54	18 to 72	10
1	17	700	452	973	42	460	125
1	18	700	213-3	442	42	460	75
1	18A	700	256-6	430	42	430	20
1	19	700	500-7	1,037	42	460	75
1	20	700	205-3	427	42	460	75
1	R-1	100	32-1	71	24	180	5

Coke Oven, continued

Coal mix contains 30% volatile material

Coal imported from West Virginia, central Pennsylvania and northern Kentucky

75% of coal mined by Mining Division of the Bethlehem Steel Co.

Coal crushed to 80% minus ⅛″ fineness.

Coal moisture controlled to 5%.

Coal treated with napthenic base coal spray oil to obtain bulk weight of 45 lbs. per cu. ft.

Coal received in 600 and 900 ton scows, and 5,400 ton barges

BATTERY PLANT

General Battery Data

Battery No.	Start of Operation	Type (Koppers)	Fuel Gas	No. Ovens	Tons of Dry Coal/Day	Tons Coke Per Month
1	1929 Original					
	1960 Rebuilt	Gun	C.O.	63	1,110	24,800
2	1914 Original					
	1936 Rebuilt					
	1960 Rebuilt	Gun	C.O.	60	1,050	23,620
3	1915 Original					
	1951 Rebuilt	Gun	C.O.	63	1,110	24,800
4	1918 Original					
	1960 Rebuilt	Gun	C.O.	63	1,110	24,800
5	1920 Original					
	1953 Rebuilt	Gun	C.O.	63	1,110	24,800
6	1922 Original					
	1953 Rebuilt	Gun	C.O.	63	1,110	24,800
7	1941	Underjet	CO or BF	61	1,460	32,590
8	1948	Underjet	CO or BF	61	1,460	32,590
9	1950	Underjet	CO or BF	65	1,450	32,360
10	1952	Underjet	CO or BF	65	1,450	32,360
11	1955	Underjet	C.O.	65	1,450	32,360
12	1957	Underjet	CO or BF	65	1,450	32,360
TOTALS				757	15,320	342,240

"A" Plant

Batteries Nos. 1, 2, 3, 4, 5, and 6.

Koppers-Gun type luted doors

Equipment

    3 Mud mills to supply mud for doors

    5 Coke pushers

    12 Hydraulic door extractors (6 on pusher side, 6 on coke side)

    5 Larry cars—14 tons capacity each

    5 Motor cars

    5 Coke pans

"B" Plant

Batteries Nos. 7, 8, 9, 10, 11 and 12

Koppers—Becker underjet type self-sealing doors

Equipment

    6 Coke pushers

    6 Door machines

    6 Larry cars—14 tons capacity each

    6 Motor cars

    6 Coke pans

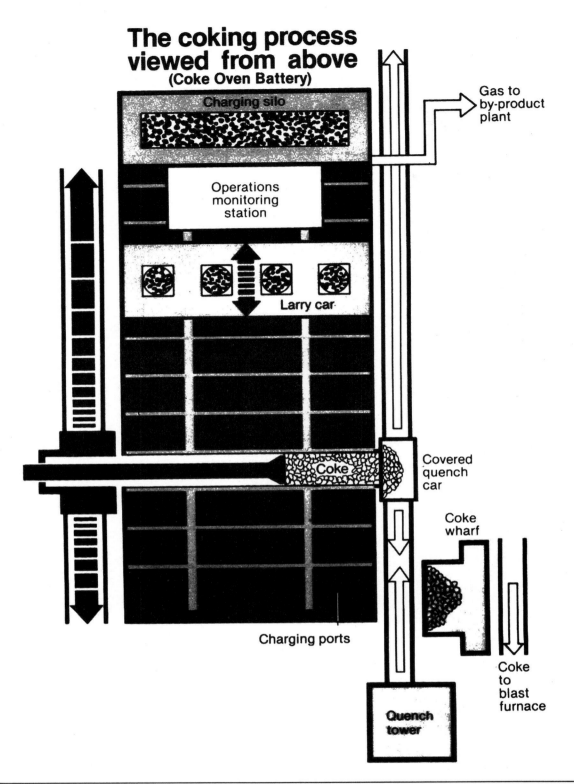

The coking process viewed from above
(Coke Oven Battery)

Charging silo

Gas to by-product plant

Operations monitoring station

Larry car

Coke

Covered quench car

Coke wharf

Charging ports

Coke to blast furnace

Quench tower

The coking operation of "A" battery at the Sparrows Point plant was similar to the representation above. The **larry car**, or charging machine, loaded up with coal by traveling beneath the charging silo and then filled an individual oven from the top through four ports. After an 18-hour cooking time at a final temperature of at least 1,800 degrees Fahrenheit, the pushing machine at left moved the coke out of the oven and into the **quench car** at right. Hot coke was then moved to the quench tower and flooded with about 16,000 gallons of water to cool it before being unloaded at the wharf to await further processing. Diagram courtesy of the Dundalk Patapsco-Neck Historical Society.

New "A" Battery Coke Oven Starts Up - 1982

In 1982, Sparrows Point began operating a new $160 million coke oven. It had **585 ovens** with a **combined capacity of 8,325 tons per day**. The new "A" Battery had an annual capacity of 900,000 tons per year. It was equipped with the latest advances in oven machinery and a computer control system which controlled the underfiring with either coke oven or blast furnace gas, as well as monitoring batteries 1 to 6, 11 and 12, and the coke handling system. **Automated larry cars** charged 32 tons of coal into each oven with minimum charging emissions. **The first push was on April 23, 1982 at 1330 hours.** There were **six quenching stations** for the **nine operating batteries**. A recirculation system was used to control coke moisture and reduce water pollution. Coke from the nine batteries was deposited onto four wharves and transported via belt conveyors to the blast furnace central receiver. Photograph courtesy of Baltimore Museum of Industry.

"A" Coke Oven Battery

A new generation of coke oven machinery was represented by the pushing machine shown above at Sparrows Point's new "A" coke oven battery. The 380-ton machine pushed coke from an oven into a receiving car on the opposite side of its 80-oven battery. It was fully automated and spanned five ovens. The machine had a computer controlled pushing schedule and performed certain environmentally oriented tasks such as cleaning coke oven doors following a coke push. Despite the upgrades to the coke works, the facility at Sparrows Point closed in 1991. It had experienced battery failure and the additional cost of installing controls to meet environmental regulations sealed its fate. Photo courtesy of Baltimore Museum of Industry.

Below is a cross-section view of the "A" coke oven battery.

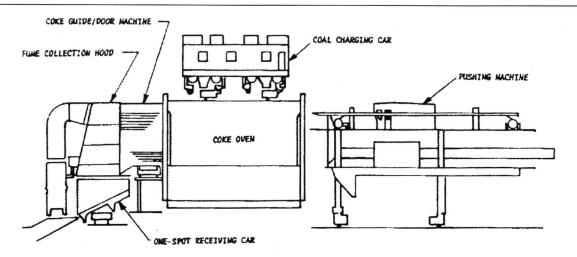

Controlling Coke Emissions

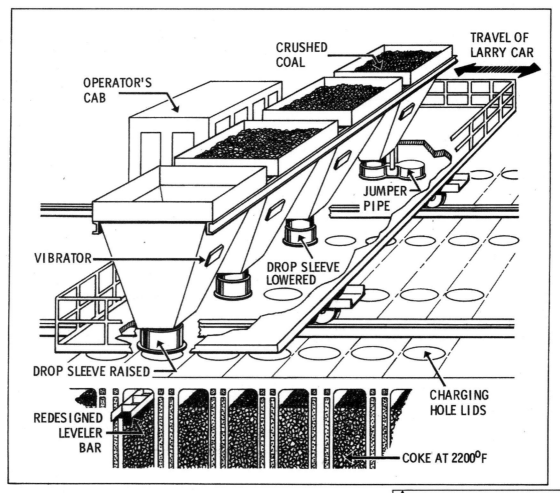

OPERATOR'S CAB

CRUSHED COAL

TRAVEL OF LARRY CAR

JUMPER PIPE

VIBRATOR

DROP SLEEVE LOWERED

DROP SLEEVE RAISED

REDESIGNED LEVELER BAR

CHARGING HOLE LIDS

COKE AT 2200°F

↑ The sketch above is of a typical larry car used for filling coke ovens with coal. It shows several retrofitted environmental controls that limited visible emissions. Bethlehem Steel worked several years to equip older ovens with controls to meet Maryland air quality specifications. Diagram courtesy of Dundalk Patapsco-Neck Historical Society.

← Full time operation began in January 1980 at the Coke Ovens for a new air pollution control system at a cost of $6 million. At the far end of the system, which operated on railroad tracks along the Coke Ovens, coke is pushed from an oven into a receiving car. Captured emissions traveled the length of a 116-foot long system through a scrub and clean process. Before cleaned effluent was released (foreground) into the atmosphere, the emissions were contained while the system moved to a tower where the coke was quenched.

In August 1982, a new $160 million coke oven battery was commissioned at Sparrows Point. It was composed of 80 slot-type side by side ovens. The 850,000 ton per year battery took more than three years to complete. To make room for the new "A" battery, Nos. 7 and 8 batteries were dismantled. Below is a map of the new "A" battery location.

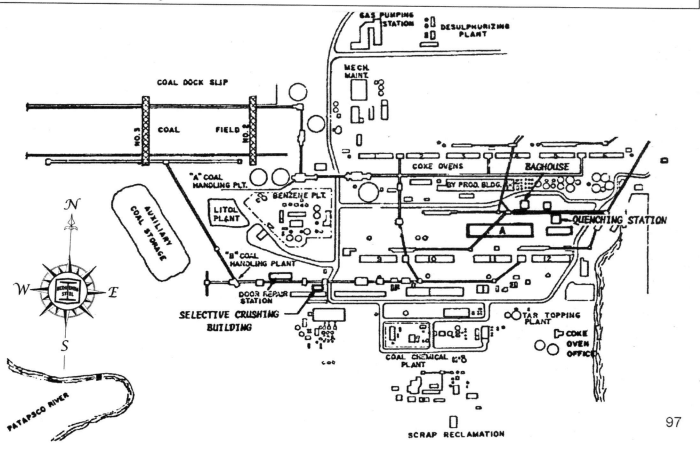

Coke, limestone, and iron ore are the basic ingredients fed into a blast furnace in the first step of the steelmaking process. Sparrows Point made its own coke, consuming at one time 5 million tons of coal a year. Coal, which has been roasted in the absence of air to drive off the volatilities, has been turned into coke and is then pushed at a white-hot temperature into a coke car. On this page are three examples of pushing coke at the Coke Ovens. Top photo dated 1949, bottom left photo dated 1968, bottom right photo dated 1959.

Pushing Coke

Coke Ovens

← A worker prepares to restart the coke ovens following the 116-day strike in 1959. This photograph was taken on top of "B" plant and shows the No. 9 Battery. No. 9 Battery was built in 1950 and had 65 ovens. It produced 1,450 tons of dry coal per day and produced 32,260 tons of coke per month. Photograph dated November 7, 1959, courtesy of Bill Goodman.

Workers prepare to start up No. 4 Battery of "A" Plant following the end of a 35-day strike in 1956. This is a side view of No. 4 Battery showing the doors of the coke oven. Note that door number 436 is open and empty. No. 4 Battery was originally built in 1918 and was rebuilt in 1960. It had 63 ovens and used 1,110 tons of dry coal per day and produced 24,800 tons of coke per month. Photo dated November 7, 1956, courtesy of Bill Goodman.

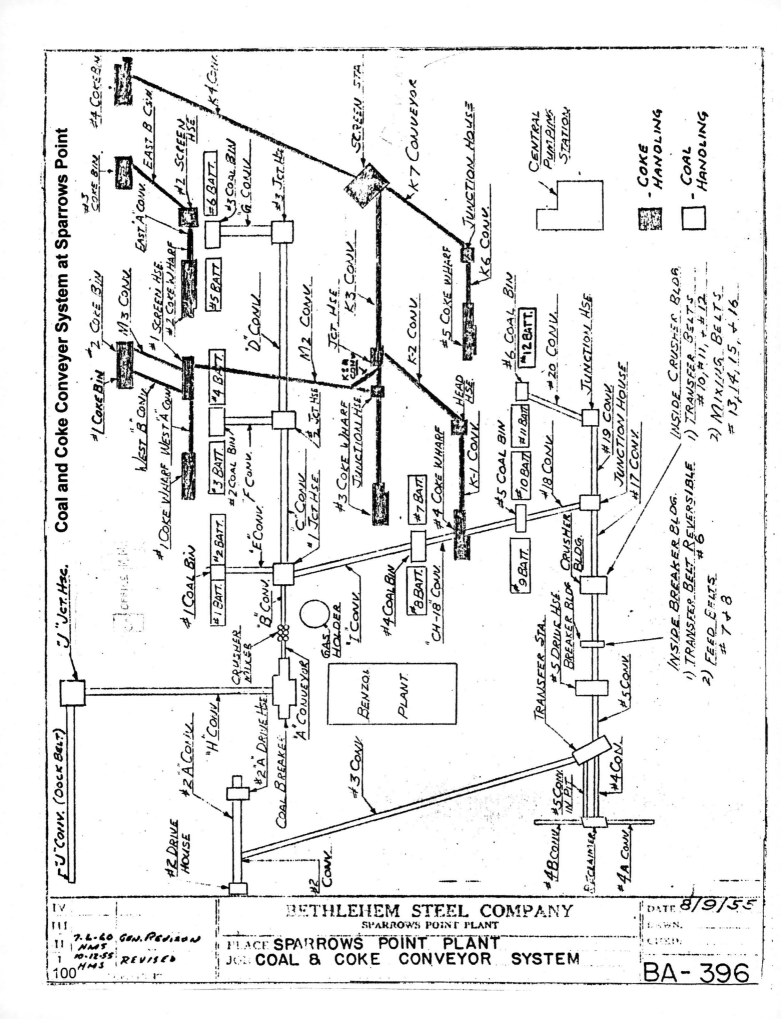

Coal and Coke Conveyer System at Sparrows Point

COKE HANDLING

COAL HANDLING

BETHLEHEM STEEL COMPANY
SPARROWS POINT PLANT

PLACE SPARROWS POINT PLANT
JOB COAL & COKE CONVEYOR SYSTEM

DATE 8/9/55

BA-396

OPEN HEARTH AND BESSEMER DEPARTMENTS

(Information compiled as of October 1960)

GENERAL

Operating personnel—2,200
Acreage—165
Annual rated capacity—8,200,000 ingot tons

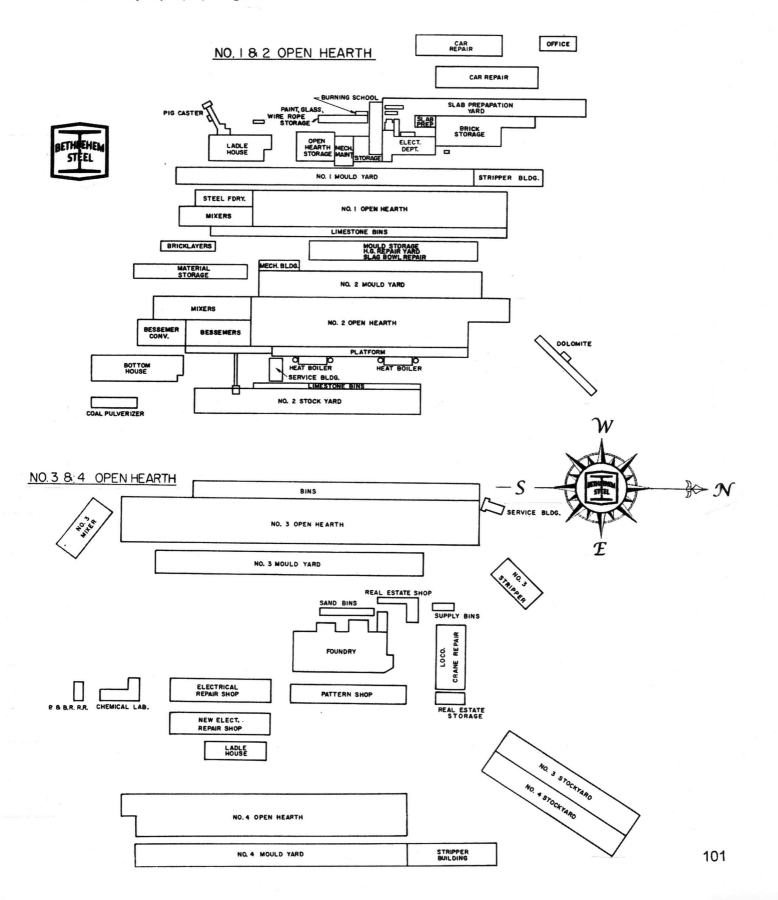

AVERAGE FUEL RATE   Open Hearth, continued

O.H. Shop	Gals. Oil per Ton of Stl.	Gals. Tar per Ton of Stl.	Cu. Ft. Gas per Ton of Stl.	Millions of BTU's/Ton
No. 1	6.8	13.2	1898	3.95
No. 2	2.1	5.9	3468	3.12
No. 3	2.3	9.5	3270	3.30
No. 4	3.8	9.0	2973	3.42

ANNUAL RAW MATERIAL CONSUMPTION

O.H. Shop	Limestone Tons/yr.	Ore Tons/yr.	Scrap Tons/yr.	Burnt Lime Tons/yr.	Dolomite Tons/yr.	Hot Metal Tons/yr.	Pig Iron (Cold) Tons/yr.	Alloys (Comb.) Tons/yr.
No. 1	120,548	163,852	633,340	11,760	114,198	1,187,958	31,116	17,508
No. 2	32,122	97,614	518,328	15,436	61,554	711,184	7,724	7,852
No. 3	88,494	251,712	888,308	17,702	123,248	1,752,828	13,458	29,719
No. 4	72,930	178,726	982,532	20,416	117,392	1,320,620	14,274	17,158
Totals	314,094	691,904	3,022,508	65,314	416,392	4,982,590	66,572	72,236

SHOP PRACTICE

O.H. Shop	Heats/Mo.	Chg. to tap time Hrs. Min.	Tons of Steel per Hr. per Fce.	Ladle Lining Life Heats/Lining
No. 1	935	8 : 10	18.3	20.4
No. 2	320	9 : 30	35.9	25.1
No. 3	780	8 : 40	28.6	22.1
No. 4	545	8 : 15	42.1	20.2

OXYGEN FURNACES

No. 75 Furnace

Two lance installation
35,000 to 50,000 cu. ft. oxygen/hr./lance
5 to 8 hrs. charge to tap time

No. 94 Furnace

Two lance installation
50,000 cu. ft. oxygen/hr./lance
5 to 8 hrs. charge to tap time

No. 96 Furnace

Three lance installation (current practice—2 lance operation)
50,000 cu. ft. oxygen/hr./lance
5 to 8 hrs. charge to tap time

HEAVY EQUIPMENT USED IN PITS

O.H. Shop	Bulldozer	Eimco	Truck
No. 1	1	1	2
No. 2	1		
No. 3	1	1	2
No. 4	1	1	2

LADLES

O.H. Shop	Steel Ladles		Iron Ladles	
	Quantity	Cap'y.-Tons	Quantity	Cap'y.-Tons
No. 1	20	170	7	65
No. 2	18	190	6	75
No. 3	18	285	9	75
No. 4	8	395	6	150
	5	430		

HOT METAL MIXER STATIONS

No. 1 Open Hearth Shop

One 1,000 ton mixer

No. 2 Open Hearth Shop

One 1,300 ton mixer
One   650 ton mixer

No. 3 Open Hearth Shop

One 1,200 ton mixer
One   450 ton mixer

MIXING HOUSE

Materials used per month (used for steel runners, etc.)

O.H. Shop	Refused Brick Lbs.	Allen Clay Lbs.	Magnesite Lbs.
No. 1	618,000	206,000	33,000
No. 2	445,000	165,000	139,000
No. 3	618,000	216,000	196,000
No. 4	618,000	215,000	73,000

STEEL FOUNDRY (1916)

Routine Production

Produces 800 to 900 tons cast items per month

3 slag bowls per week ⎫
3 charging pans per day ⎭ 645 tons per month

Miscellaneous items as per plant order (150 to 250 tons per month)

Equipment

4,000 patterns
32 flasks (10 charging pan, 2 bowl, rest are standard)
1 core oven

Miscellaneous

Uses 500 to 700 tons New Jersey silica type foundry sand per month

MISCELLANEOUS EQUIPMENT

8 hot metal cars (power units)—two per shop
1 idler
51 — 260 cu. ft. slag bowls (No. 1 and No. 2 Open Hearths)
49 — 375 cu. ft. slag bowls (No. 3 and No. 4 Open Hearths)
Ingot mould trucks
    742 trucks
    24 idlers
    14 coffins
    3 stopper rods
    1 weight car
2,370 charging pans (33 cu. ft. pans in No. 1 and No. 2 O.H.)
    (45 cu. ft. pans in No. 3 O.H.)
    (60 cu. ft. pans in No. 4 O.H.)
5,340 average ingot moulds on hand (sizes range from 22" x 34" x 80" to 42" x 81" x 96")
512,000 tons refractories used per year
4,000 average stools on hand (8,000 to 60,000 lb. each)
680 mould caps
116 bottom pour runners
550 charging buggies
7 standard gauge railroad engines (P&BRRR)
Narrow gauge diesel engines and track
    3 — 90 ton
    4 — 70 ton
    8 — 50 ton (normally used as 100 ton tandem units)
16.3 miles of N.G. track (some track services Blooming Mills)

Open Hearth Ladles

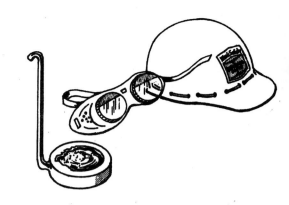

← The first of 18 Open Hearth ladles built for Sparrows Point were completed in April 1953 by the Bethlehem Pennsylvania Plant. The **265-ton capacity steel ladles** were among the largest in the industry and part of Sparrows Point's expansion program in the late 1950s. The ladles were **16 feet high and weighed 44 tons** a piece. The riveted band shown in the photograph at left around the mid-section was removed so that the ladle could be shipped in two pieces. **Footnote 19**

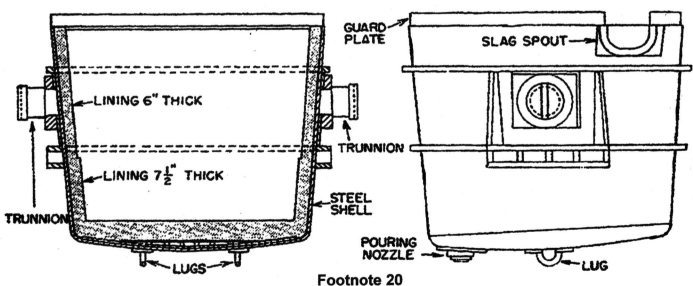

Footnote 20

In the diagram above left is the **vertical section of a steel ladle through the trunnions** showing the increased thickness of the lining in its lower portions. The diagram at right illustrates a side view of the same ladle. The ladle shell itself was fabricated from steel plate by riveting or welding. The diameter of the ladle increases toward the top to facilitate the removal of the shell of metal that occasionally solidifies on the sides and bottom of the interior of the ladle, which is commonly referred to as a **skull**.

The massive arched roof center of the No. 4 Open Hearth is being replaced in this photograph. Forklift operators from the 406 Department are shown raising the pallets of brick over the seven open hearth doors. Once the bricks were in place, the 404 Labor Gang would pass the bricks to the bricklayers who then replaced the roof center. The 55-gallon drum at right held a slurry of mortar mix. Notice the criss-cross of timber used to support the structure. Once the arched roof center was completed, the brick layers would tear out the timbered scaffolding. An open hearth roof would have to be replaced every six months to a year, depending on wear and tear. Photo dated December 5, 1970. Special thanks to Al Hastings.

"I graduated from Penn State and came to the Point in 1953. My first job was Assistant Ceramic Engineer in the Fuel and Steam Department. We were responsible for the most economical use of refractories that included high temperature brick work, mortar, cement, and plastics throughout the plant. These items were used in all furnaces, the BOF, the open hearths, and the finishing side. We were always on the lookout for new refractories that might be more cost effective and give more life to the furnaces.

"Each month we issued reports on the consumption of refractories in various departments. We also issued specialized reports on trials of refractories. For example, if a new brick was to be used, we would get permission to install it and then monitor its potential and cost-effectiveness to determine if it would be used or not used. We also compiled an annual report that included the consumption of refractories for each department for the entire plant. I subsequently became a Ceramic Engineer. The duties were similar.

"In 1970, I moved out of the Steam Department and into the Mechanical Department and became Assistant General Foreman of the Brick Department. We repaired and rebuilt various types of furnaces throughout the plant from the coke ovens to the Rod and Wire Mill. I eventually became General Foreman of the Brick Department.

"In 1979, I went to the Environmental Control Department as the Assistant Superintendent. We were responsible for air and water pollution abatement, plant safety, and environmental health. We monitored air quality at the plant and reported our results to the State. We had specific emissions guidelines that we would put out. Financial penalties could be imposed by the State if we exceeded the limits. We were also responsible for monitoring the water quality throughout the plant. There were several water outfalls around the plant. One was near Pennwood Wharf, which went into Jones Creek and another was located at the waste water treatment facility on the Humphrey's Creek side of the plant. Environmental control was also responsible for plant safety. We set up the policies and then enforced them. We compiled monthly plant safety statistics for every department at Sparrows Point. We also set up and reported to the General Manager at regularly scheduled monthly safety meetings. We also set up safety inspections for every department throughout the whole plant. Our department was also very active in the area of environmental health. We were always on the lookout and testing for asbestos, mercury, lead, and other environmental contaminants.

"In 1982-83, there was a major realignment of departments at the plant. The Environmental Control Department was divided in two. Air and water pollution abatement was separated from safety and environment, and they became separate entities. I went with the safety and environment group to Human Resources. I then became Senior Safety Engineer and remained in that capacity until I retired in 1989. The highlight of my career at Sparrows Point was having the luxury of traveling around the entire plant. I visited every department and got to meet and know a lot of wonderful and interesting people. It was a fantastic experience." ~Bill Wilhelm, Senior Safety Engineer, 1953 -1989

The Pouring Operation

The pouring operation was critical in controlling molten steel so that it did not endanger personnel or damage equipment. It was also critical because poor practice in the assembly, adjustment or manipulation of pouring equipment could seriously and adversely affect the surface quality of the product. Shown above, the steel from the Open Hearth was poured into a train of ingot molds which would then be sent to the **soaking pits**. Photograph dated 1938, courtesy of Rich Glenn.

Cross-Section of the No. 4 Open Hearth Furnace

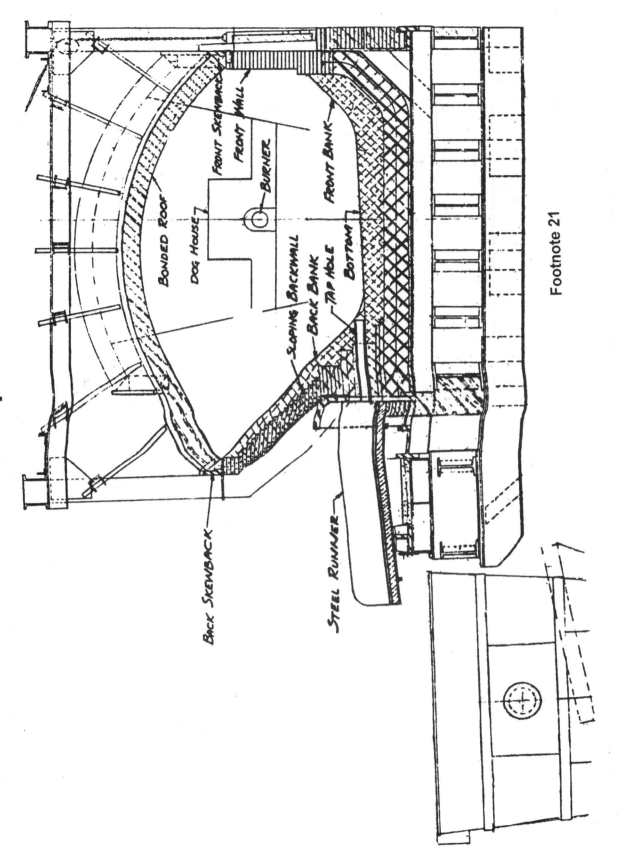

Footnote 21

Charging Machine at the No. 4 Open Hearth

The above photograph shows a **charging machine** at the No. 4 Open Hearth on August 3, 1959. **Charging** was the procedure of **loading the furnace with limestone, ore, burnt lime, scrap, and cold pig iron.** This operation was performed by a charging machine which dumped these materials into the furnace. The charging machine picked up a steel pan, or **charging box**, filled with one of these materials, then pushed it through an open doorway and emptied the contents by turning the box upside down.

The preliminary steps to charging began in the **Stockyard**. It was there that the limestone, ore, and other materials were loaded into the charging boxes. The boxes had to be filled to capacity. If they were delivered to the furnace partially filled, the time to charge a furnace would be lengthened because more boxes would be needed to complete the charge. It was important for the **First Helper** to realize that the fewer boxes needed for a charge, the shorter the charging time required.

Sequence of Operations for a Charging Machine

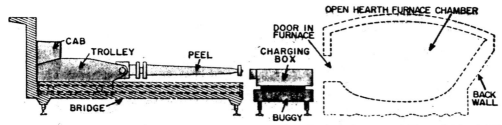

A. POSITION OF TROLLEY, PEEL AND CHARGING BOX AT START OF CHARGING OPERATION. (SEE INSERT AT BEGINNING OF THIS CHAPTER, SHOWING HOW CHARGING MACHINE AND BUGGIES CAN MOVE FROM DOOR TO DOOR AND FURNACE TO FURNACE ON TRACKS PARALLEL TO FRONT OF THE FURNACES.)

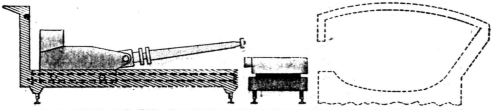

B. PEEL IS RAISED AND TROLLEY MOVES FORWARD TO POSITION HEAD OF PEEL OVER RECESS IN END OF CHARGING BOX

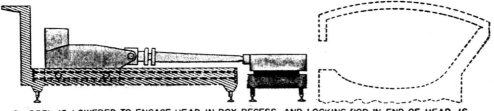

C. PEEL IS LOWERED TO ENGAGE HEAD IN BOX RECESS, AND LOCKING ROD IN END OF HEAD IS ADVANCED TO LOCK BOX ONTO HEAD OF PEEL.

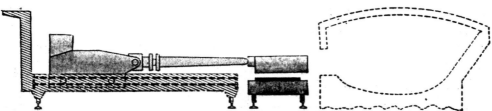

D. PEEL IS RAISED TO ELEVATE BOX ABOVE LEVEL OF SILL OF FURNACE DOOR.

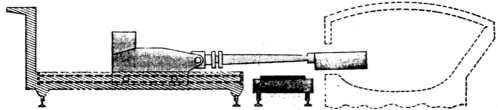

E. TROLLEY ADVANCES TO MOVE BOX ON END OF PEEL INTO FURNACE.

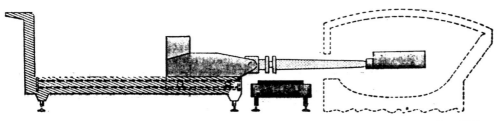

F. PEEL REVOLVES TO TURN BOX UPSIDE DOWN AND DUMP ITS CONTENTS ONTO HEARTH. THE ABOVE SEQUENCE OF OPERATIONS IS THEN REPEATED IN REVERSE ORDER TO WITHDRAW EMPTY BOX FROM FURNACE AND REPLACE IT ON BUGGY. THE BUGGY IS THEN MOVED FORWARD TO POSITION ANOTHER LOADED BOX BEFORE THE DOOR (IN SOME PLANTS, THE CHARGING MACHINE PEEL IS LOWERED AGAINST THE END OF THE BUGGY, AND THE SELF-PROPELLED MACHINE MOVES TO SHIFT THE BUGGY.) THE ABOVE OPERATIONS THEN ARE REPEATED WITH SUCCEEDING BOXES.

Footnote 22

Molten Pig Iron Pour at the No. 4 Open Hearth

Molten pig iron from the Blast Furnace was poured into a 395-ton Open Hearth furnace. The pig iron mixed with scrap will be refined into steel at the No. 4 Open Hearth. The **rate of flow** of the hot metal was controlled by the rate at which the crane hook attached to the rear of the ladle near the bottom was raised. Photo dated December 15, 1962, courtesy of Bill Goodman.

Teeming

By manipulating a lever as shown in the photograph above, the **pourer** opened and closed the **nozzle of the ladle** to control the flow of molten steel from the ladle to the **ingot molds**. This operation was called **"teeming" or "pouring."** Photograph dated 1938, courtesy of Bill Goodman.

Open Hearth Pouring Floor

The **pouring floor**, or pit side, of the furnace building extended along the tapping side of the furnaces. It was usually about 70 to 80 feet wide and as long as the charging floor, but at general yard level. The **pouring platforms** were situated along the inside of the wall of the building, opposite to the back, or **tapping side**, of the furnaces. Two to four such platforms were installed at a height convenient to the tops of the ingot molds standing on mold cars ready to be filled. Photo dated 1938, courtesy of Bill Goodman.

A Piece of the Town Disappears…
Again and Again

Section by section, **the town of Sparrows Point** would eventually succumb to the expansion of the steel mill. It began in the late teens and early twenties with the demolition of the **Shipyard community**. This was followed in 1930 with the demolition of the **West End community** to make room for the No. 3 Open Hearth. Shown above is an area that comprised the 200, 300, and 400 blocks of "B", "C", "D", "E", and "F" Streets.

Tenants were evicted from this area to make room for the **No. 4 Open Hearth**. The broad street running diagonally across the photograph was "D" Street. The empty lot at left was where the homes in the 200 block of "D" Street were located. The steam locomotive (used in the pile driving process to build No. 4 Open Hearth) is sitting in the 300 block. The kindergarten is at top center (slightly to the right). It was located on the southwest corner of 5th and "E" Streets. No. 4 Open Hearth was operational in 1957.

In 1972-1973, the entire town of Sparrows Point was demolished to make room for the **"L" Furnace**. In 2013, a process was begun to demolish the steel mill itself. Nothing lasts forever. Photo dated April 10, 1956, courtesy of Hillard "Digger" O'Day.

113

Skull Cracker

Shown above, Morris Jones stands next to a giant steel ball located in an area known as **"The Drop."** Here, Morris and his skull cracking giant ball broke up scrapped ingot molds shown in the background. The **five- to nine-ton balls** were lifted by a crane using a magnet to a height of 50 feet and then dropped. In addition to ingot molds, Morris and his crew also broke up Open Hearth doors, caster butts, frozen caster tundish steel, frozen ladle steel, and mill rolls. In a single turn, Morris could break and load more than 400 tons of busted up pieces into scrap cars. Most of the scrap was recycled back into the mill at Sparrows Point, and some was sold to outside sources. Some of the scrap was also sent to other Bethlehem Steel plants. In 1989, about one million tons of scrap was processed at Sparrows Point. Although the steel mill at Sparrows Point generated a lot of scrap, it bought more than it sold. Photo credited to Phil Szczepanski.   **Footnote 23**

DEPARTMENT OF THE NAVY
OFFICE OF THE UNDER SECRETARY
WASHINGTON

October 8, 1942

Mr. Eugene G. Grace, President
Bethlehem Steel Company
Sparrows Point, Maryland

Dear Mr. Grace:

This is to inform you that the Army and Navy are conferring upon you the Army-Navy Production Award for your great work in the production of war equipment.

The award consists of a flag to be flown above your plant, and a lapel pin, symbolic of distinguished service to America, for every individual in your plant.

You men and women of the Bethlehem Steel Company at Sparrows Point are making an outstanding contribution to victory. You have every reason to be proud of the record you have set, and your accomplishment stands as an example to all Americans.

Sincerely yours,

James Forrestal

Sparrows Point Steel Mill Receives the Prestigious Army-Navy "E" Award

Seal of the Department of the Navy

Sparrows Point General Manager Stewart Cort displays the prestigious Army-Navy "E" Award for wartime production on November 6, 1942. The award consisted of a flag (shown above), which was to be flown above the plant and a lapel pin was given to every individual in the steel plant. Both photographs courtesy of the Dundalk Patapsco-Neck Historical Society.

Flag of the Secretary of the Navy

More than 20,000 proud Sparrows Point workers and guests attended the Army-Navy "E" Award presentation on November 6, 1942. Shown here on the "B" Street field, many flash the "V" for **"VICTORY"** sign. Note the Company Store on "C" Street in the background.

Left: Chester M. Broski, Millwright-Welder, bought a thousand dollar bond as the fourth war bond drive got underway at the Sparrows Point Plant. Charles Quigley, center, was the Solicitor, and Hugh Thomas, Mechanical Foreman, in the Hot Strip Mill looked on. Photo courtesy of Baltimore Museum of Industry. Photo dated 1944.

A war bond was both an investment in one's country and an investment in one's financial future. Americans could purchase a war bond for $18.75. The government immediately paid for tanks, planes, ships, uniforms, weapons, medicine, food, and everything else the military needed to fight during World War II. Americans purchased about $185 billion worth of bonds during World War II.

George S. Greenwood, General Foreman, (second from right in tie) sold war bonds to the men on his turn at the Sparrows Point Plant in 1944. Photo courtesy of Dundalk Patapsco-Neck Historical Society.

VICTORY!

The Steel Workers Organizing Committee, C. I. O., has again scored another victory. 10c per hour increase in wages has been secured for all Steel Workers including

SPARROWS POINT

Effective April 1st, 1941

COME TO THE

MASS MEETING

THURSDAY, APRIL 17th, 1941

at 7:30 P. M.

—— at the ——

DUNDALK S. W. O. C. HALL

Dundalk and Patapsco Avenues

DUNDALK, MARYLAND

"It's Up to Us to Vote 'SWOC'."

The photo below shows polling place #10, located in the southeast corner of the Sheet Mill Warehouse, September 25, 1941.

BETHLEHEM EDITION

Steel Labor

THE VOICE OF THE STEEL WORKERS ORGANIZING COMMITTEE—C. I. O.

| Vol. VI | Indianapolis, Ind., September 25, 1941 | | No. 9 |

SWOC VICTORY IN SPARROWS POINT ELECTION IS ASSURED; BETHLEHEM MEETS UNION TO DRAW UP CONTRACT

"Your Place Is in the SWOC," Says Baltimore Priest

Rev. John F. Cronin, S. S., well-known Catholic priest of Baltimore, has thrown his support to the Steel Workers Organizing Committee, which will be involved in a Labor Board election at the Sparrows Point, Md., plant of Bethlehem Steel.

"I am asking you to join the union for the future of America by getting men interested in unionism and no other 'ism,'" said Father Cronin, professor of economics at St. Mary's Seminary, Baltimore.

"Whatever you have received in the last four years in the way of better wages or improved working

Contract Parleys Started in 'Little Steel'; SWOC Asks 10-Point Program

MEET IN FOUR CITIES

Union Shop, Check-off Included in Proposals Now Being Discussed

Conferences to cover 170,000 steel workers in four "Little Steel" companies are now under way, based on a 10-point union program which includes the union shop and the check-off.

Union officials and management officials of Bethlehem Steel, Republic Steel, Youngstown Sheet & Tube,

Twenty Thousand to Vote in Election Sept. 25 in Last Big Bethlehem Mill

VAN BITTNER TO SPEAK

Parade and Mass Meeting on Sept. 23 to Climax SWOC Organizing Campaign

Another Labor Board election victory for the SWOC in Bethlehem Steel was certain, as final preparations were under way for the voting at the huge Sparrows Point, Md., plant.

Upwards of 20,000 workers will vote on Sept. 25 in the last large

On September 25, 1941, Sparrows Point employees voted by an overwhelming majority to be represented by the **Steel Workers Organizing Committee (SWOC).** Ballots were cast at 10 polling places similar to the one shown at left at the Open Hearth Services Building.

Note: The honeycombed structures overhead contained baskets that Open Hearth employees used to keep their street clothes and valuables in during their shift. The baskets were lowered and raised by chains (at left) which were secured by personal locks.

120

STRIKE!

The Steelworkers Strike of 1952
On December 31, 1951, the **Steelworkers Union** announced that its 650,000 members would walk off the job unless they got a raise. **President Truman** turned the situation over to the **Wage Stabilization Board**. The union agreed to hold off a strike until April 8, 1952, while the Board tried to work out a compromise. After weeks of hearings, they agreed to a 26 cent an hour raise. The Union agreed and steel companies were willing to oblige as long as they could raise the price of steel $12 a ton. Truman opposed the price hike. The interests of the nation in wartime (Korean War) were too important to be jeopardized by a strike. When a strike seemed imminent. "Give 'em Hell Harry" took over the mills to keep them running. On June 2, 1952, the Supreme Court called the takeover illegal and voided Truman's order. Steelworkers immediately set picket lines and the strike lasted seven weeks. The Steelworkers Union ultimately settled for a pay increase of 21 cents an hour.

The Steelworkers Strike of 1956
In July 1956, the Steelworkers Union went on strike for 35 days. They were asking for a three year contract and the first cost of living escalator clause. They were also asking for a little-known passage called 2B. This was the past practices clause. In short, it is defined as laborers' fears of being replaced by machines. For example, if a job required three workers to perform it, three workers would always be assigned to that job, even if the technology available did not require it. The clause also demanded that the company could not change the pay rate. This clause would cause Bethlehem Steel Company a great deal of trouble in the future. **Footnote 24**

Top photograph: Steelworkers mingle along the picket line at the Sparrows Point Plant on April 30, 1952. Note the presence of a significant number of Sparrows Point Policemen.

Bottom photograph: John Hamric holds a sign stating that "This plant on strike." Note the idle blast furnace in the background.
Photos courtesy of Bill Goodman.

Sparrows Point Police Officers Joe Robertson and Raymond Gable maintained a lonely vigil at the Tin Mill Clockhouse during the strike of 1952. Both photographs courtesy of Bill Goodman.

Steelworkers Local #2610 manned a picket line in front of the Main Office on March 28, 1968. Robert Schweiger, union member, passed out picket signs as union members protest.

In 1958, Fortune Magazine put six Bethlehem Steel Company executives on the top 10 list of the nation's highest paid executives. Arthur B. Homer, Chairman of the Board, topped the list with a salary of $511,249. That year, Bethlehem boasted profits of $137 million dollars and Homer proposed that steelworkers take a one year wage freeze. At the time, the average steelworker was making $1.96 an hour. Tired of the discrepancies, steelworkers at the Sparrows Point Plant and across the nation went on strike on July 15, 1959. The strike lasted for 116 days.

BLAST FURNACE DEPARTMENT

GENERAL

(Information compiled as of October 1960)

- Operating personnel—1,190
- Acreage—146
- Annual rated pig iron capacity—5,480,000 tons
- Annual rated sinter capacity—4,380,000 tons

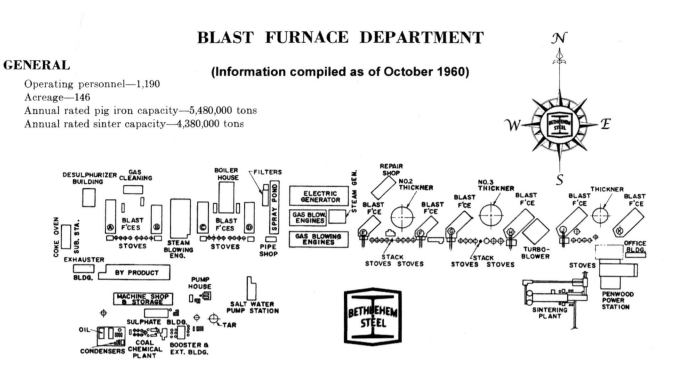

FURNACE PHYSICAL DATA

	FURNACES									
	A	B	C	D	E	F	G	H	J	K
Built	11/87	11/87	3/89	3/89	3/20	7/20	10/41	4/48	7/53	3/57
Rebuilt	3/28	3/29	7/33	4/37	—	—	—	—	—	—
Hearth										
Type	Carbon	Carbon	Carbon	Carbon	Carbon	Carbon	Carbon	Carbon	Carbon	Carbon
Diameter	25'6"	25'6"	28'0"	28'0"	19'9"	19'9"	28'0"	28'9"	28'9"	28'9"
Thickness	3'5½"	3'5½"	3'7"	3'7"	3'1½"	2'4½"	3'3½"	3'8"	3'8"	3'8"
Height	11'11"	12'1"	11'11"	11'11"	11'9"	13'5"	11'11"	11'11"	11'11"	11'11"
Volume—cu. ft.	6,090	6,170	7,294	7,294	3,542	4,110	7,294	7,709	7,709	7,709
Area—sq. ft.	511	511	615	615	306	306	615	649	649	649
Bosh										
Diameter	28'9"	28'9"	31'3"	31'3"	23'9"	23'9"	31'3"	32'4½"	32'4½"	32'4½"
Thickness	1'10½"	1'10½"	1'10½"	1'10"	1'10½"	1'10½"	1'10½"	2'3"	2'3"	2'3"
Height	12'9"	12'9"	12'9"	12'9"	12'4"	12'4"	12'9"	12'9"	12'9"	12'9"
Slope	82°44'12"	82°44'12"	82°44'12"	82°44'12"	80°47'20"	80°47'20"	82°44'12"	81°54'33"	81°54'33"	81°54'33"
Volume—cu. ft.	7,377	7,377	8,772	8,772	4,595	4,595	8,772	9,365	9,365	9,365
Stack										
Slope—in./ft.	1.002	1.002	1.287	1.287	0.968	0.968	1.074	1.060	1.060	1.060
Stockline Dia.	20'0"	20'0"	20'8"	20'8"	16'9"	16'9"	21'2"	22'0"	22'0"	22'0"
Volume—cu. ft.	31,624	31,624	34,710	34,710	20,436	20,436	38,935	41,200	41,200	41,200
Thickness	2'9½"	2'9½"	3'9½"	3'½"	3'⅝"	3'⅝"	3'7-15/32"	3'10½"	3'10½"	3'10½"
Ratio—Hearth Area : Stack Vol.	1:61.89	1:61.89	1:56.44	1:56.44	1:66.78	1:66.78	1:63.31	1:63.48	1:63.48	1:63.48
Bell										
Diameter	15'0"	15'0"	15'8"	15'8"	12'0"	12'0"	15'8"	16'6"	16'6"	16'6"
Slope	50°	50°	50°	50°	45°	45°	50°	50°	50°	50°
General										
Offtake Dia.	4'6"	5'0"	5'6"	5'6"	3'6"	3'6"	5'6"	5'6"	5'6"	5'6"
Height—Taphole to Fce. Ring	99'8"	99'8"	95'0"	95'0"	94'10"	95'5"	102'0"	105'3"	105'3"	105'3"
Type Top	Neeland	Neeland	McKee	McKee	Neeland	Neeland	Neeland	McKee	McKee	McKee
No. Tuyeres	16	16	20	16	12	12	16	20	20	20

STOVES

Blast Furnace, continued

Furnace	No. of Stoves	Size (Ft.)	Heating Surface (Sq. Ft. Total)
A	4	22 x 125	545,601
B	4	22 x 125	526,901
C	4	22 x 125	543,040
D	4	22 x 125	524,340
E	4	22 x 100	400,000
F	4	22 x 100	368,530
G	4	22 x 125	524,340
H	3	28 x 133	825,939
J	4	28 x 135	881,708
K	4	28 x 135	881,708

AUTOMATIC MOISTURE CONTROL

Furnaces A, B, C, D, H, J, K.

HIGH TOP PRESSURE

"C" Furnace—Conventional blower, 100,000 CFM @ 30 lbs
"J" Furnace—*New blower, 125,000 CFM @ 35 lbs.
    *To be installed during 1961

FURNACE RELINING STATUS

Furnace	In Blast Since	Last Relined Hearth & Stack
A	7/57	7/57
B	5/57	5/57
C	1/59	1/59
D	2/56 Presently down for stack repairs	2/56
E	3/53 Presently down-sealed	3/53
F	Idle Being relined	4/60
G	11/54	11/54
H	7/55 Presently down-sealed	7/55
J	Idle Not started up after reline	6/60
K	3/57	3/57

BLOWING ENGINES

Quantity	Unit	Kind	Capacity CFM	Rated Pressure PSI
2	Recip. Double	Steam	58,000	30
9	Two Cylinder Single	Gas	189,000	30
5	Two Cylinder Single	Gas	113,000	30
3	Blowers	Turbo	240,000	30
*6	Blowers	Turbo	600,000	30

*1 turbo-blower to be replaced with new 125,000 CFM @ 35 psi blower.

FLUE DUST RECOVERY SYSTEM

Dry

> 10 Dust catchers (1 at each blast furnace)
> Furnaces A, B, C, D, E, F and G have 30′ diameter dust catchers
> Furnaces H, J, and K have 41′-6″ diameter dust catchers

Wet

> 1 — 170′ diameter thickner serving furnaces A, B, C and D
> 1 — 130′ diameter thickner serving furnaces E and F
> 1 — 130′ diameter thickner serving furnaces G and H
> 1 — 90′ diameter thickner serving furnaces J and K
> 1 — 80′ diameter final thickner at Sinter Plant
> 2 — 8′-6″ diameter filters at Sinter Plant

ANNUAL RAW MATERIAL CONSUMPTION

Ore	8,775,200 tons (approximately 3,000,000 tons are sinter)
Coke	4,086,000 tons
Limestone	1,554,000 tons

TYPICAL FURNACE MATERIAL BALANCE (depends on ore quality, etc.)

In	Out
2.00 tons ore, sinter, etc.	1.00 ton pig iron
0.40 tons limestone	0.45 tons slag
0.70 tons coke	5.05 tons blast furnace gas
3.50 tons air	0.10 tons flue dust
——	——
6.60 tons	6.60 tons

ORE HANDLING FACILITIES

Main Field—2,500 ft. x 350 ft. (2,000,000 tons capacity)

> 1 Mead Morrison bridge and unloader—24 ton bucket
> 1 Mead Morrison bridge and unloader—28 ton bucket
> 1 Wellman bridge and unloader—28 ton bucket
> 1 Brown hoist bridge and unloader—24 ton bucket
> 2 Dravo unloaders—24 ton buckets
> 1 Hoover Mason bridge—15 ton bucket
> 2 Heyl and Patterson unloaders—12 ton buckets

Auxiliary Field—1,517 ft. x 350 ft. (1,500,000 tons capacity)

> 1 Heyl and Patterson bridge—23 ton bucket

Belt System

> The conveyor system is fed by five bridges and unloaders
> Stocking out—6,200 tons/hr.
> 48″ belt length—900 ft. long
> 60″ belt length—1 mile long

DEPARTMENT EQUIPMENT

> 43 — 125 ton mixer type ladles (3 more on order)
> 55 — 800 cu. ft. twin pot cinder cars (6 more have been approved)
> 60 — 50 ton flue dust cars
> 6 — 75 ton trestle transfer cars (ore)
> 5 — 50 ton trestle transfer cars (coke)
> 1 Double strand (Heyl and Patterson) pig casting machine—800 tons/day capacity

MISCELLANEOUS

Blast Furnace, continued

Approximately 4,800 feet of elevated ore trestle
Ore unloading pier—2,200 feet long
Approximately 250 ore ships unloaded annually (average 30,000 tons/ship)
48,263,000,000 cu. ft. blast furnace gas produced in March 1960.

SINTERING FACILITIES

Dwight Lloyd Type of Strands

Number	6
Installation	No. 1—Dec., 1952; No. 2—Jan., 1953; No. 3—May, 1956; No. 4—Sept., 1956; No. 5—June, 1957; No. 6—July, 1957
Length	102 feet
Width	6 feet
Speed—min.	3 feet/min.
Speed—max.	10 feet/min.
Size manifold	6 in.
Type burner	¾ in. pipe pinched at end to $\frac{3}{16}$"
Ignition fuel	Coke oven gas
Bed depth	10 in.
Tons sinter/day/strand	*2,000
Tons sinter/day/sq. ft. of wind box	3.2 to 3.6
Wind box	
Static pressure	—27 in. water gauge
Number	16 per strand
Area	612 sq. ft.
Air—CFM	127,000 to 144,000
Fans	
Type	Flat paddlewheel
Number	1 each strand
HP	1,000
CFM	144,000
Screens	
Type	Vibrating, screen building; minus ⅜" to storage bins. Plus ⅜" to minus 3" to lump storage bins. Plus 3" to Open Hearth. Vibrating after coolers; minus ⅛" return to storage bins, plus ⅛" to lump storage.
Coolers	
Type	Rotary
Number	One each strand
Time holding	Approximately two hours
Pug mills	Double shaft, two in series
HP	60 each
Ore screen rate	1,600 tons/hr.

*To be increased to 2,500 tons/day/strand (15,000 tons/day total)

SCALES

Quantity	Capacity	Type
1	600,000 x 20	Track Scale
1	400,000 x 20	Track Scale
2	180,000 x 20	Hopper Scales
3	85,000 x 100	Track Scales
1	80,000 x 100	Track Scale
2	80,000 x 20	Hopper Scales
1	60,000 x 100	Track Scale
1	60,000 x 50	Track Scale
1	50,000 x 250	Crane Scale
8	50,000 x 50	Track Scales
10	10,000 x 25	Hopper Scales
16 Miscellaneous small scales		

CRANES

10-15 ton cranes (one at each furnace)

Clean Sweep

The photograph above shows "A" Furnace on February 20, 1948 and the crew who completed the reline. Note the broom with a 26 on it, indicating the amount of time it took to complete the job from start to finish. Photo courtesy of Al Hastings.

"I started to work at the Point in February 1947. I was an **Apprentice Bricklayer** when we did a **reline** of "A" Blast Furnace. The 404 Labor Department tore it down from the top to the bosh where the metal starts. Then, we relined it. The whole job took **26 days from start to finish**. At that time, it was a world record." ~Al Hastings, Division Foreman - Brick Department, 1947 – 1983.

Blast Furnace Reline

"The first step in a blast furnace reline is to **pull the wind off** of the furnace. All of the gas and air are turned off. This keeps the pressure out of the **bustle pipe**. Once this is done, you remove the top housing mechanism that includes the **hopper and the bell**. These are lifted from the top of the furnace by a crane. The next step is to cut a hole in a section of the **bosh** so that debris can be pulled out of the old lining. **Riggers** come next and install a swinging scaffold. Four cables hold the **swinging scaffold** in place. The Labor Gang comes next and they get on the swinging scaffold and begin tearing down the brick lining of the furnace from top to bottom. As they work their way down, they use a ladder to climb back to the top when their shift changes. The ladder has a tubular basket attached to it for safety purposes.

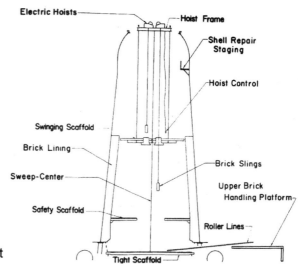

"After the labor gang has torn down the old lining and it has been cleaned out, the **carpenters** come and install a **safety scaffold** at the **mantle level**. Another hole is cut above the mantle to receive the new lining material and it is placed on the safety scaffold. The swinging scaffold is now located just above the safety scaffold and the bricks are ready for installation. A 1 ½ inch cable was installed top to bottom as a center line. The bricks are tapered to accommodate the circumference of the furnace as well as the sloping walls. **Three brick sizes were used – 18 inch, 15 inch, and 9 inch**. They are laid in a **slurry**. We had a wooden pail with a U-shaped yoke on it. For every foot we went up the wall, we would cut off an inch of the pole. The pole was swung around from the center line to the furnace wall to make sure the new lining was uniform all the way around. Also, each foot we went up, the riggers would install **stack coolers** which were used later when the furnace was running as a cooling device. As we proceeded up the furnace wall on the swinging scaffold, bricks were placed on slings and hoisted up to us. There were two hoists. As a rule, we would try to install two vertical feet on each turn. When we finally reached the last ten feet of the furnace reline, **wear plates** would be installed. Wear plates lined the inside of the furnace at the top to reduce damage that was caused when the **burden** (coke, ore and limestone) were dumped into the hopper and made their way down

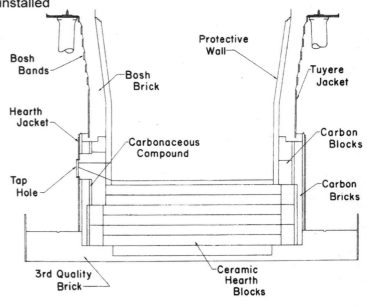

into the stack. There were two gangs at work on a furnace reline. One that relined the stack and another group that worked on the bosh area. The bosh reline started with eight courses of bottom block that was twelve feet high. It was a solid layer of brick covering the entire bottom of the furnace floor. Then, we would start the **bosh sidewalls**. This was a 22-inch thick wall that went up the mantle. When we got to the **tuyeres**, we had to make 24 holes to accommodate them. The riggers would come in next to install the **bosh coolers**. There were 30 of them – one every foot. Once that was done, the carpenters came back in and took out the safety scaffolding. We then continued up to where we started at the underpinning. At this point, the entire furnace had been relined from top to bottom. In addition to relining blast furnaces, we also relined blast furnace stoves, the open hearths and hot metal sub cars." ~ Al Hastings, Division Foreman – Brick Department, 1947 – 1983.

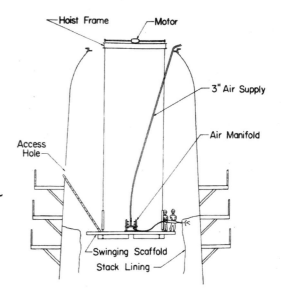

No. 8 ("H") Blast Furnace Excavation

Blast furnaces were sometimes referred to in number form and sometimes in letter form. The foundation for **No. 8 Furnace, also known as "H",** was being prepared in the photograph above on April 28, 1947. Note the steam-driven pile driver and the wooden timbers being driven into the ground. The houses in the background were located in the 500 block of "B" Street, a very close proximity for a residence to the blast furnace. Photograph courtesy of Dundalk Patapsco-Neck Historical Society.

A Lot of Progress on No. 8 Blast Furnace

Significant progress had been made on No. 8 Blast Furnace since the excavation in April 1947. Shown here on December 2, 1947, the **casthouse** has begun to take shape around the **furnace stack**. No. 8 Blast Furnace was blown in during April 1948. Photo courtesy of Dundalk Patapsco-Neck Historical Society.

"H" Furnace, Circa 1950

"H" Furnace, looking northwest, shortly after it was blown in. The furnace was only two years old when this photograph was taken. **Hoppers of limestone and Open Hearth slag** are shown on the center track at the base of the furnace. **Coke and ore** were distributed on the two tracks on each side of the **center track** on the **trestle**. For perspective, note the man in the lower right hand corner of this photograph. **Footnote 25**

World Record for "H" Furnace

"H" Furnace looking southwest circa 1950. The large structure in the foreground is the casthouse. On the left is an inclined skip. The inverted Y shape structure in top of the furnace are **furnace uptakes**. In August 1951, "H" Furnace set a **world record** of 55,835 tons of hot metal in one month.

← "K" Furnace looking west on Blast Furnace Row. Also visible are "J" and "H" Furnaces. "K" Furnace was blown in during March 1957 and would be the last furnace built at Sparrows Point until "L" Furnace was completed in 1978. "K" Furnace was razed in 1990.

"I went to work at the Point in 1974. My first job was in the 56-66 Inch Cold Sheet Mill. I worked as a Laborer and eventually moved up to **third feeder** on a mill. My job was to break the tail of the coil down and flatten it out so that it could be started in the mill. Using a six button remote, you would unwind the coil a few feet. The tail had an arc in it and I would step on it and bounce up and down several times to straighten it out. I got laid off from that job and bid on a job in the Pipe Mill. The Pipe Mill is one of the noisiest places in the whole plant. When I first started, they said they had enough work to last for seven years. I worked there for 30 days and got laid off. My first eight years at the Point, I was laid off for six. One of my jobs in the Pipe Mill was to maintain the **bullies**. Bullies were large cylindrical pieces of pipe used for heating pipes to keep them from freezing. I would have to shake them down to get the ashes out of the bottom and then refill it with coke. After leaving the Pipe Mill, I went to the 68 Hot Strip Mill as a Mechanical Helper. My job was to change the bearings on work rolls. I did that job for two years.

"In 1978, I applied for and was accepted into the Ironworker Apprenticeship Program. At that time, it was known as an erector apprenticeship. It was a four year program. We received instruction in algebra, geometry, sheet metal layout, rigging, burning, and welding. When I finished the program, I was a "C" Rate Ironworker. We were primarily maintenance ironworkers. We worked all over the plant from the unloading towers to finishing. Most of the work was at the "L" Furnace and No. 7 Strand. We worked in gangs. Each gang had three Ironworkers: **a Fitter, a Burner, and a Welder.** Each morning, the boss came out and lined us up for the day. The Fitter was in charge of the gang. I was a Fitter. My job was to take measurements and lay the job out. The Burner would use a torch to burn a steel plate and the Welder would do the attachment of the parts. I was an "A" Rate Fitter. Each job had to be coordinated. A crane, tool wagon, welding machine, and gas and iron had to be brought to each job site. We also called in a jock strap – three bottles of oxygen and a bottle of mapp gas.

"An example of the type of work we did was to repair the 120-inch diameter gas main used by the Blast Furnace. An inspector would walk the catwalk to check the line for leaks. Once he found a leak, he would mark it and put in a job order. Before the job could be started by our gang, the fire department came out to the site to conduct three tests. One for toxicity, one for explosiveness, and one for oxygen deficiency. If it passed these inspections, we were given the okay to proceed with the repair. Once we got the job order, we would check it out. It might require a crane with a man in a basket. We might have to build scaffolding under the job. Depending on the size of the hole, we could sometimes drive a wooden peg into the hole and cut it off flush with the pipe. We then determined how far back from the hole we had to go before we found solid metal. Once that was determined, we cut a square bar and welded it over the hole. The square bar also had a hole in it. A fitting was attached to the hole to allow an air hose to be attached. This hose was extended through the ground to allow the gas in the pipe to escape. Once the gas was out, the welder would close the hole with a permanent plug. Wherever something needed to be repaired involving metal, we could be called in to fix it." ~Les "Buck" Rabuck, "A" Rate Fitter – Rigging Department, 1974 - 2003

The Casthouse

Frank Weiskopf is shown looking into the mouth of a **hot metal sub** to watch the level of iron as it rises in the sub. When the sub was almost full, another worker would **throw a gate** and let iron flow down a runner to the next spout and fill another sub. Timing was crucial during this operation. It was important to fill each sub as much as possible so as to never run out of space to put the flowing iron. It was also important to never spill liquid iron over a sub and down onto the tracks below the casthouse floor.

Below, George Toth is shown taking a sample of liquid iron and pouring it into a small mold. Once the iron had solidified, the sample would be taken over to the **Chem Lab for analysis of silicon, carbon, and sulfur**. This information would then be passed on to the Open Hearth so that they would know the chemistry of the hot metal that would be coming over to them from this particular cast.

Both photographs courtesy of Bill Goodman and dated April 1952. Special thanks to John Lovis for his technical advice.

"K" Furnace on Blast Furnace Row

"K" Furnace was blown in during March 1957. That year, Blast Furnace Row produced a record 4.6 million tons of metal. "K" Furnace had a 28 foot, 9 inch hearth diameter. The bosh was 32 feet, 4 ½ inches. It had 20 tuyeres and was rated at 1,800 to 2,400 tons per day.

Salamanders and Carbon Bottoms

"After continual use, the solid bottom of a furnace would erode into a **concave bowl** shape where the last metal tapped out of the furnace would collect and be trapped. This mass of metal was known as a **salamander**. In order to get this metal out you had to **jackhammer** into the furnace floor until you reached a red hot area. You then used a series of **oxygen lances** to push into the pool of molten metal to release it.

"After World War II, it was discovered that the Germans were using **carbon bottoms** in their blast furnaces. These were much more durable and longer lasting. We then changed over to carbon bottoms at Sparrows Point. They measured 22 ½ inches by 22 ½ inches and were placed on the bottom in a long-short-short-long series to span the 32-foot diameter of the furnace. Once one course was laid a second course was installed. This **course was shifted 22 ½ degrees** so that the overlap would not meet at a joint. Each layer was subsequently shifted 22 ½ degrees until five layers were installed. I never recall going in to change a carbon bottom." ~Al Hastings, Division Foreman - Brick Department, 1947 – 1983. Diagram courtesy of Al Hastings

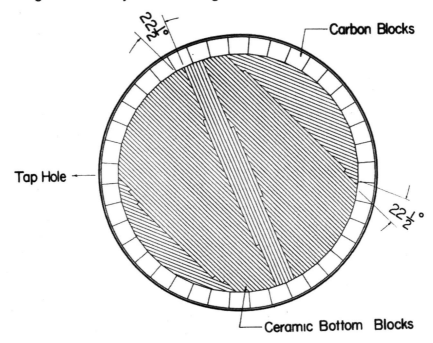

Radioactive Isotopes and Furnace Relines

"In the early days, there was a lot of guess work in **determining the thickness of a blast furnace wall.** You had to look for **red spots** which told you that the lining of the furnace was getting thin. Pipe fitters and millwrights would install a water spray system and concentrate it on the red spot.

"In the 1970s, **Geiger counters** replaced the guesswork. As a furnace was relined, a line of **isotopes** were placed in a ring around the furnace wall at different depths in the wall. When they first used the isotope method, signs were placed around the area with skull and crossbones indicating danger. At first, the bricklayers refused to work in the area because rumors had spread that the radioactive isotopes would make you sterile. However, with time, they overcame their fears and the method of using isotopes and Geiger counters for determining the thickness of a furnace wall became commonplace.

"Before the isotopes were installed, holes were driven in the reline bricks by the Machine Shop. As the wall of the reline went up, the isotopes were taken from a lead pot with tweezers and dropped in each hole. Then, a trowel of mud was placed over the hole and sealed. Later, when it came time to check the thickness of the furnace wall, a guy came with a Geiger counter. There were a series of six or eight catwalks outside of the furnace. He would then read the placement of isotopes and accurately determine the thickness of the furnace wall." ~ Al Hastings, Division Foreman - Brick Department, 1947 – 1983.

Blast Furnace Row

A view of "K" Furnace (center) and the other nine furnaces that made up the nearly 1 mile long "Blast Furnace Row." "K" Furnace was blown in during March 1957. The view is looking west towards the Patapsco River.

Looking west, "H" Furnace is in the center of the top photograph. The building just in front of the casthouse is the new **blower house**. At far right on the horizon is **No. 3 Open Hearth**. The building just to the left of No. 3 Open Hearth is the **Mixer Building**, where liquid iron was stored prior to being sent to the Open Hearth. At far left are the ore fields, bridges, and a portion of the blast furnace trestle. The large diameter pipe being installed was the blast furnace gas main that was extended east to the new **Pennwood Power House**. Below is a similar view looking northwest from the **ore basin**. Both photos circa 1948, courtesy of Dundalk Patapsco Neck Historical Society.

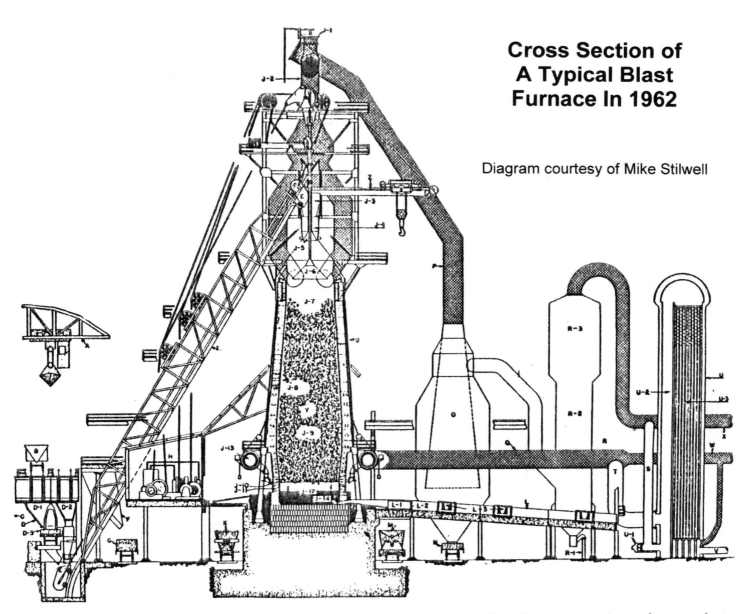

Cross Section of A Typical Blast Furnace In 1962

Diagram courtesy of Mike Stilwell

Idealized cross-section of a typical modern blast-furnace plant. Details may vary from plant to plant.

Legend

A. Ore bridge
B. Ore transfer car
C. Ore storage yard
D. Stockhouse
    D-1 Ore and limestone bins
    D-2 Coke bin
    D-3 Scale car
E. Skip
F. Coke dust recovery chute
G. Freight car
H. Skip and bell hoist
I. Skip bridge
J. Blast furnace
    J-1 Bleeder valve
    J-2 Gas uptake
    J-3 Receiving hopper
    J-4 Distributor

J-5 Small bell
J-6 Large bell
J-7 Stock line
J-8 Inwall
J-9 Bosh
J-10 Tuyeres
J-11 Slag notch
J-12 Hearth
J-13 Bustle pipe
J-14 Iron notch
K. Slag ladle
L. Cast house
    L-1 Iron trough
    L-2 Slag skimmer
    L-3 Iron runner
M. Hot-metal ladle
N. Flue dust car
O. Dust catcher

P. Downcomer
Q. Hot blast line to furnace
R. Gas washer
    R-1 Sludge line to thickener
    R-2 Spray washer
    R-3 Electrical precipitator
S. Gas offtake to stove burner
T. Hot blast connection from stove
U. Stove
    U-1 Gas burner
    U-2 Combustion chamber
    U-3 Checker chamber
V. Exhaust gas line to stack
W. Cold blast line from blower
X. Surplus gas line
Y. Stock—Iron ore, coke, limestone
Z. Jib boom crane

Diagram of Blast Furnace Department Operations

Circa 1962

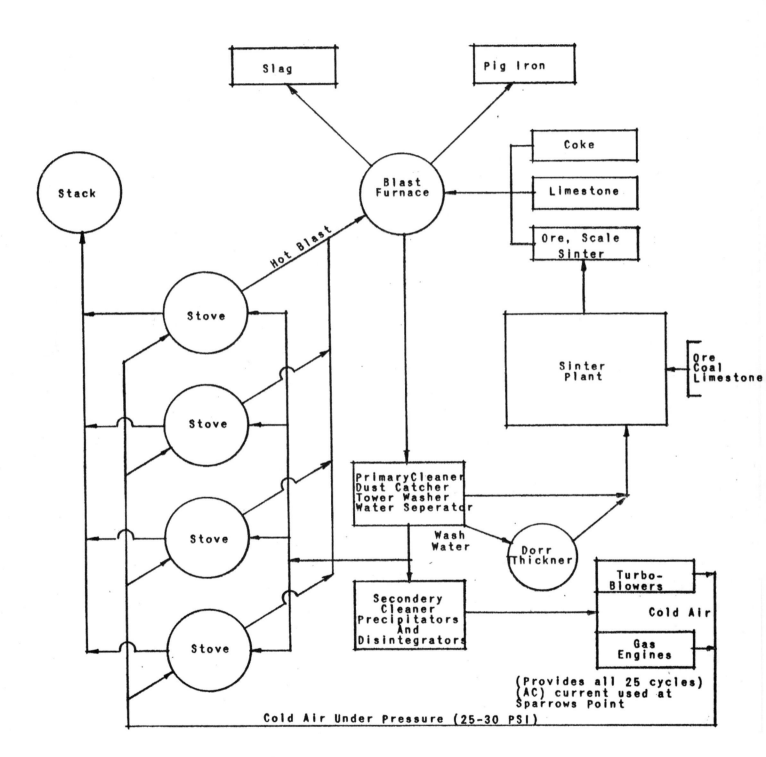

Diagram courtesy of Mike Stilwell

Flushing the Monkey

In the photograph above, the two men are in the process of **draining slag from the cinder notch** before it was time to make a **cast**. This process was also known as **"flushing the monkey."** As the slag hit the **gate**, it would be directed outside of the **casthouse** to **cinder bowls** located on the tracks below. Prior to a cast, two to four cinder bowls could be filled with slag. The cloud that is visible above the runner was a combination of fumes from the burning coke breeze that lined the slag runners and sulfur coming out of the slag itself. It appears that the men are poking the runner to keep the slag flowing continuously. On the left side of the photograph you can see the **skimmer plate** that stands at the end of the iron trough and tap hole. Photo circa late 1940s, courtesy of Baltimore Museum of Industry.

Left to right: Mike Cerreta, Joe Papa, and Vince Stevens are showing a new type of insulation that was to shield "L" Furnace tap hole drills from intense heat and molten slag. Photo dated 1989.

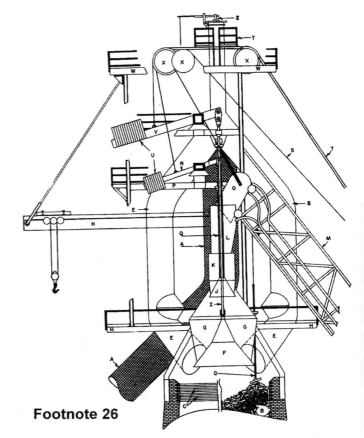

Footnote 26

Schematic diagram showing the principle operating parts of an oxygen blast furnace top of the1950s.

Legend

A. Downcomer	J. Small bell	S. Skip cables
B. Stock—Iron ore, coke, limestone	K. Distributor	T. Bell cables
C. Protection armor	L. Receiving hopper	U. Bell counterweights
D. Stock indicator	M. Skip bridge	V. Large bell beam
E. Gas uptake	N. Jib boom crane	W. Bull wheel platform
F. Large bell	O. Skip	X. Bull wheels
G. Hopper	P. Receiving hopper platform	Y. Bleeder platform
H. Main platform	Q. Small bell rod	Z. Bleeder valve
I. Large bell rod	R. Small bell beam	

"I started out as a **Millwright Helper** in the Blast Furnace Department. At first, I was a **Runner**. If they needed materials for a job, I went and got them. I also hooked up burning outfits. I put the gauges and torches on them. Whatever needed to be done to maintain the mechanical equipment for the blast furnaces, our department did it. I was a helper for 12 years. Then I took a test for an **A, B, or C Technician**. These replaced the Millwright name. I passed everything and qualified for "B" Technician. I had to stay in that position for 1,040 hours before I could take another test. I passed the lubrication test and moved up to "A" Technician in the Blast Furnace Department. Now, I was running a gang. **We changed hot blast valves on the blast furnace stoves, burner shut-off valves, regulating valves, repaired chimneys, replaced cast floor parts, and repaired bucket cars to name a few of the things we did.**

"Material from the **Stockhouse** was put in a **bucket hoist** and sent to the furnace top. There it was dumped into the top of the furnace where it landed on the **McKinley Hat**. The McKinley Hat is actually the **double bell and hopper**, which regulated the flow of raw materials into the top of the furnace. Prior to a furnace reline, we had to remove many of the hopper parts. We took out upper and lower seal valves, flow control valves, equalizer valves, relief valves, check valves, the rotating chute, wear plates, and stack rods. There were **three hoppers on top of the "L" Furnace**. We were the first gang to ever change the rotating chute inside of the "L" Furnace top.

"When I became Foreman, I had a crew of 25 men. Sixteen were from the Mechanical Department and the rest were from Fuel & Electrical. Our job was to take care of the blast furnace, the stock house, and ore handling. I retired in 1994." ~Joe Papa, "L" Furnace Maintenance Foreman, 1957 – 1994.

Pennwood Power Plant
Under Construction - 1947

The above photograph shows the **Pennwood Power Plant** under construction in December 1947. When completed, the plant's generating capacity would be raised to 114,000 KW. Prior to this, the plant's equipment included six 3,000 KW gas engine sets, one 10,000 KW turbo generator, and one 20,000 KW turbo generator, all operating at 25 cycles. Photo dated December 30, 1947, courtesy of Butch Johnson.

The Gas Engine House

← Gas Engine – Electric Power House and Blowing Engine House looking southwest.

↓ In 1938, approximately half of the total power consumption used at Sparrows Point was generated in the plant. The other half was purchased. The photograph shows the interior of the Gas Engine House with six generators which were driven by four-cylinder twin tandem gas engines. Photo courtesy of Rich Glenn.

Two tracks of railcars at right in the photograph below delivered **coke breeze** into the roofed structure that covered the tracks. There, the coke breeze was dumped into a pit where it was transferred on a conveyor to the top of **Pennwood Power (above)**. When the coke breeze arrived at the top, it went into **hoppers**. These hoppers fed the **stoker** on No. 1, No. 2, and No. 3 Boiler. Also shown in the photograph are canals separated by a steel bulkhead

The canal on the right was the **inlet canal**. It brought salt water in to cool the condensers on No. 1, No. 2, and No. 4 Generators. Once used, the water fell by gravity and exited into Jones Creek via the **outlet canal**. The saltwater also fed the high pressure pumps that fed water to the high pressure salt water system. The water was also used to feed some of the fire hydrants in the plant as well as the coke quenchers. It also fed three low pressure pumps that cooled condensers at No. 1 and No. 2 Turbo Blower buildings and No. 7 and No. 8 Generators.

Pennwood Power Station was completed in 1948. It burned **coke breeze and blast furnace gas**. The addition of this station increased generating capacity to a point where 80% of the power requirement was generated at the plant. The station contained two 400,000 pound per hour boilers operating at 900 psi, 900 degrees Fahrenheit. Each boiler contained 26,660 square feet of heating surface, 10,515 square feet of water wall surface, 11,400 square feet of super heater surface, 12,860 square feet of economizer surface, and 45,500 square feet of tubular air pre-heaters. The boilers were fired with coke breeze on **traveling chain grate stokers** and with blast furnace gas or fuel oil through combination burners. In 1953, No. 3 Boiler was added. In 1957, No. 4 Boiler was added. Photo dated 1948, courtesy of Butch Johnson.

"I started in the Rail Mill in 1947. I worked there for one year. I was a **Mechanical Helper**. I repaired machinery. Anything that broke down, we fixed it. I left the Rail Mill in 1948 and went to the **Gas Engine House** located between No. 3 and No. 4 Blast Furnaces. In there were huge generators for making electricity. I worked on **turbines and turbos**. The turbos were located in the No. 1 Blower Room and the No. 3 Blower Room. These turbos were used for blowing air to the blast furnaces.

"The Pennwood Power Plant would shut down some part of the facility every year. They brought in factory men from General Electric. We did what they told us to do. We would tear down the equipment, see what was worn, and put it in, for example, new bearings if needed. Some of the tools that were used were pipe wrenches, hammers, chisels, and impact wrenches. When working on turbines, we used a crane to lift the cap off to expose the **spindle blades**. Then, we took out the spindle and sand blasted it. We also had to clean the carbon off of the shell. Turbines were used to make electricity.

"In 1960, I got laid off. When I returned to work, I was loaned out to the 56-Inch Cold Mill as a Mechanical Bearing Changer. I worked between the 56-Inch Cold Mill and the 42-Inch Cold Mill. After that, I went to the Bull Gang. We set new machinery in the mills. I then became a Mechanical Repairman. I repaired and installed new machinery. I helped build the new Pipe Mill and rebuilt the Plate Mill. We did a variety of jobs. Anyone that had a job to do, they'd call us. It could be a job like setting a new roll grinder or doing repair work to the coke ovens. I worked all over Sparrows Point."

~Ralph Wilson, Repairman "A" – Mechanical Department, 1947 - 1988

The Humprey's Creek Water Treatment Facility, above, utilized **aerators, chemical devices, a thickener, and three football size settling basins** to treat the effluence that flowed from the plant's finishing mills. In the background above are the No. 3 Rod and Wire Mill, the No. 2 Rod and Wire Mill, and the Pipe Mills. The view is looking northeast. Below is a diagram of the treatment facility showing the mechanical aerators that are in the photo above. A new waste treatment facility was built in 2004 to meet environmental standards. Photo circa 1975, courtesy of Bill Goodman.

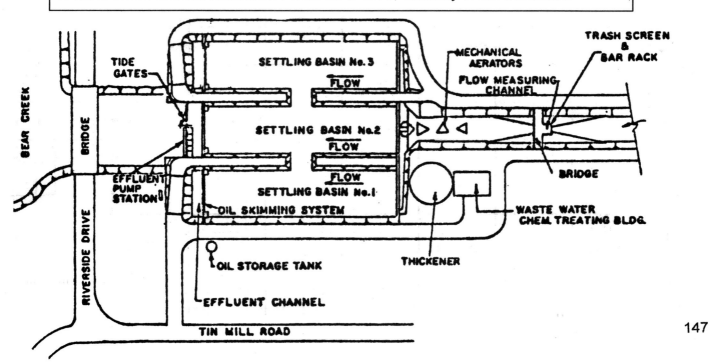

Twenty-Second Annual First Aid Meet

Bethlehem Steel began its **First Aid Competition** in 1915 – a year before they purchased the Sparrows Point property. However, records indicate that the event was not held at Sparrows Point until 1926. All departments at the steel plant participated and sent a team. Shown below is a seven man team from the **Fuel and Steam Department**. The teams were presented with a specific injury or trauma and were graded on how they "treated" the injury. This event was held between the "F" Street alley and the rear of the **Dispensary**. These events were held annually into the early 1970s.

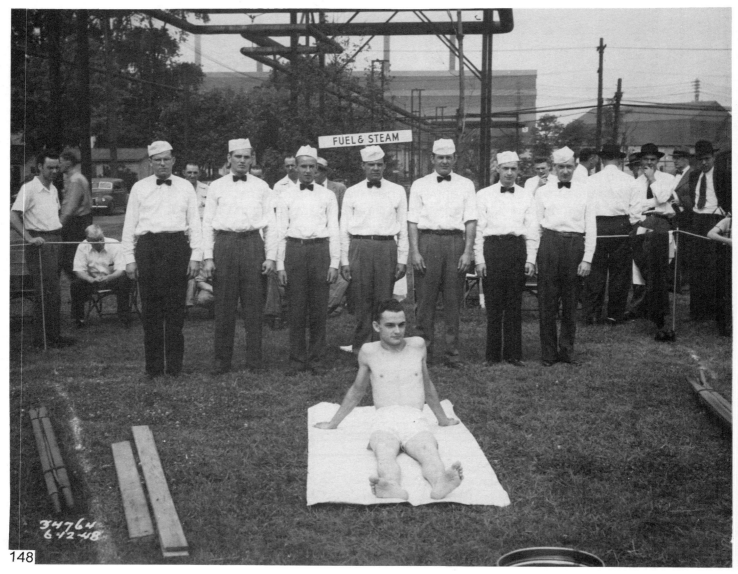

Pattern Shop

L to R: Milt Fenlock, Ed Hamill, ?, ?, Charlie, Nevin Gintling, Vernon Zephir, McFall

"I graduated from Sparrows Point High School in June 1943. I was 16 years old at the time. In order to get a job at the Point, you had to be 17, so I had to fib about my age. I started out in the Metalurgical Lab but was transferred to the Pattern Shop when an apprenticeship became available. I completed the apprenticeship when I was 18.

"The Pattern Shop was located on the west side of 2nd Street. Directly across from our shop were the company houses on "D" and "E" Streets. These houses would later be torn down when they built the No. 4 Open Hearth in 1956. Our shop remained between the No. 3 Open Hearth and the No. 4 Open Hearth after that. The job of the Pattern Shop was to make quality castings that would be used in the steel plant and in the Shipyard. We made a variety of patterns. Some small, but some very big ones such as ladle cars that carried slag. A lot of this work was done on a lathe. A lot of our patterns were made of wood but some were made of metal or plastic. After we made a pattern, it was sent to the foundry, where they made a mold from different types of sand, and then they would melt and pour hot metal into them to make whatever the order called for. Eventually, I became an "A" Pattern Maker. I worked in the Pattern Shop for 31 years. I retired in September 1974." ~Milton Fenlock, "A" Pattern Maker, 1943 - 1974

"We would go down our back alley to the Pattern Shop, which was only about a half block away. We would knock on the second window of the shop and one of the workers there would come out and ask us what he could do for us today. We would ask him if they weren't real busy, could they make us a pair of stilts. Then, he would measure us how tall we were and ask our name and tell us to come back about 4 o'clock. When we came back, the stilts were ready. They would also make Dutch wooden shoes for us to hang on the wall. I wish I still had them today. The men working at the Pattern Shop were very good to us children who lived on the Point. We had hours and hours of fun walking on our new stilts made by these men. The Point sure was a wonderful place to live." ~Regina Ewing Rosenberger, former Sparrows Point resident.

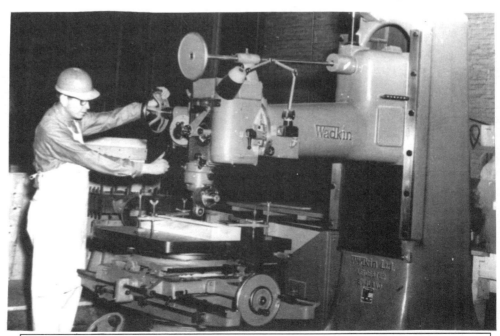

Milt Fenlock at work on a drill press in the Pattern Shop. Photo dated April 27, 1966. All photos on this page courtesy of Milt Fenlock, dated April 27, 1966.

← Pattern makers employed by the Maryland Steel Company pose for a photo circa 1905. Photo courtesy of Jack McCardell.

"John Boland McCardell was born in Hampstead, MD in 1893. His parents, two brothers – Albert and Howard, three sisters – Mary Alice, Ruth, and Elizabeth, moved to Sparrows Point in 1902. My father John worked for his father as a water boy on the railroad at the old sintering plant. My father John left school in the 5th grade to work as a pattern maker. He worked for the Maryland Steel Company and later the Bethlehem Steel Company. He lied about his age which was 11, and said he was 12 in order to get hired on. John worked for the next 56 years before retiring in 1960. I still have a wooden bucket given to him at a retirement dinner at the Sparrows Point Country Club because of his days as a water boy for his father. Until his passing, he would go to Oriole games and the Balco Club in Fort Howard and keep company with my family. John passed away in 1976." ~Jack McCardell, former resident of Sparrows Point

Iron and brass workers of the Maryland Steel Company pose for this photo taken on May 26, 1913.

Pattern Shop Floor Plan

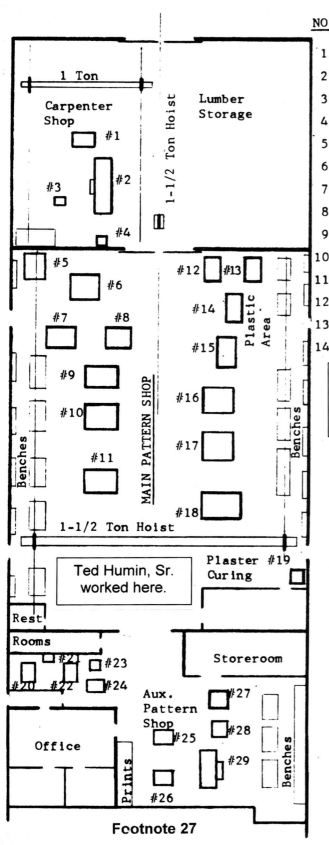

NO.	MACHINE		
		15	Face Plate
1	Table Saw	16	Face Plate
2	Cross Cut & Rip Saw	17	Double Disc Sander
3	Drill Press	18	Pattern Milling Mach.
4	Band Saw Filing Mach.	19	Curing Oven
5	Knife Grinder	20	Lathe
6	Disc & Spindle Sander	21	Tool Grinder
7	Planer	22	Lathe
8	Jointer	23	Spindle Sander
9	Table Saw	24	Disc Sander
10	Band Saw	25	Table Saw
11	Drill Press	26	Planer
12	Lathe	27	Band Saw
13	Lathe	28	Core Box Mach.
14	Band Saw	29	Jointer

"I met a secretary who worked in the Pattern Shop office. Her name was Elnora West. We married in 1951." ~Milton Fenlock, "A" Pattern Maker, 1943 - 1974 (Milton passed away in 2008. He and Elnora were married for 58 years.)

Milton Fenlock (left) and Vernon Zephir, working in the Pattern Shop in 1964. The caption on the photo read, "A row boat! You're kidding – aren't you?" Photo courtesy of Milton Fenlock.

Footnote 27

Layout of the Blacksmith Shop

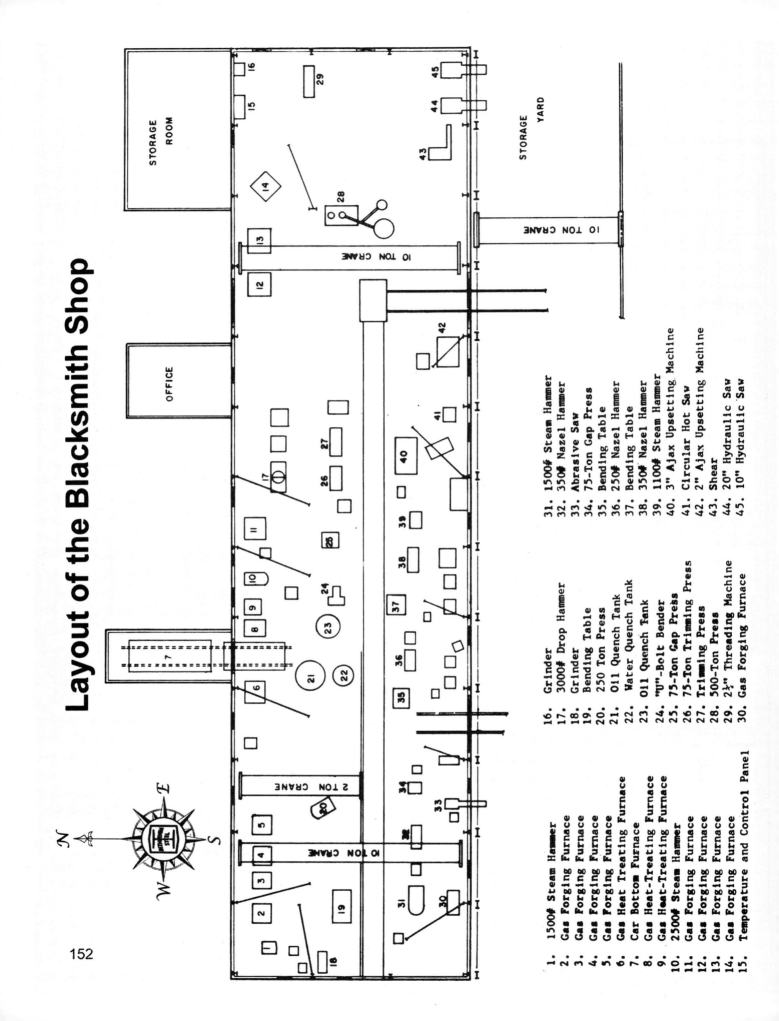

1. 1500# Steam Hammer
2. Gas Forging Furnace
3. Gas Forging Furnace
4. Gas Forging Furnace
5. Gas Forging Furnace
6. Gas Heat Treating Furnace
7. Car Bottom Furnace
8. Gas Heat-Treating Furnace
9. Gas Heat-Treating Furnace
10. 2500# Steam Hammer
11. Gas Forging Furnace
12. Gas Forging Furnace
13. Gas Forging Furnace
14. Gas Forging Furnace
15. Temperature and Control Panel

16. Grinder
17. 3000# Drop Hammer
18. Grinder
19. Bending Table
20. 250 Ton Press
21. Oil Quench Tank
22. Water Quench Tank
23. Oil Quench Tank
24. "U"-Bolt Bender
25. 75-Ton Gap Press
26. 75-Ton Trimming Press
27. Trimming Press
28. 500-Ton Press
29. 2½" Threading Machine
30. Gas Forging Furnace

31. 1500# Steam Hammer
32. 350# Nazel Hammer
33. Abrasive Saw
34. 75-Ton Gap Press
35. Bending Table
36. 250# Nazel Hammer
37. Bending Table
38. 350# Nazel Hammer
39. 1100# Steam Hammer
40. 3" Ajax Upsetting Machine
41. Circular Hot Saw
42. 2" Ajax Upsetting Machine
43. Shear
44. 20" Hydraulic Saw
45. 10" Hydraulic Saw

Iron and Brass Foundry

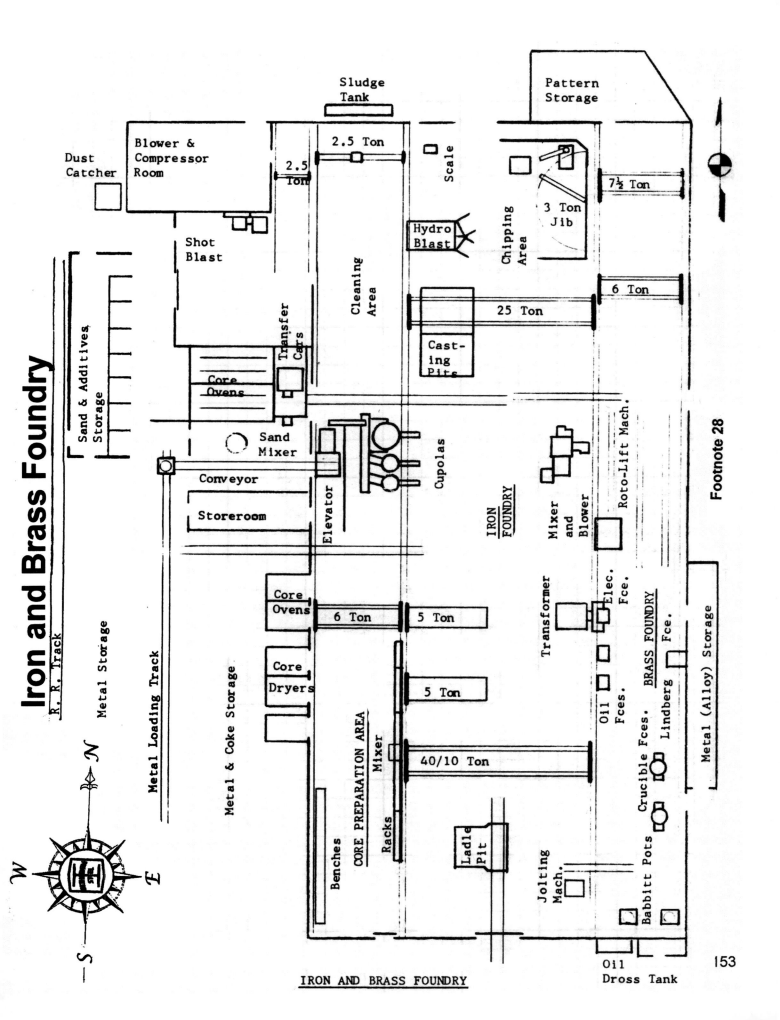

R.R. Track

Metal Storage

N

W E

S

Dust Catcher

Blower & Compressor Room

Shot Blast

Sand & Additives Storage

Metal Loading Track

Metal & Coke Storage

Sludge Tank

2.5 Ton

2.5 Ton

Scale

Cleaning Area

Transfer Cars

Core Ovens

Sand Mixer

Conveyor

Storeroom

Elevator

Cupolas

Core Ovens

Core Dryers

Benches

CORE PREPARATION AREA

Mixer

Racks

6 Ton

5 Ton

5 Ton

40/10 Ton

Ladle Pit

Jolting Mach.

Pattern Storage

7½ Ton

3 Ton Jib

Chipping Area

Hydro Blast

25 Ton

6 Ton

Casting Pits

IRON FOUNDRY

Mixer and Blower

Roto-Lift Mach.

Transformer

Elec. Fce.

Oil Fces.

Crucible Fces.

BRASS FOUNDRY

Lindberg Fce.

Metal (Alloy) Storage

Babbitt Pots

Oil Dross Tank

Footnote 28

IRON AND BRASS FOUNDRY

153

Steps to Making a Sand Casting in the Iron and Brass Foundry

"In **foundry work**, the terms **'cope' and 'drag'** refer to the upper and lower parts of a two-part casting **flask** used in **sand casting**. Shown above, the flask is the wooden box containing the molding sand and is known as the drag. The **skeleton pattern** has been bedded and is shown halfway into the drag. Sand is packed around the skeleton pattern to fill the voids. Then, the sand is swept around the skeleton pattern to take the shape of the pattern. (The man in the middle of the photograph is using a brush. The man at right is holding a piece of wood that contained the pattern number.) This particular sand casting looks like a three-way pipe. After sweeping, the excess sand is blown away and a **parting agent** is applied. This is a non-sticking powdered silica.

"At this juncture, the top part of the flask would be set in place. This part is called the cope. Now you set your **sprue**. A sprue is where you pour the molten metal into. **Risers** are put in for shrinkage, especially around the heavy parts of the pattern. Risers allow gas to come off and feeds the molten metal back into the heavy parts of the casting to keep them from cracking.

"Now you pack sand into the cope and all around the pattern until it is up to the top part of the cope. The risers are pulled out next and the sprue is enlarged to make a funnel to pour the molten metal. Then, you lift the cope off and roll it back and coat the casting with **graphite**. Now you pull the skeleton pattern out and do some sweeping away of sand to get the right thickness of the metal. Next the core is pulled out. This is the inside cavity of the pipe. Now the bottom half of the skeleton is pulled out and you cut your **gates** in. The sprue comes down and hits the **runners**. The runner feeds the gates, which go to the casting. Now the bottom is ready to be coated with graphite. The **core** is then set back in, which makes the cavity. The cope is set in place on the drag and lined up with pins. The flask is clamped down and you are ready to pour the metal.

"Whenever you did a **pour**, you always had firemen there because the flask was wooden and would often catch on fire when it came in contact with the molten metal. There were always buckets of water on hand just in case."
~Gary "Hon-Bun" James, Foundry Supervisor, 1958 – 1987
Photo dated April 14, 1948, courtesy of Dundalk Patapsco-Neck Historical Society

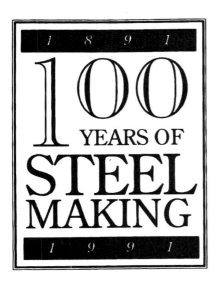

John Boeren, Foreman, came to the ⟶
ladle house as a laborer in 1950, when the
Blast Furnace Department was still using
ladles like the one shown at right.

Above: In 1950, Sparrows Point had 52 **open top ladles** for transporting hot metal. At that time, the plant was just converting to **sub cars**. The original "H" and "J" furnace subs were only 41 feet long with a 125-ton capacity. When steelmaking ended at the Lackawanna plant, some of their medium-size 230-ton subs were transferred to Sparrows Point. These subs were 64 feet long.

Below: **Double slag pots** that were used at Sparrows Point sit in the car repair area near "K" furnace **casthouse**. When the "L" furnace came on-line, it was equipped with granulated slag facilities that produced a by-product material that was sold to the cement industry. Slag no longer had to be transported as a liquid for dumping in pits or filling in the shoreline. Bottom photo courtesy of John Glaab, dated March 2006.   **Footnote 29**

Hot Metal Subs

Above is an old **Treadwell hot-metal sub**. Treadwell was a major supplier to Bethlehem Steel. These subs were equipped with a motor operated drive that rotated the ladle for dumping. The subs at Sparrows Point had a capacity of 90 to 120 tons. This particular sub was also used as a **test car**. The car to the extreme left was also a scale test car. It was made from two old Treadwell end platforms and slabs were laid across it to get the desired weight. Note the unusual six wheel trucks. The building in the background was the "K" Furnace casthouse.

Below: In 1978, "L" Furnace subs were put into service. They were built by **Pecor** and had a capacity of 330 tons. Note that No. 206 below is equipped with **16 axles**, compared to six axles on the old Treadwell sub above. Sixteen axles were required to distribute the greater weight along the rail. Both photographs courtesy of John Glaab, dated March 2006. **Footnote 30**

Sparrows Point Pistol Range

The above photograph shows the Sparrows Point Police Department Pistol Club in operation in its final year. The last year of operation was 1964. Photo courtesy of Bill Goodman.

"The Pistol Range was located near Gray's Station on Bear Creek. It opened in the late 1930s and closed in 1964. Law enforcement and security personnel from all over the country would come to Sparrows Point to compete. As many as 600 people at one time would show up. The range had a large grove of trees. Some would come in campers and set up in the grove. Thursday was practice day. On Friday, the competition would start with .22 caliber. On Saturday, they would move to .38 caliber and finish on Sunday with .45 caliber. **The range had 164 targets**. All of the targets were controlled from the target house. An operator there could control all 164 targets by pulling a single lever which would open or close them to the shooters. **The Sparrows Point Police Department had its own traveling pistol team**. **Chief Miles** was passionate about his pistol team. One of the first questions he would reportedly ask a new applicant was, 'How well do you shoot?'" ~Bob Falk, Sparrows Point Police Department, 1962-1984

A four-man team was selected to compete in matches from the six Sparrows Point policemen shown at left. Left to right standing: Lieutenant H.H. Leland, Officers Carroll LaMar, Albert Fewster, and Charles Lipscomb. Kneeling: C.A. Marshall, R.C. Clemson. Photo dated 1951.

The Sparrows Point
Police Department Pistol Club

The **Sparrows Point Police Department Pistol Club began in 1934** with two targets tacked against a stack of railroad ties. From this primitive beginning, a program of pistol instruction was developed. All Sparrows Point police officers were required to take the instructional program. This eventually evolved into the Sparrows Point Police Department Pistol Club. In 1939, the **Maryland State Pistol and Revolver Championships** were held at Sparrows Point. They continued to be held there for **25 consecutive years**. Over the years, the Club was enlarged several times. In 1951, they expanded to 120 firing points and added a club house. Sparrows Point's pistol club was comprised of 50 officers who also maintained the club. In 1951, the Sparrows Point police department employed 170 officers. The Sparrows Point Police Department Pistol Club was described as "among the finest in the country."

The Sparrows Point Police Department Pistol Club sponsored two tournaments a year – **the Maryland State Pistol and Revolver Championship and the Maryland Police Revolver Tournament**. This meet at Sparrows Point was **considered one of the more prominent events in the pistol shooting world.** Teams came from law enforcement agencies all over the country, including the US military. The outdoor range was used daily by the Sparrows Point Police Department, Baltimore County Police Department, Anne Arundel County Police Department, Baltimore City Police Department, and the Maryland State Police. The **range closed in 1964**. Footnote 31

A Brief History of the Sparrows Point Police Department

Sparrows Point Police Department, June 16, 1916. Seated, left to right: Off. Patrick Allen, Chief James Robb, Lt. George Scott. First row, left to right: Sgt. Warfield Anderson, Sgt. Charles Jones, Off. Charles James, Off. Sam Neal, Lt. Edward English, Off. Sam Kirby, Guard John Watson, Guard Robert Cox. Second row, left to right: Sgt. Harry Morrison, Off. John Campbell, Off. Carroll Jones.

After the Pennsylvania Steel Company purchased the Sparrows Point property in 1887, the mill and town grew quickly. At the time, there was no state or county police in existence, so the company hired its own police force to maintain law and order in the plant and in the town. Although the exact date of the creation of the Sparrows Point Police Department is not known, it has been verified that a security force was in existence prior to 1890. They were not, however, commissioned policemen.

As the town and plant continued to grow, there was a concern for police protection. The first special police commissions were issued on January 14, 1901 by the Governor of Maryland to seven officers. They were Patrick Allen, John Campbell, William Hughes, Frank Larrimore, McKenzie Magnadier, John Strasbaugh, and Warren VanBuskirk. On December 31, 1901, George Warren and Thomas Hughes were added and Henry Pfaff on February 5, 1902. With Pfaff as chief, these ten men constituted the new Sparrows Point Police Department in 1902. It was the second oldest police department in the state of Maryland. Baltimore City was the oldest.

The Special Police of Sparrows Point were commissioned to protect the property of the Maryland Steel Company, and later the Bethlehem Steel Company, within the state of Maryland. They were authorized to carry weapons and make arrests within their legal jurisdiction. By 1915, the Department had 29 commissioned officers, with James Robb as chief. In 1933, there were 56 police officers on the force and during World War II, the number exceeded 300.

The original headquarters of the Sparrows Point Police Department was located on the east side of 4th Street between "B" and "C" Streets. Its cell block had wooden bars. The station then moved to a building located behind the old Company Store. In 1937, the headquarters relocated to the corner of 4th and "D" Streets. They shared that facility with the Sparrows Point Fire Department. In 1957, the station moved to a new building located on 9th Street between "F" and "H" Streets. It remained there for 30 years. In 1987, the police headquarters moved over to the PBR building on North Point Boulevard.

In 1981, the Sparrows Point Police force had 154 officers. Due to economic hardships in the steel industry, that number was reduced to 17 commissioned officers by 1986. Gate security was maintained by Pinkerton's Inc., with the commissioned officers patrolling the plant and other Bethlehem property in Maryland. Between 1987 and 2012, there were seven commissioned police officers on the Sparrows Point Police Department, including the chief. The force ceased to exist in 2012 when the mill was sold at auction to liquidators who planned to dismantle the entire steel plant at Sparrows Point. Photo courtesy of the Dundalk Patapsco-Neck Historical Society. **Footnote 32** 159

BETHLEHEM STEEL COMPANY
Sparrows Point Plant
1962

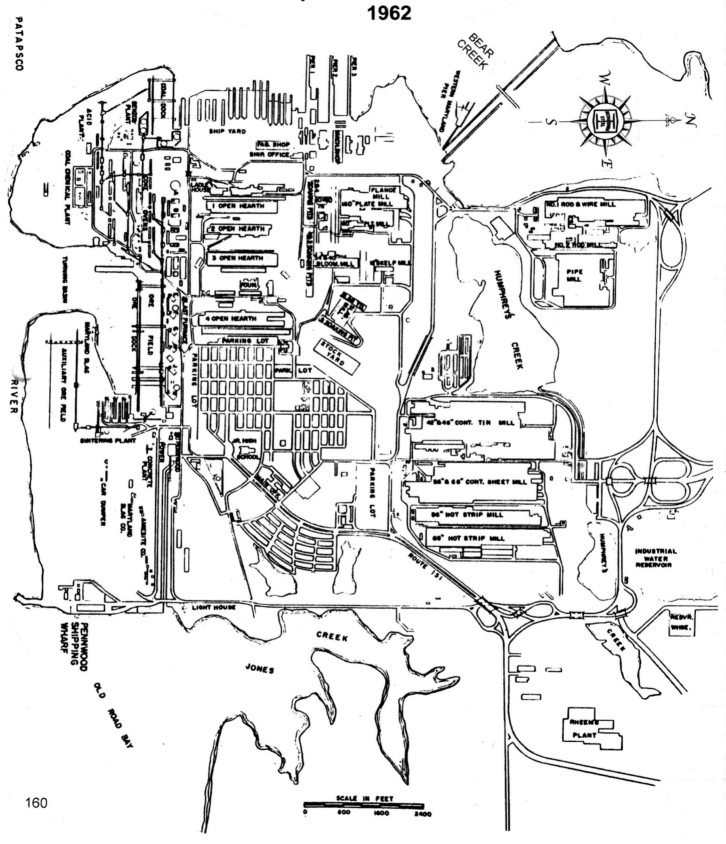

FLOW DIAGRAM – SPARROWS POINT PLANT
(As of 1960)

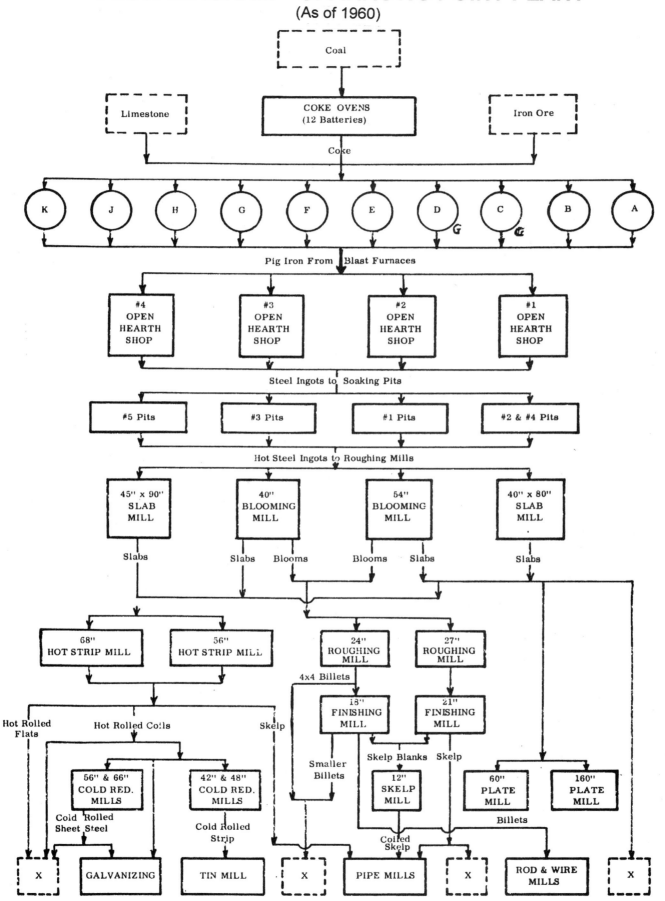

X ---- Products shipped direct to customers without further processing.

History of the Sparrows Point Shipyard

The **Maryland Steel Company** built the Shipyard at Sparrows Point in **1889.** It delivered its first ship in 1891. Between 1891 and 1917, Maryland Steel Company built 176 ships – almost all commercial, but including three torpedo destroyers, six naval colliers, and the dry dock Dewey.

Bethlehem Steel Corporation purchased the Sparrows Point Shipyard in **1917.** It continued to build tankers, ore carriers, coastal passengers, and cargo ships when other big yards were reduced to barge building. By the time the **Emergency Shipbuilding Program** for WWII started up at the Sparrows Point Shipyard, they were up to Hull #(4)327.

During WWII, the Sparrows Point Shipyard was extremely productive. Between 1939 and 1946, it built 116 ships – 68 tankers, 26 cargo, 20 refrigerated cargo, 6 ore carriers, and 6 passenger/cargo. Many of the ships built at the Sparrows Point Yard came into harm's way during the war. Thirty-four were sunk, 50 others received **Battle Stars** for heroism in places like Iwo Jima, Guadalcanal, and the Invasion of Normandy.

Following WWII, many shipyards struggled to find work, but the Sparrows Point Yard kept busy. In the 25-year period between WWII and the passage of the "Merchant Marine Act" in 1970, the Yard built 128 ships – 83 tankers, 11 ore carriers, 3 lakers, 21 general cargo ships, 7 ammunition ships, and 3 miscellaneous types.

1971 was a transition period for the Shipyard. As ships began to grow exponentially in size, the traditional method of launching a ship down an inclined way was fast becoming obsolete. That year, the Yard added a 1,200-foot long by 200-foot wide **graving dock**, served by four 200-ton cranes. During the next 20 years, the Yard produced 21 tankers, 6 container ships, 8 jack-up drill rigs, 6 tank barges, 3 container barges, 2 survey ships, and a dry dock. The largest of the ships built at the yard were five **265,000 DWT** tankers.

In 1986, Bethlehem Steel abandoned the new construction of ships at the Sparrows Point Yard. It continued in the ship repair business and moved a floating dock from the Key Highway Yard to Sparrows Point for this purpose. In 1996, Bethlehem Steel Corporation announced a comprehensive restructuring plan that included selling Beth Ships – Sparrows Point Shipyard. On October 3, 1997, the Shipyard was sold to **Veritas Capital Fund.**

Baltimore Marine Industries (BMI) was the successor to Bethlehem Steel Corporation as the owner and operator of the Shipyard at Sparrows Point. It was in operating for 2 ½ years. Due to a sluggish economy, and a general downturn in the ship repair business, the company filed for Chapter 11 bankruptcy in 2003. On November 5, 2003, BMI was sold at auction for $11.25 million to **Barletta-Willis LLC,** who indicated that they planned to use the facility to build barges and repair and build light ships. **North America Ship Recycling**, a subsidiary of Barletta-Willis, did receive nearly $3 million in contracts to dismantle a few retired ships from the US Department of Transportation's James River Reserve Fleet in Virginia. 162   Footnote 33

The 48-Inch Farrel Betts Tracer Lathe

Carlton Stuckey, Machinist "A" lathe traces a profile of a wheel tread by using a template of the tread design. Any profile could be used to suit a job requirement. Forty-eight inches is the diameter that the machine could swing over the machine ways. The length was determined by the machine's capacity.

"On August 10, 1950, I became employed at Bethlehem Steel Company's Sparrows Point plant as a Mechanical Helper. For the first 30 days, I was assigned to the 25 cycle gas engine generator building as an Oiler on No. 3 Gas Engine Generator. After 30 days, I was assigned to a repair gang but I asked the General Foreman if I could stay as an Oiler. He granted me permission but I was still classified as a Mechanical Helper, however, I still had to attend Mechanical Helper school to learn the course. During this class, an instructor asked why I was not in the apprentice program as a machinist apprentice. I told him I was not permitted to take the test as I was a high school dropout who enlisted in the Marine Corps in February 1946. He said if my General Foreman would grant me permission to take the test in writing, then I could take the test. Permission was granted and I passed the test with a grade of 87.

"On December 10, 1951, I started my four year apprenticeship in the No. 2 Machine Shop. I had to serve 8,000 hours in the Machine Shop and four hours each week in school maintaining a 70 grade average or better in both shop and classroom study. During that apprenticeship, I had to work in the mill for six months – first in the Coke Oven Department for three months and then in the Plate Mill for three months. I worked with a Millwright Gang as a Mechanical Helper. I finished my apprenticeship in December 1955 as a Machinist "C". I worked 2,000 hours in each grade, "C" and "B", before becoming a Machinist "A". I was assigned to the large machine section known as the Center Aisle. My first assignment was to work on the Five-Inch Horizontal Boring Mill where I worked most of the time. The jobs were large so they had to be handled by an overhead crane. We did a lot of boat work for the Shipyard on this machine, such as bushings, line shaft, stern tubes, etc. You were given a drawing of the job to be machined along with a planning route card with instructions of machining. You set the job on the machine, secured it, and selected the tools to machine the job. Setting up the machine was the most physical part of the Horizontal Boring Mill. The machine process was the easy part. I was also required to work other Horizontal Boring Mills when necessary.

"In 1962, I was given the opportunity to fill in as a Foreman on an as-needed basis. I worked a good bit of my time on the floor where jobs were stripped for repair and later assembled. I also filled in for the other machine sections as well – all on the 11 to 7 turn. One other thing you did as a Machinist was to go into a mill with portable machinery to repair specific parts of the mill that could not be sent to the Machine Shop. This was interesting and challenging work as very seldom was it a simple job. You were on a crew and a Foreman and you worked as a team. The mill, of course, was not an operation, so you worked thirteen hour shifts until the job was completed.

"On May 7, 1965, I became an exempt Foreman in the No. 2 Machine Shop. I was assigned to the South Aisle section on the 3 to 11 shift. Machines in this area were planers, slab millers, drill presses, and small layout tables. Shortly after, I was given the Center Aisle layout machine section with the responsibility to be the Turn Foreman. I became Quality Foreman in 1984. This required checking jobs before they were shipped to customers. It also required going to the mill when there was a problem with a job that the Machine Shop had done. This was a tough part of the job. In February 1986, Bill White became General Foreman and I was asked to be his Senior Foreman. My responsibility was to take care of the Machine Shop repair, adjust the schedule for mill break downs, handle emergencies and outages. Much of my job was now working at a computer and on the telephone to handle any problems the Machine Shop was given. On August 31, 1989 I retired. I always felt that the men in the No. 2 Machine Shop were very intelligent and could meet any challenge they were given. 'If you could get it through the Center Aisle door, we could do the job.'" ~Mike Punko, Senior Foreman, 1950 - 1989

L7A Build Up Lathe - No. 2 Machine Shop

L7A Build Up Lathe 72 Inches Over Ways – Shown in the lathe is a frame that holds an **open hearth ladle pot**. The **journals** are being machined on each end. Notice the build-up blocks under the tailstock and headstock to get a swing over 72 inches. Photo dated November 16, 1966, courtesy of Dundalk Patapsco-Neck Historical Society.

"I worked in the No. 2 Machine Shop in the **floor area**. Our job was to repair steel mill mechanical equipment. For example, in the Hot Mills, they had **mandrills** which rolled up coils. If there was a mechanical problem, they would send the unit to us and we would strip it all the way down and assess the repairs needed. We would do what we could and send the part to be repaired to a machinist or to a particular machine. The Cold Mill had similar breakdowns. A coiler might need bearings, seals, gears, or a shaft repair. We repaired equipment for the entire steel plant. It could be **backup chucks** that housed backup rolls, **coiler frames** that housed the mandrills, **reduction units** from the blast furnace, or door machines from the coke ovens.

"Sometimes I would be sent out to the mill to repair something on the job. One time, I went to **Pennwood Power**. On that job, they had a factory man. He would tell us what to do and we would assist him. The No. 2 Machine Shop was a very efficient place. There wasn't too much that we couldn't do." Ed Kraemer, "A" Rate Machinist, 1952 - 1994

KEEP THINGS Shipshape FOR SAFETY

All of the safety slogans and posters used in this publication were originated by the Bethlehem Steel Company.

You're never too old to learn about SAFETY

← 90" x 90" Ingersoll Milling Boring Machine – Adjustable rail. This machine had two overheads and two sideheads for milling and boring tools. The machine required a machinist and a machine tool helper.

↓ North Center Aisle – small lathe aisle.
▼ Both photographs dated November 16, 1966, courtesy of Dundalk Patapsco-Neck Historical Society.

"I worked in the No. 2 Machine Shop. I was upstairs on the third floor next to the tool makers. Also on that floor were the welders, hydraulic repair, and chain fall. Below the second floor were lockers and scale repair. I was hired as a Learner. After two years, I became an "A" Mechanic. Our department was divided into two parts. One part was torch repair. We repaired all of the bearing and scarfing equipment, torches, regulators, and hoses. The second part required pneumatic tools. They were called air tools such as impact wrenches, sump pumps, hoists, tampers, jackhammers, and grinders. Anything run by air we repaired for the whole plant. After a while, you would get to know these tools so well you could take them apart without looking at a drawing. There was a lot of variety in this job. It was never the same thing every day." ~Ken Fowler, Tool and Torch Repair, 1956 - 1998

No. 2 Machine Shop North Ctr. Aisle

Main Drive Bull Gear and Pinion Gear

The **main drive bull gear and pinion gear** are being matched up by **bluing the teeth** on the small gear and rotating the bull gear one revolution. After inspecting the gear teeth for pressure against each other's gear tooth, the machinist will then grind any tooth that needs to be relieved of excess pressure. The machinist shown is Edward Kunkel. Photo dated November 16, 1966, courtesy of the Dundalk Patapsco-Neck Historical Society.

"I went through a **four year apprenticeship**. It totaled 8,000 hours of work experience. When I finished, I was a **Machinist with a "C" rate**. To get to "B" and eventually "A", you had to complete 1,000 for each step. I worked on lathes, planers, slotters, shapers, and milling machines. I worked different shifts when I first started. You needed a lot of seniority to get on day shift.

"Sometimes I would get a **fabrication job**. You'd have to put it on a **layout table**. For example, it could be a ship's rudder which could weigh 80 tons. It's a three dimensional object and the job is asking for a tapered bore where the **pintle pin** goes. First, you would have to make a reference line. This would require scribing a line around the perimeter of the rudder to establish a **center line**. Then you would have to make a vertical line perpendicular to the horizontal line to determine the exact position for the pintle bore. Once this was done, the rudder goes to the **Eight-Inch Horizontal Boring Mill**. This move required a rigger and a crane operator. This was an intricate move and a precise maneuver. The 80-ton rudder would have to be lifted and moved to the Horizontal Boring Mill and placed on the **platen**, which was like a large steel floor. It was part of the Boring Mill. Once it was set, a surface gauge was used to align the rudder. Once alignment was completed, it was clamped and ready to bore. After the tapered bore was completed, the rudder then went to the **12-Inch Morton Boring Machine**. They had to set up to the bore and a slotted keyway was cut into the bore. Once this was completed, it went to the floor area where the rudder was again set up in preparation to be fitted with the rudder stock. Then, the machinist would align both pieces and coat the rudder stock with **high-spot bluing**. The rudder stock sat on two trolleys so that it could be inserted and removed from the rudder. Then, you would refine the bore hole, and then fit up the key to go into the key slot.

"Once the job was done, you would have to call in the inspectors. They would use a thousandths and a half feeler stick to check the measurements. A feeler stick is something like a spark plug gauge. Sometimes there would be several inspectors. One from the owner's people, one from the Coast Guard, and one from the insurance company. After the final inspection, the rudder was returned to the Shipyard for installation." ~Ernie Walter, Machinist "A", 1951 - 1984

The Cavernous No. 2 Machine Shop

The No. 2 Machine Shop was located between the Plate Mill and the Shipyard. It was one of the best equipped facilities and contained machines not found anywhere else on the east coast. Credit photo to Phil Szczepanski.

No. 2 Machine Shop – South Aisle

Photo dated November 16, 1966, courtesy of Dundalk Patapsco-Neck Historical Society

Sparrows Point – 1944

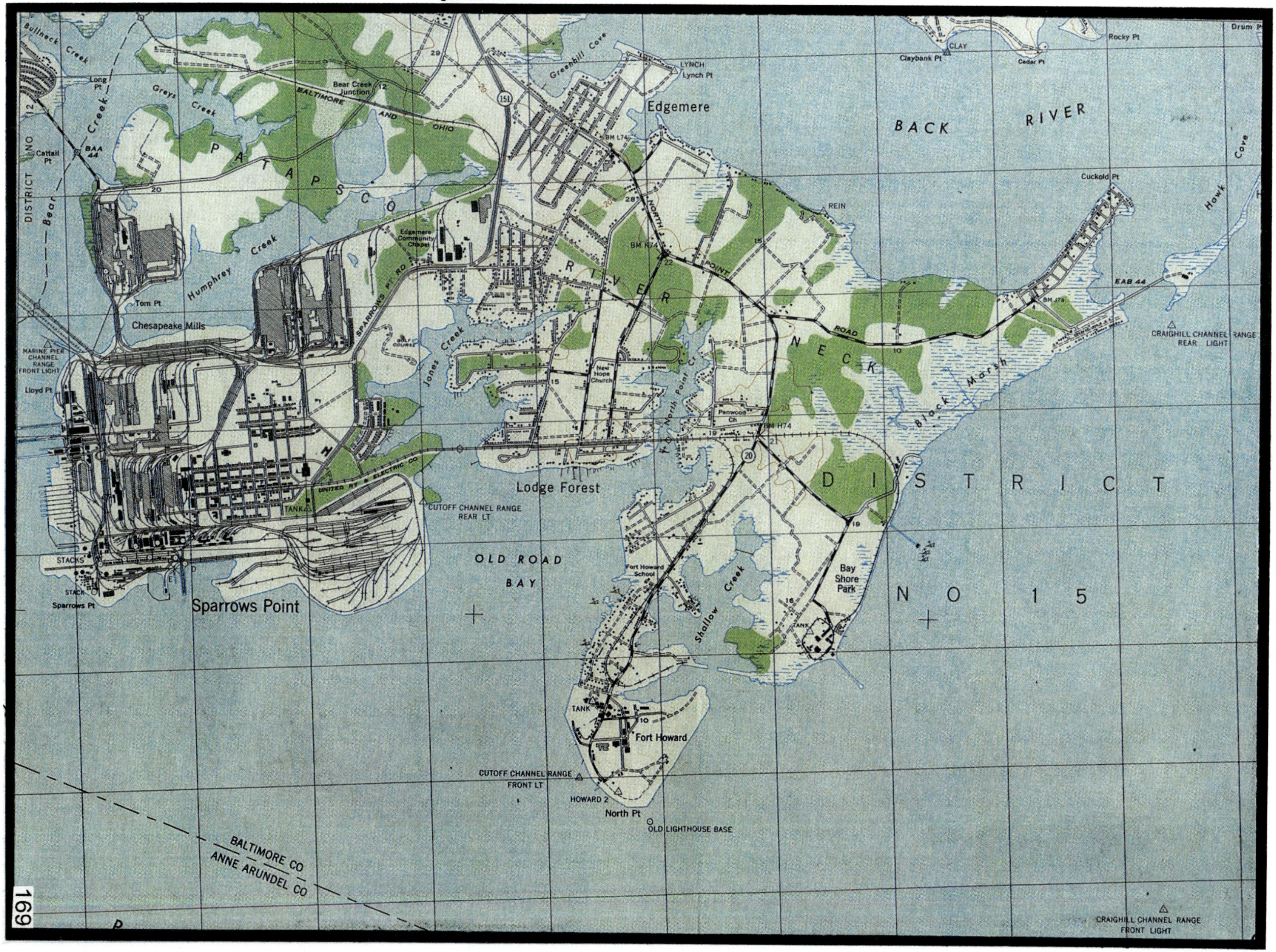

BACK RIVER

Drum Pt
Hawk Cove
Rocky Pt
Cedar Pt
CLAY
Claybank Pt

Black Marsh

EAB 44

Cuckold Pt

CRAIGHILL CHANNEL RANGE REAR LIGHT

CRAIGHILL CHANNEL RANGE FRONT LIGHT

DISTRICT NO 5

NECK DISTRICT

REIN

ROAD

Bay Shore Park

Shallow Creek

Edgemere

LYNCH
Lynch Pt

NORTH POINT

RIVER

North Point Rd

BM

Hope Church

Fort Howard School

Fort Howard

Old Lighthouse Base

TANK

North Pt

HOWARD 2

Lodge Forest

OLD ROAD BAY

CUTOFF CHANNEL RANGE REAR LT

CUTOFF CHANNEL RANGE FRONT LT

Greenbank Co

Elementary Community School

Jones Creek

BALTIMORE AND OHIO

Bear Creek Junction 1/2

SPARROWS PT RD

UNITED

PATAPSCO

Humphrey Creek

Greys Creek

Tom Pt

Chesapeake Mills

TANK

Sparrows Point

BALTIMORE CO
ANNE ARUNDEL CO

Bullneck Creek

Long Pt

Carroll Pt

BAY 44

Bear Creek

MARINE PIER CHANNEL RANGE FRONT LIGHT

Lloyd Pt

STACKS

Strick Pt

Sparrows Pt

DISTRICT NO 12

169

In 1958, Sparrows Point was the largest steel plant in the United States. It was capable of producing more than 17 tons of steel every minute. At peak operation, the workforce of about 30,000 employees received an annual payroll of about $225 million. Daily rates of water consumption: 125 million gallons of industrial water, 10 million gallons of fresh water, 500 million gallons of salt water. About 14,000 tons of coal was used daily, enough to heat 1,850 Baltimore homes for a year. Some 150,000 gallons of paint and 30,000 gallons of mastic material were used to protect the plant's 1,500 buildings, machinery, and other facilities.

1. Coal storage
2. Coke oven area
3. Coal chemical plants
4. Ore storage
5. Blast furnaces
6. Open-hearth furnaces
7. Slabbing and blooming mills
8. Soaking pits
9. Plate mills
10. Rod and wire mills
11. Pipe mills
12. Tin mills
13. Cold sheet mills
14. Hot sheet mills
15. Shipbuilding yard (Adjoins steel plant)
16. Main office building

Before...

The tree-lined tranquil scene above is the 900 block of "D" Street (looking west) in Sparrows Point in 1971. At right is Dr. Farber's office. In the far right distance in Nick's Restaurant and beyond that, Caplan's Department Store and the elementary school. Although the streetcar tracks are still there, it was more than a decade prior that the No. 26 made its last run. In less than a year, this tranquil scene would be shaken to the core as Bethlehem Steel announced that the town had to be vacated to make room for the massive "L" Furnace that was to be built over this exact location. In less than two years, the entire town of Sparrows Point was systematically demolished and carried away. A town that had its beginnings in 1887 would become nothing more than a memory for those who lived and worked there.

And After...

The massive "L" Furnace, shown here looking east in 2007, sits atop the 700 and 800 blocks of "D" Street. At left in the grassy field, was the location of St. Luke's Catholic Church and Rectory. The field at right was an open space used by children who attended the elementary school, which was located just east of the Catholic Church. The streetcar tracks remain, nearly a half century after the last car made its way down the street. A silent reminder of a bygone era. This photograph was taken at the intersection of 6th and "D" Street by Clarence "Chuck" Kuser.

Spectacular Bessemer Display

Showers of sparks, smoke and flame combine to make the **Bessemer steelmaking process** at Sparrows Point one of the most spectacular sights at the plant. Photo dated 1951, courtesy of Baltimore Museum of Industry.

Open Hearth Furnace

Tapping molten steel from an Open Hearth furnace at the Sparrows Point plant in 1951. The small ladle shown at left catches the slag overflow.

No. 4 Open Hearth

The No. 4 Open Hearth became operational in 1957.

Pennwood Power: Photo dated March 15, 2007, courtesy of Bill Goodman.

No. 7 Strand Mist Eliminator: The large red building in the background was the "L" Furnace Stockhouse. The twin structures in the foreground were the **No. 7 Strand Mist Eliminator**.

Photo courtesy of Bill Goodman.

The Ore Field: Showing the Ore Pier and three of the seven **junction houses.** Photo dated March 15, 2007, courtesy of Bill Goodman.

The Ore Fields: At right, the black pile was **coke**, the gray pile was **wasabi**, and the white pile was **limestone**. The view is looking east towards Old Road Bay and Fort Howard. Photo courtesy of Bill Goodman.

The Stockhouse: The large red building at right was the **Stockhouse**. The "L" **Furnace** is in the background. The blue building at left was the **coal pulverizing building**. The view is looking north from the Ore Basin. Photo dated March 15, 2007, courtesy of Bill Goodman.

Bessemer Remnants

Above: All that is left is the riveted framework of Sparrows Point's first Bessemer shop in this photograph taken in 2002. At the time, the structure was 111 years old. **Bessemer operations began at Sparrows Point in 1891**. Upon close inspection (not visible in the photograph), are the steel rails used for bracing columns which are inscribed with: **PS CO 89 (Pennsylvania Steel Company 1889).** Photo courtesy of Ruth Stilwell.

Bill Zablocki – Truck Driver

"Before coming to the Point, I had several jobs. I worked for Crown Cork & Seal for three years and then went to the Key Highway Shipyard. I was an Outside Machinist Helper. The job required climbing down inside the holes of ships. It was scary work. I moved on to Cross and Blackwell and was a forklift operator. Then I drove a truck for the City. In 1956, I went to the Point. My wife's parents had a friend named Mr. Sam Savage. He was head of the Safety Department for the whole Point. They talked to him and he put in a good word for me and I got hired.

"I started out in the **Sorting Room** working with the ladies. They were **Tin Floppers**. I was a **Pile Puller**. When the tin came from the shears, it was on a skid. The ladies would flip each piece of tin and check them to get the bad ones out. They saved the good ones.

When they'd get a pile of tin, I would take a hook and pull the skid out slow and then put a new skid in its place. I'd pull the skid to the **Wire Man** who wrapped the tin in cardboard to get it ready for shipment. Then a forklift took it to Shipping, and from there it went to a customer.

"I worked in the Sorting Room until the strike of '59. When I got laid off at the Tin Mill, I went to the Plate Mill and then to the Pipe Mill. My job at the Pipe Mill was to clean two furnaces they had there. They had to be cleaned everyday. I used a 25-foot long bar to chip off residue. There were three of us on each side. The furnaces had to be clean when the slabs went through. It was a very hot job and I was always glad that I got called back to the Tin Mill.

"In March 1960, an opening came up on the **Motor Pool**. I had some connections. My only experience was driving the dump truck for the City. They wanted someone for flatbeds, Yukes, and everything else. Mr. Jack Yard was the boss of the Motor Pool. He gave me the driving test. He said, 'You're a little rusty, aren't you?' He said he was going out on a limb, but he gave me the job.

"After a while, I got experience with other equipment and started driving a tractor trailer. At first, I worked at Penwood Wharf at Truck Dock 70. At first I worked daylight, then 3 to 11. A little while later, I traded a guy for midnight. I stayed on midnight for 40 years.

"After a while, I started to drive for the **Roll Shop**. At the beginning of the turn, I'd go to Dock 6 or 9 at the Hot Mill to see if they had any dirty rolls. I'd blow the horn and get a Mechanic to load the rolls. He'd get a crane operator to load them. Then I took the rolls back to Dock 15 at the 68-inch Hot Strip Mill. You had to pull in there, not back in. Harold Gribble and some guys would unload the rolls. If they had good rolls there, I'd take them back. I'd work one mill at a time, depending on the needs of the mill. Sometimes, I hauled work rolls, sometimes I hauled backup rolls.

"Dock 54 was near the Tin Mill. They had a buggy to haul rolls. They would hook it up to a wagon and take it to wherever it was needed. If it broke down, then they would call for a truck driver. Sometimes you had to do this so the mill wouldn't go down. Sometimes, I got called to the No. 2 Machine Shop to haul rolls. You went wherever you were needed. A lot of times, when I went somewhere else besides the Roll Shop, it was when I worked a double. I worked lots of doubles. Sometimes I went to the Coke Ovens to drive a Yuke. Sometimes I went to the Ore Docks. When I wasn't working a double at the Point, I worked a second job hauling for A&P. The wife said the kids needed a pair of shoes or the boys' tuition at Curley was due. I'd come home from midnight and sleep from 8 a.m. to noon and then get up and go to work for the A&P. Sometimes, I'd go to DC or Virginia, but mostly worked in Maryland. Usually, I'd work two times a week for them. I did that for 15 years.

"I worked at the Point for 43 ½ years. I never missed a day of work the first 39 years, and only one day in 43 ½ years. Whatever needed to be done, I did it. That's what I got paid for." ~Bill Zablocki, Truck Driver, 1956 to 1998.

Photo courtesy of Jack Yard.

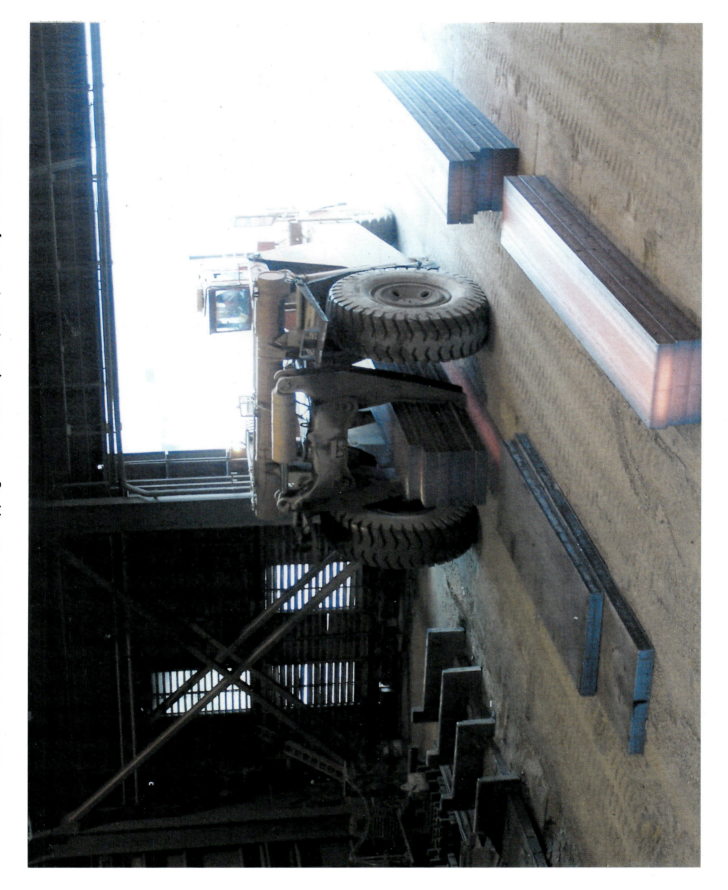

Slab Hauler at Continuous Caster Shipping. Photo dated April 30, 2005, courtesy of Bill Goodman.

Components of a Blast Furnace

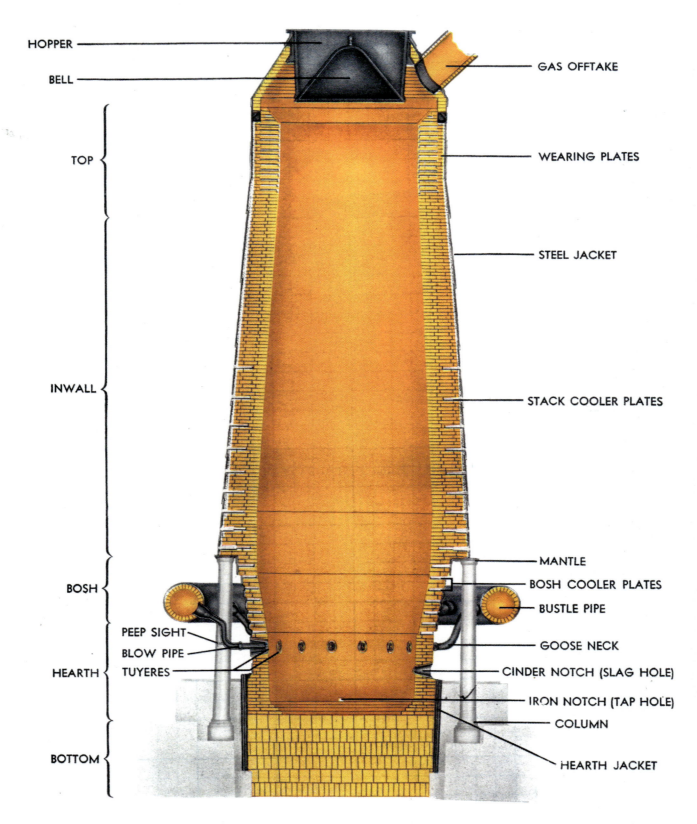

HOPPER

BELL

GAS OFFTAKE

TOP

WEARING PLATES

STEEL JACKET

INWALL

STACK COOLER PLATES

MANTLE

BOSH

BOSH COOLER PLATES

BUSTLE PIPE

PEEP SIGHT

BLOW PIPE

HEARTH

TUYERES

GOOSE NECK

CINDER NOTCH (SLAG HOLE)

IRON NOTCH (TAP HOLE)

COLUMN

BOTTOM

HEARTH JACKET

IRON BLAST FURNACE

Schematic Drawing

Courtesy of Al Hastings

FIRECLAY BRICK   STEEL

Components of a Hot Blast Stove

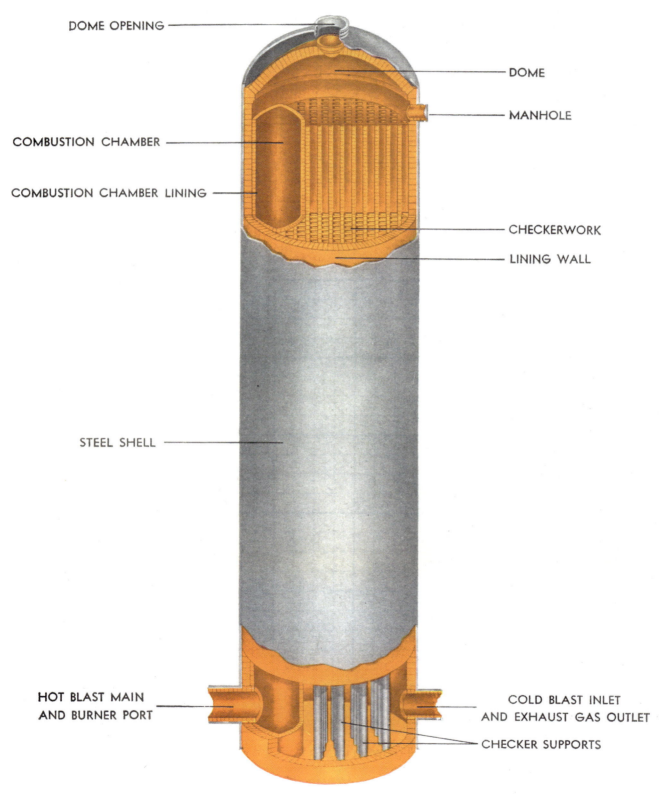

DOME OPENING

DOME

MANHOLE

COMBUSTION CHAMBER

COMBUSTION CHAMBER LINING

CHECKERWORK

LINING WALL

STEEL SHELL

HOT BLAST MAIN
AND BURNER PORT

COLD BLAST INLET
AND EXHAUST GAS OUTLET

CHECKER SUPPORTS

Courtesy of Al Hastings

HOT BLAST STOVE
Schematic Drawing

FIRECLAY BRICK   STEEL

Red Hot Glowing Ingots

A train of ingot buggies moves the still-glowing ingots from the Open Hearth to the soaking pits.

Photo courtesy of Baltimore Museum of Industry.

"Red hot glowing ingots used to be transported on flat cars. Sometimes two to four ingots at a time. Each ingot weighed 66,000 pounds. They were a beautiful sight to behold at night, especially when it was snowing." ~Jack Yard, General Foreman, Motor Pool

186

"K" Furnace Aglow in the Evening Light

"K" Furnace was blown in during March 1957. Shown here in 1970, the Cast House is lit by the glow of liquid iron flowing down the runners. "K" Furnace was banked in 1980 and razed in 1990.

No. 2 Machine Shop

Mrs. Jean Fraser   August 27, 1987
Bethlehem Steel Corporation
Sparrows Point Plant

Dear Jean:

I would like to pass on some information of a big savings,
that we recently accomplished in No. 2 Machine Shop.

The Landis 60" x 240" Type 30 Roll Grinder located in the
48" Tandem Mill was in very bad need of an overhaul after
30 or more years of service. John Taylor, Maintenance
Foreman of the Roll Shop sent out for bids to overhaul
this grinder. A copy of the bid from the Delaware Valley
Machinery, Inc. is enclosed. $740,782.00 plus 44 weeks.

John contacted the tool room of No. 2 Machine Shop and
asked for our opinion and guidance. We then sent a tool-
maker to check out the repairs required. It was checked
and found that we could handle this job in the shop.
After considering our shop rate, etc., we told John that
we could take the grinder out, transport it to No. 2 Shop,
do all the machining repairs, liners etc. and put it back.
in the mill. Our estimate for all this work was $120,000.00
and approximately 6 weeks shop time.

The grinder was released on May 26th. A week later we had
it stripped, off its foundation and in the shop. The work
progressed until July 22nd when it was shipped back to
the mill. 7 weeks in the shop at this point no overtime
was worked in the shop.

The final total of hours worked by toolmakers and machinists
in the shop and mill came to 1623.50 hrs. x shop rate of
$38.50 equals $62,504.75. Your may check with John Taylor
on other time, electrical etc.; considering that 95% of
the work was done by No. 2 Machine Shop. This is a big
saving.

Shown in the photographs – top left: Mike
Punko; top right: Harry Pugh; bottom left:
Dennis Evans; bottom right: J.A. Jakowski.
Below: graphic of metal working lathe from a
1911 illustration.

Lathe.

The Basic Oxygen Furnace Process

Iron from the blast furnace was poured into the Basic Oxygen Furnace at Sparrows Point where it was refined into steel. Photo circa 1978, courtesy of James Kidd.

Late in 1965, two 200-ton **Basic Oxygen Furnaces** were installed at Sparrows Point. Basic oxygen steelmaking is a process for **making steel from molten pig iron, scrap, basic fluxes, and gaseous oxygen** in a pear-shaped vessel lined with basic refractories. The furnace actually resembles the old Bessemer Converter with the exception that the bottom was closed and **pure oxygen was injected** into the molten bath from a **water-cooled lance** positioned above the bath.

The operation was simple and rapid. The furnace was tilted to receive scrap which was approximately 30% of the total charge. This took only one or two minutes. Molten pig iron from the blast furnace was added immediately by means of a specially designed ladle with a built in pouring spout. The entire charging operation was completed in less than 5 minutes and the furnace was then rotated to the vertical position. The oxygen lance was lowered and the refining process began. **Footnote 34**   189

BOF Vessel No. 2: Ken Robinson, shown as he guided the vessel tilt operation. Photo dated June 2, 2005, courtesy of Bill Goodman.

Heat Colors

Temper Colors

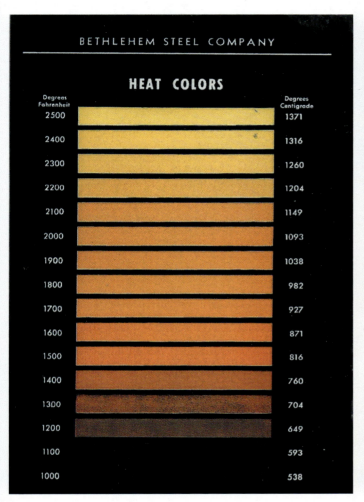

BETHLEHEM STEEL COMPANY

HEAT COLORS

Degrees Fahrenheit		Degrees Centigrade
2500		1371
2400		1316
2300		1260
2200		1204
2100		1149
2000		1093
1900		1038
1800		982
1700		927
1600		871
1500		816
1400		760
1300		704
1200		649
1100		593
1000		538

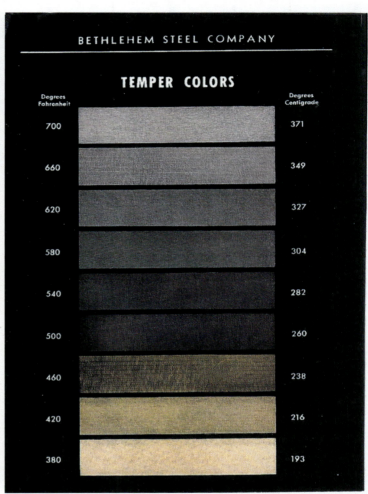

BETHLEHEM STEEL COMPANY

TEMPER COLORS

Degrees Fahrenheit		Degrees Centigrade
700		371
660		349
620		327
580		304
540		282
500		260
460		238
420		216
380		193

The above heat colors represent colors that were observed on pieces of 31-40 steel when viewed through peep holes in enclosed furnaces during average daylight conditions.

The above temper colors were observed on tempering 0.95% carbon steel at the temperatures shown.

Footnote 35

191

No. 1 Strand – Continuous Caster: Shown above, Chris Pope was putting a **temperature probe** into a tundish at No. 1 Strand at the Continuous Caster. Photo dated November 10, 2009, courtesy of Bill Goodman.

Continuous Caster: Shown below is Tracy Bowers as he prepared a **tundish fly** on No. 2 Strand. Photo dated October 11, 2009, courtesy of Bill Goodman.

Lancing A Shroud: Chris Pope, shown below, as he **lanced a shroud** at No. 1 Strand at the Continuous Caster. Photo dated October 3, 2009, courtesy of Bill Goodman.

Pennwood Wharf

Coils of sheet steel were ready for shipment at the plant's Pennwood Wharf in 1970.

Sparrows Point Tinplate for Campaign Buttons

Sparrows Point Tinplate for Campaign Buttons

Normally we think of tinplate as the material from which tin cans are made. That's the biggest single use for it. About five million tons of tinplate went into nearly 45 billion cans last year. A less familiar application of tinplate is its use in campaign buttons. Large quantities of tinplate, and some blackplate, are going into campaign buttons.

Shown here are small sections of the lithographed tinplate sheets. After lithographing, buttons are stamped out and formed.

Many tons of tinplate and blackplate for these buttons are coming from Bethlehem's Sparrows Point tin mill — the largest tin mill in the world.

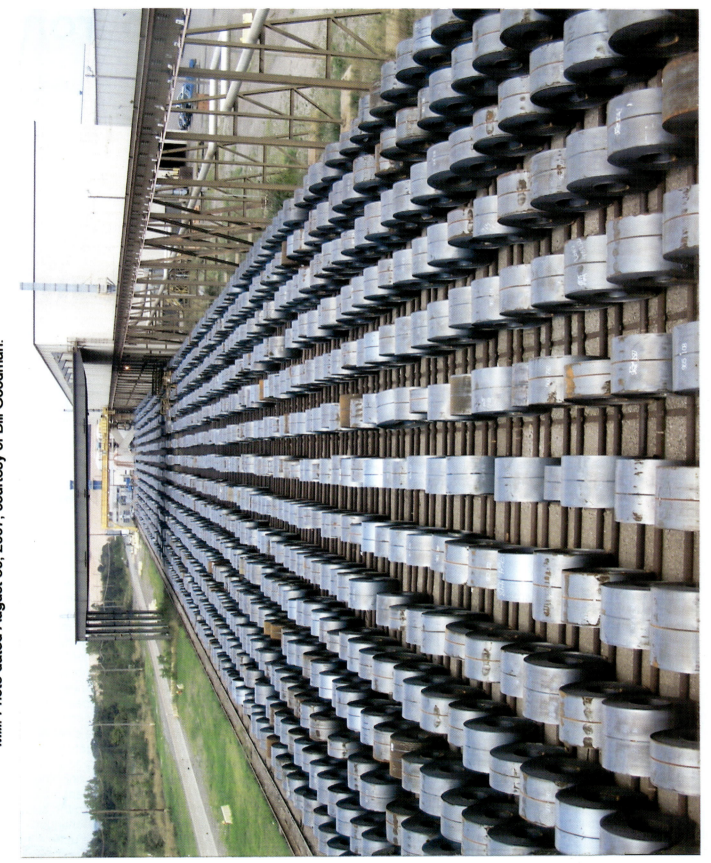

New Cold Mill Stockyard: This multitude of coils were hot band that came from the 68-Inch Hot Strip Mill. Photo dated August 30, 2007, courtesy of Bill Goodman.

Ore...To Iron

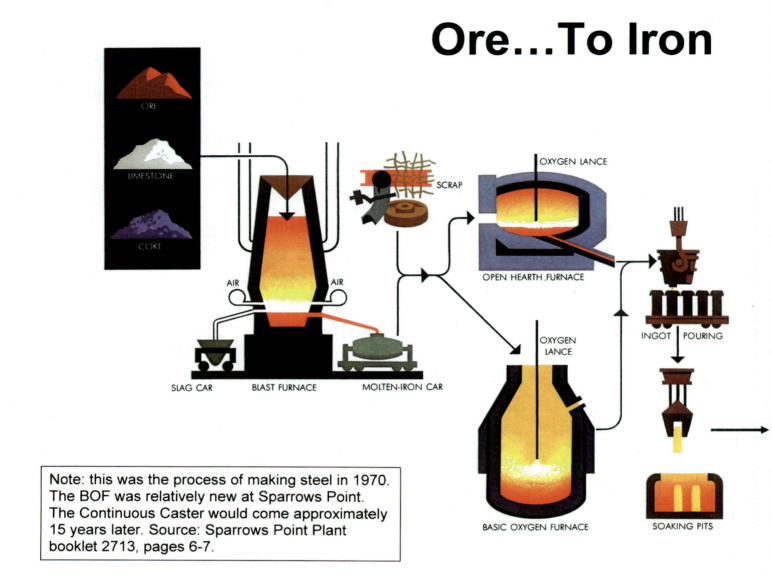

ORE

LIMESTONE

COKE

SCRAP

OXYGEN LANCE

OPEN HEARTH FURNACE

AIR   AIR

OXYGEN LANCE

INGOT   POURING

SLAG CAR   BLAST FURNACE   MOLTEN-IRON CAR

BASIC OXYGEN FURNACE

SOAKING PITS

Note: this was the process of making steel in 1970. The BOF was relatively new at Sparrows Point. The Continuous Caster would come approximately 15 years later. Source: Sparrows Point Plant booklet 2713, pages 6-7.

Blast furnaces produced iron to be refined into steel. Iron ore, coke, and limestone were charged continuously into the top of the hot furnace. As the solid materials descended, they were blasted with preheated air. The coke burned, forming gases that reduced the ore to iron. Lime from the limestone combined with the ore's impurities to form slag, which floated on top of the iron and was drawn off separately. Every few hours, the iron was tapped from the bottom. **Open hearth furnaces** were charged principally with molten iron from the blast furnaces, and cold steel scrap. Flames from liquid gas fuel or gas, using preheated air for combustion, swept across the shallow hearth to supply the heat for melting the charge, refined it into steel, and reduced the amount of such elements as carbon, manganese, phosphorus, and sulphur. In some furnaces, lances directed a stream of oxygen into the charge to speed up the steelmaking process. **Basic oxygen furnaces** used large quantities of high-purity oxygen to speed combustion. They made steel much more rapidly than open hearths. **Ingots** were made by pouring liquid steel from the steelmaking furnaces into ingot molds, where it cooled and solidified. After the molds were removed, the steel ingots were reheated in special furnaces called soaking pits, until each ingot was of uniform temperature throughout, ready for rolling. **Blooming or slabbing mills** rolled the bulky ingots down into smaller semi-finished forms which the finishing mills could handle. This "hot rolling" (working the hot material) improved the structure of the steel. **Slabs** went on to the plate and sheet mills, where they were processed into a variety of flat-rolled products. **Blooms** went to the billet mills for further hot rolling. Some of the resulting billets were then rolled into reinforcing bars and rods on continuous mills. **Pipe** was made from skelp, a flat-rolled product produced on the sheet mill. For continuous-weld pipe up to 4 inch diameter, the skelp was welded into an endless strip. It was then fed through a furnace into a series of rolls which formed and then welded the pipe by pressing the heated edges together. Electric resistance-weld pipe up to 16 inch diameter was made by cold forming skelp to circular shape, then welding the edges together with the heat generated by an electric current passed across them.

...To Finished Steel

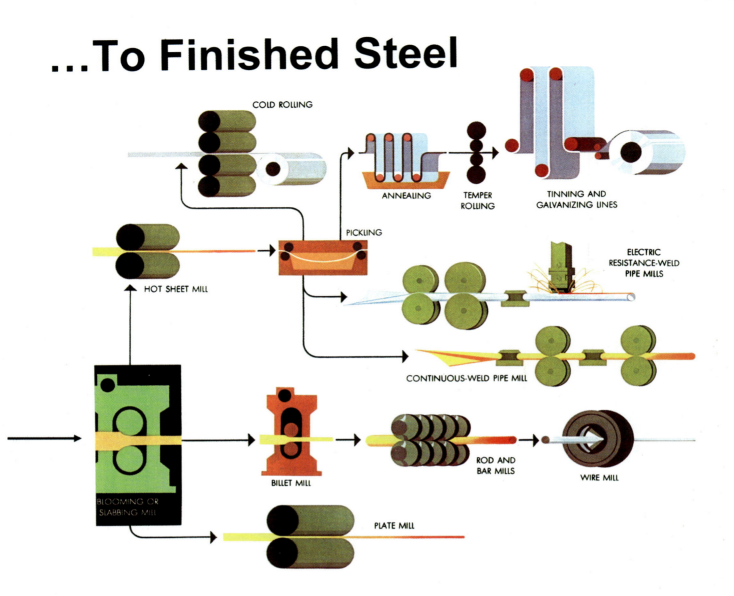

COLD ROLLING

ANNEALING

TEMPER ROLLING

TINNING AND GALVANIZING LINES

PICKLING

HOT SHEET MILL

ELECTRIC RESISTANCE-WELD PIPE MILLS

CONTINUOUS-WELD PIPE MILL

BILLET MILL

ROD AND BAR MILLS

WIRE MILL

BLOOMING OR SLABBING MILL

PLATE MILL

Wire was made from coiled rods produced on the high-speed continuous rod mills. The rods were cold drawn through a series of dies of gradually diminishing size, to produce wire of the required gauge. Most wire was furnished bright. Some was zinc-coated, either by the hot-dip method or the Bethanizing (electrolytic) process. **Rod and reinforcing bars** were also produced on the rod mills. The rods were processed by customers into wire or directly into finished products. Reinforcing bars, used widely in concrete construction, were rolled in a variety of sizes. **Plates** were rolled from reheated slabs on either of two types of plate mills: sheared or universal. Plates produced on sheared-plate mills must be cut on all sides to the desired dimensions after rolling. Universal-plate mills, having a set of vertical edging rolls in addition to their horizontal ones, rolled plates to the desired width, with the straight and parallel edges, so that side shearing was not necessary. **Sheets** were hot rolled from slabs on high-speed, continuous mills in one continuous passage through the roll stands, ending up as a coil .Much of this output was pickled prior to processing into cold rolled sheet. Cold reduced to obtain an improved surface, this sheet may also have received additional treatment to impart special qualities. Other sheet was galvanized (zinc-coated) for applications were corrosion resistance was important. **Tinplate** was made from blackplate (a light-gauge, cold-reduced sheet) by applying a thin tin coating via an electrolytic process. "Tin-free" steel for can stock was made in the same way, except that a chromium treatment was applied. Duo-Bethcolite, an extremely thin, strong sheet, was manufactured by cold reducing the blackplate a second time. It too, may have been produced uncoated, or plated with tin or chromium.

Track and Stud Galvanized Steel Framing

"This **track and stud galvanized steel structure** was erected right behind the Main Office at Sparrows Point. I helped to put it together. It was around 1995. Duane Dunham, who was then Plant Manager, became interested in this type of construction and sent us out to find a market for steel framing. He saw it as another way to expand our business. The market emerged mainly in the deep southern states, primarily Florida. Steel framing could be used instead of lumber in places that had high termite damage, where lumber was scarce, and in places that experienced frequent hurricanes. Bethlehem eventually found a manufacturer of steel framing, a company called Pro-Con, and bought half interest in them. We built a house for Disney in a town called Celebration and many homes for Habitat for Humanity in Homestead, Florida. When Bethlehem declared bankruptcy in 2003, Pro-Con bought back Bethlehem's interest in the company. They are still in business today."
~ Steve Painter, Bethlehem Steel Sales, 1964 – 2003
Photo credited to Robert Smith.

68-Inch Hot Strip Mill Coilbox
Mechanical Arrangement

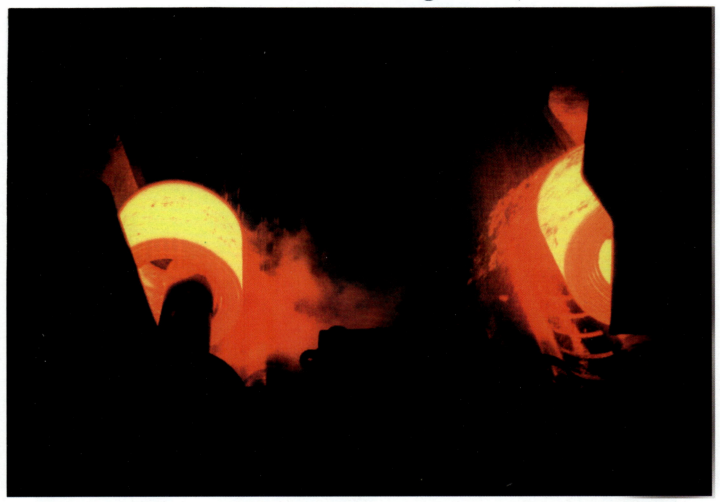

The **Coilbox** solved the basic problem of temperature loss of the transfer bar before rolling in the finishing stands. After the last **roughing mill** pass, the **transfer bar head** end was directed into the **Coilbox entry chute** and through the **bending rolls** to form a coil on **cradle rolls** with the assistance of the **coil forming roll**. After the tail-end of the bar exited the bend rolls, the coil was stopped and the tail-end was peeled and fed into the finishing mill by reversing the direction of the supporting cradle rolls. Once the bar was in the finishing mill, the coil could be transferred by means of the **transfer mechanism** to another set of cradle rolls. This allowed the Coilbox to receive another transfer bar while decoiling the previous one. The Coilbox was part of the remodernization of the 68-Inch Hot Strip Mill in 1990. Photo courtesy of Ruth Stilwell, dated 2002.

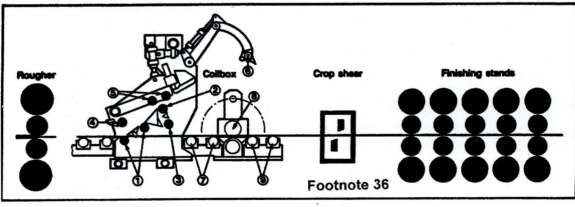

Coilbox Arrangement and Design

1 Entry rolls
2 Bottom bending roll
3 Coil forming roll
4 Deflector rolls
5 Top bending rolls
6 Peeler
7 Coiling station (cradle rolls)
8 Transfer mechanism
9 Uncoiling station (cradle rolls)

Footnote 36

68-Inch Hot Strip Mill Reversing Rougher

A glowing steel slab is rolled into sheet as it passes through the reversing rougher of the 68-Inch Hot Strip Mill.

Last Bar Through the 68-Inch Hot Strip Mill

Shown above are the finishing stands 6, 7, 8, 9, 10, and 11 of the Hot Strip Mill. Note that the photograph shows the relative speeds of the mill stands as they ran faster due to an increased length of the strip caused by its decreasing thickness. The ends of the top backup rolls on stands 9, 10, and 11 at far right show this effect.

This is a significantly historical photograph with respect to the history of the steel mill at Sparrows Point because it shows the last bar ever to go through the mill. The date was June 15, 2012 at 7:21 a.m. Photograph is looking south and was taken by Mike Homa.

56-Inch Cold Strip Skin Pass

No. 2 Skin Pass 56-66 Inch Cold Mill Left to right: Cecil Tingler, John Corso, Joe Kerry, Dan Yeager, and Frank Usher. Photo courtesy of Dan Yeager, circa 1980.

"In the **56-Inch Cold Mill**, there were three Skin Pass Mills. No. 1 and No. 2 were 50 inches wide and ran coils from the 56-Inch Tandem Mill. No. 3 Skin Pass was 60 inches wide and ran coils from the 66-Inch Tandem Mill. Both Tandem Mills were located at the north end of the 56-Inch Cold Mill and ran north to south. The three Skin Pass Mills were located in the center of the 56-Inch Cold Mill and ran west to east."

"I was a **Roller** on the **No. 2 Skin Pass** located in the **56-Inch Cold Mill**. A Roller is the boss of the crew. A crew consisted of a **Roller, a Feeder, a Catcher, and an extra Feeder Helper**. The No. 2 Skin Pass was a two-stand mill, each consisting of two huge backup rolls which applied pressure to two work rolls. The Feeder and the Roller would start a coil at the entry end of the mill. Then the Catcher would go to the middle section of the mill and start the coil through the second stand. The Feeder and the Catcher would then attach the coil to the delivery end. Sometimes I had to stand in the middle to bring up the tension. If all went well, you could average 40 coils on a turn. If it was really bright stuff, a specialty product, you'd get 20 coils if you were lucky."
~ Dan Yeager, Skin Pass Roller, 1947 – 1988

"L" Furnace and the Star of Bethlehem

"L" Furnace and the Star of Bethlehem – photo dated December 26, 2007, courtesy of Bill Goodman.

New Cold Mill: The New Cold Mill started up in 2000. Shown here was the Tandem Entry. Photo dated January 9, 2005, courtesy of Bill Goodman.

No. 4 Continuous Galvanizing Line: The No. 4 Line was located inside of the Tin Mill complex. Photo dated March 6, 2008, courtesy of Bill Goodman.

Changing Signs of the Times

Between 2003 and 2012, ownership of the Sparrows Point Steel Mill changed several times. The signs above reflect those changes. After Bethlehem Steel sold the property in 2003, it was occupied by International Steel Group, Mittal Steel, Severstal, RG Steel, and finally liquidators Hilco Trading. Photo courtesy of Mike Stilwell

A Brief History of the Patapsco & Back Rivers Railroad

PBR #306 works at the coal fields. The view is looking north towards Blast Furnace Row. Photo circa 1960.

The **Pennsylvania Steel Company** purchased the Sparrows Point peninsula in early 1887. On March 1st of that year, surveyors landed and within days, signs of industry could be seen. A receiving wharf was built 900 feet out into the water and railroad tracks were laid on the pier. On July 18, 1887, five months after the surveyors arrived, **the first locomotive landed** on the shores of Sparrows Point. In October 1887, ground was broken for the first blast furnaces. Two years later, the fledgling steel mill was producing pig iron. The railroad was a beehive of activity, with trains bearing coke, ore, and limestone coming from Lower Canton wharves to the stackhouse.

In 1918, the Patapsco & Back Rivers Railroad was formed. Its name is derived from the two rivers that border the Sparrows Point peninsula. To the west, is the Patapsco River. To the east, is the Back River. Although the railroad is an integral part of the steel mill's operations, it is required by law to run its operations as a separate entity. This was an outcome of President Teddy Roosevelt's desire to break up monopoly ownership and control by the railroads of the country's coal mines. For this to occur, the Interstate Commerce Act of 1887 was amended in 1906 to disallow ownership of a railroad by a company whose products were transported.

At one time, **Bethlehem Steel Corporation** had **nine subsidiary railroads**. The **Patapsco & Back Rivers Railroad (PBR)** was one of them. Other subsidiary Bethlehem Steel railroads included the Philadelphia, Bethlehem and New England **(PB&NE)**; Conemaugh & Black Lick **(C&BL)**; Steelton & Highspire **(S&H)**; Brandywine Valley **(BVRY)**; Upper Merion & Plymouth **(UMP)**; Cambria & Indiana **(C&I)**; South Buffalo **(SB)**; and Lake Michigan & Indiana **(LMI)**.

From the very beginning of the railroad's existence at Sparrows Point, all of its switchers were steam locomotives. In the 1930s, the **steam era** began to wane as the newer diesel locomotives began to emerge. In January 1937, **PBR purchased its first diesels**. They were three new SC models built by Electro-Motive Corporation (EMC). Also in 1937, PBR purchased seven **ALCO HH600's**. The highhood model would prove unpopular largely because of design flaws, the primary one being poor visibility. Although this was later corrected, PBR never purchased another ALCO. In 1941, PBR purchased its first Baldwin – a VO660 model. It would continue to purchase Baldwins, new and used, until the mid-1960s. The last new Baldwins purchased were **Baldwin Lima Hamilton** S-12's. Other models owned by PBR included the VO1000, the DS44660, and the DS441000. (PBR continued on the next page.)

209

To prepare for the diesel age, PBR built a new **Locomotive Repair Shop** in 1946. For its time, the Locomotive Repair Shop was a state-of-the-art facility. It could handle four locomotives. It had three inspection tracks, one jack track, and one track for leveling trucks. In 1963, the shop was expanded. This provided space for four additional locomotives, a paint shop, and a two-bay garage.

In 1956, Baldwin Locomotive Works went out of business. That year and the year following, PBR purchased ten new **Electro-Motive Division of General Motors Corporation (EMD)** SW1200's. The only other new purchase of EMD's occurred in 1969, when PBR purchased two SW1500's.

In 1966, PBR began to rebuild several aging Baldwins with EMD engines. Five of them were rebuilt with 12/567 engines and three of them were rebuilt with 12/645C engines. EMD quickly filled the void left by Baldwin. Many of the locomotives were purchased used from the other Bethlehem shortlines, such as PB&NE, C&I, C&BL, SB, and S&H. Models owned by PBR included the SW1, NW2, SW7, SW9, SW900, SW1200, SW1500, and the GP9. In 2005, EMD closed its doors and another chapter in railroad history ended.

In the early 1970s, PBR found another use for its aging Baldwin fleet. It began to convert several of them into **slugs**. Although cut down from Baldwin frames, slugs were considered locomotives by the Federal Railroad Administration **(FRA)** and must have a **cab card**. Between 1971 and 1978, PBR converted 10 Baldwins into slugs. In 2010, only two of the original slugs, #15 and #19, remained at Sparrows Point. #15 was still in service as of 2010.

The 1980s brought some serious changes to PBR. As the steel mill began its decline, it impacted directly on the railroad. In 1983, the **Rod, Wire, Pipe, and Nail Mills closed**. In 1990, another big change occurred. This was the **introduction of slab carriers**. These giant rubber-tired carriers took away a significant percent of PBR's railroad business and had a substantial impact on its workforce.

Despite the disheartening struggle to downsize because of mill closures, reduced capacity, and the impact of modernization, a bright star shone over PBR in 2001. PBR was the recipient of a **gold medal** award for being the safest shortline railroad in America. The **H.H. Harriman Award** is given out annually for the best employee railroad safety records in the country. It was the fourth consecutive year that PBR won a medal. In 1998 and 2000, they won a bronze medal. In 1999, they took the silver, and in 2001, they won the gold.

When Bethlehem Steel was sold to **International Steel Group (ISG)** on April 30, 2003, the Patapsco & Back Rivers Railroad officially closed its doors as well. The railroad, however, was not bankrupt. When ISG purchased Bethlehem's assets, it emerged as **ISG Railway Inc.** On April 13, 2005, ISG sold the Sparrows Point plant to **Mittal Steel Company** and the railroad officially became **Mittal Steel Railway Inc.** In February 2007, the Department of Justice ordered Mittal to sell the steel mill and it changed hands once again. This time, the Russian company **Severstal** purchased the mill and the railroad became **SSP Railroad Holding LLC (SRHL).** In March 2011, Severstal sold the Sparrows Point facility to RG Steel. This company lasted approximately one year before declaring bankruptcy. The steel plant was then auctioned off and subsequently purchased by Hilco Trading Company – a liquidator – on August 7, 2012. Hilco then sold off and auctioned whatever they could and began a 40 month plan to bring the entire steel mill at Sparrows Point and all of its structures to the ground. They have negotiated an agreement with the current owner of the railroad – MCM Management Corporation – to utilize the rail services at the plant during their 40 month demolition phase. Beyond that, the future looks bleak for the old Push, Bump and Ram. **Footnote 37**

BLOOMING MILL DEPARTMENT

(Information compiled as of October 1960)

GENERAL

Operating personnel—765

Acreage—84

Annual rated capacity—9,000,000 tons

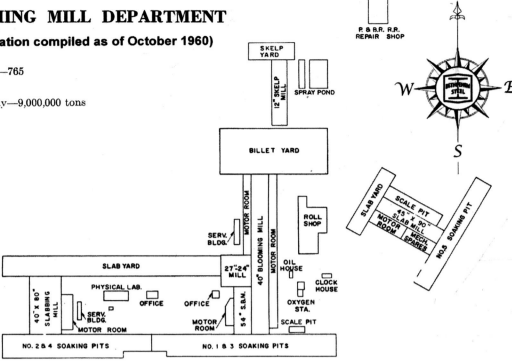

SOAKING PITS

Shop No.	Type	No. of Pits	Pit Size Ft.	Pit Area Sq. Ft.	Total Area Sq. Ft.
*1	Regenerative	4	16 x 17	272	1,088
1	Regenerative	4	16 x 17	272	1,088
1	Regenerative	20	13 x 17	221	4,420
2	Regenerative	22	12 x 17	204	4,488
3	Regenerative	8	9¼ x 20	185	1,480
4	Recuperative	5	7½ x 20½	154	770
5	Regenerative	16	16 x 20	320	5,120
*5	Regenerative	6	16 x 20	320	1,920

Total Area—20,374

*Pits being revamped or constructed.

All pits fired with mixture of Blast Furnace and Coke Oven gas (110 BTU/cu. ft.)—Recuperative (135 BTU/cu. ft.)

3 to 5 hrs. to bring hot ingots to rolling temperature } 2250°F to 2450°F
8 to 14 hrs. to bring cold ingots to rolling temperature

No. 5 pits—largest ingot 40 tons

Nos. 1 and 3 pits—largest ingot 15 tons (occasionally 25 tons)

Nos. 2 and 4 pits—largest ingot 25 tons

40" BLOOMING MILL

First steel rolled in 1919

Two-high electric driven reversing mill

5,000 HP drive

Rolls 40" dia. x 95" long

Maximum mill opening—47"

Rolls designed with four passes—8", 10", 14" and 48"

Pinion 40" P.D. x 48" long, 18 teeth

Chief product—10" x 10" bloom for continuous billet mills

1,200 tons per turn average production rate (record 2,364 tons per turn)

211

30″ CONTINUOUS MILL

First steel rolled in February 1955
Reduces 10″ x 10″ blooms to 8″ x 8″ blooms
One horizontal stand driven by 800 HP motor
One vertical stand driven by 800 HP motor
    No. 1 (H)—Pinion 30″ P.D. x 42″ long, 30 teeth—rolls 31″ dia. x 52″ long
    No. 2 (V)—Reduction drive—rolls 43″ dia. x 18¾″ long

24″ CONTINUOUS MILL

First steel rolled in 1919
Reduces 8″ x 8″ blooms to 4″ x 4″ billets
Six horizontal stands driven by single 4,000 HP motor. Each stand—Pinion
    24″ P.D. x 30″ long, 30 teeth— rolls 27½″ dia. x 60″ long

18″ CONTINUOUS MILL

First steel rolled in 1919
Billets from 24″ mill reduced to a minimum of 2″ x 2″
Six horizontal stands driven by single 3,250 HP motor. Each stand—Pinion 18″
    P.D. x 20″ long, 25 teeth—rolls 18⅝″ dia. x 27″ long.

27″ CONTINUOUS MILL

First steel rolled in 1927
Blooms from 40″ mill reduced for 21″ mill
Four horizontal stands driven by single 4,000 HP motor
One vertical stand driven by single 250 HP motor
    No. 1 (H)—Pinion 27″ P.D. x 32″ long, 27 teeth—rolls 30⅝″ dia. x 54″ long
    No. 2 (H)—Pinion 27″ P.D. x 32″ long, 27 teeth—rolls 30⅝″ dia. x 54″ long
    No. 3 (H)—Pinion 24″ P.D. x 32″ long, 24 teeth—rolls 30⅝″ dia. x 54″ long
    No. 4 (V)—Reduction drive—rolls 29″ dia. x 7″ long
    No. 5 (H)—Pinion 24″ P.D. x 32″ long, 24 teeth—rolls 30⅝″ dia. x 54″ long

21″ CONTINUOUS MILL

First steel rolled in 1927
Rolls skelp 6″ to 12½″ wide, 1⅛″ to 2½″ thick
Seven horizontal stands and two vertical stands
Horizontal stands Nos. 6, 7, 9 and 10 driven by single 6500 HP motor
Horizontal stands Nos. 12, 13 and 14 driven by single 5,000 HP motor
Vertical stands Nos. 8 and 11 driven by two 150 HP motors
    No. 6 (H)—Pinion 21″ P.D. x 32″ long, 21 teeth—rolls 21¼″ dia. x 28″ long
    No. 7 (H)—Pinion 21″ P.D. x 32″ long, 21 teeth—rolls 21¼″ dia. x 28″ long
    No. 8 (V)—Reduction drive—rolls 22¼″ dia. x 6″ long
    No. 9 (H)—Pinion 21″ P.D. x 32″ long, 21 teeth—rolls 21¼″ dia. x 28″ long
    No. 10 (H)—Pinion 21″ P.D. x 32″ long, 21 teeth—rolls 21¼″ dia. x 28″ long
    No. 11 (V)—Reduction drive—rolls 22¼″ dia. x 6″ long
    No. 12 (H)—Pinion 21″ P.D. x 32″ long, 21 teeth—rolls 21¼″ dia. x 28″
      long
    No. 13 (H)—Pinion 21″ P.D. x 32″ long, 21 teeth—rolls 21¼″ dia. x 28″
      long
    No. 14 (H)—Pinion 21″ P.D. x 32″ long, 21 teeth—rolls 21¼″ dia. x 28″
      long

54″ BLOOMING MILL

First steel rolled as 46″ Mill in 1926
First steel rolled after rebuild in 1954
Two-high electric driven reversing mill
7,000 HP drive (two 3,500 HP armatures)
Rolls 43″ dia. x 106″ long
Maximum mill opening—68″
Rolls designed with three passes—8″, 12″ and 69″
Pinion 54″ P.D. x 65″ long, 21 teeth
2,000 tons per turn average production rate (record 3,335 tons per turn)

40″ x 80″ UNIVERSAL SLABBING MILL

First steel rolled in 1936
Universal, two-high reversing mill
7,000 HP horizontal drive
2,500 HP vertical drive
Horizontal rolls 40″ dia. x 82″ long
Vertical rolls 27″ dia. x 66″ long
Number of passes vary from 17 to 25
Average reduction per pass—1½″ horizontal surfaces
                                    ½″ vertical surfaces
Pinion 46″ P.D. x 55″ long, 18 teeth
Slabs range from 4″ to 22″ thick, 16″ to 60″ wide
60% tonnage to strip mills, 40% tonnage to plate mills
2,600 tons per turn average production rate (record 3956 tons per turn)

45″ x 90″ UNIVERSAL SLABBING MILL

First steel rolled in 1957
Universal, two-high reversing mill
12,000 HP horizontal drive
4,000 HP vertical drive
Horizontal rolls 45″ dia. x 90″ long
Vertical rolls 37″ dia. x 96″ long
Maximum mill opening 78″ x 78″
Number of passes vary between 9 and 28
Average reduction per pass—2″ horizontal surfaces
                                    ¾″ vertical surfaces
3,200 tons per turn average production (record 4,475 tons per turn)

12″ SKELP MILL

First steel rolled in 1927
330 tons per turn average production (record 443 tons per turn)
Eight horizontal and four vertical stands
No. 1 vertical stand and Nos. 1, 2, 3 and 4 horizontal stands driven by a single
    1,800 HP motor
Nos. 2, 3 and 4 vertical stands each are driven by 150 HP motors
Nos. 5 and 6 horizontal stands are driven by a single 1,800 HP motor
Nos. 7 and 8 horizontal stands each have a 1,100 HP motor
    No. 1 (V)—Rolls 14½″ dia. x 10½″ long
    No. 1 (H)—Pinion 13″ P.D. x 15″ long, 24 teeth—rolls 12¼″ dia. x 15″ long
    No. 2 (H)—Pinion 13″ P.D. x 15″ long, 24 teeth—rolls 13″ dia. x 15″ long
    No. 2 (V)—Rolls 13½″ dia. x 8¾″ long
    No. 3 (H)—Pinion 12″ P.D. x 15″ long, 22 teeth—rolls 12″ dia. x 15″ long
    No. 4 (H)—Pinion 12″ P.D. x 15″ long, 22 teeth—rolls 12″ dia. x 15″ long
    No. 3 (V)—Rolls 13⅜″ dia. x 7⅞″ long
    No. 5 (H)—Pinion 12″ P.D. x 15″ long, 22 teeth—rolls 12½″ dia. x 15″ long
    No. 6 (H)—Pinion 12″ P.D. x 15″ long, 22 teeth—rolls 12¼″ dia. x 15″ long
    No. 4 (V)—Rolls 13⅜″ dia. x 7⅞″ long
    No. 7 (H)—Pinion 12″ P.D. x 15″ long, 22 teeth—rolls 12⅜″ dia. x 15″ long
    No. 8 (H)—Pinion 12″ P.D. x 15″ long, 22 teeth—rolls 12⅛″ dia. x 15″ long

SHEARS

1 — 500 ton hydraulic upcut shear (after 40″ Blooming Mill)
1 — 1,200 ton steam hydraulic down-cut shear (after 40″ Blooming Mill)
1 — 500 ton steam hydraulic down-cut shear (after 24″ Continuous Mill)
1 — 30″ steam flying shear (after 18″ Continuous Mill)
1 Rotary crop shear, 2″ x 22″ product
2 Rotary shears for finished product, ½″ x 22″ product
1 — 3,000 ton steam hydraulic down-cut shear (54″ Blooming Mill)
1 — 3,000 ton steam hydraulic down-cut shear (40″ x 80″ Slabbing Mill)
1 Electric driven slab shear, 2 — 1,000 HP motors (45″ x 90″ Slabbing Mill)

213

FURNACES

Shop No.	Fce. No.	Refractories			Rated Capacity	Record Tonnage	
		Roof	End Walls	Uptakes		Month	Year
No. 1 O.H.	58	silica	basic	silica	167 tons	15,170	162,368
(12 fces.)	59	silica	basic	silica	167 tons	15,315	162,977
	60	silica	silica	silica	167 tons	15,715	164,325
1910—Md. Steel	61	silica	basic	silica	167 tons	14,530	157,674
1916—Beth. Steel	62	silica	silica	silica	167 tons	15,314	151,298
	63	silica	basic	silica	167 tons	15,108	154,725
	64	silica	silica	silica	167 tons	14,719	156,108
	65	silica	basic	silica	167 tons	15,596	150,840
	66	silica	basic	silica	167 tons	15,560	158,471
	67	silica	basic	silica	167 tons	15,557	164,886
	68	silica	basic	silica	167 tons	15,201	162,872
	69	silica	basic	silica	167 tons	15,675	167,133
Record tonnages—No. 1 Open Hearth Shop						169,783	1,894,384
No. 2 O.H.	71	silica	silica	silica	380 tons	30,651	299,183
(5 fces.)	72	silica	silica	silica	380 tons	30,870	294,609
	73	silica	silica	silica	380 tons	28,659	299,192
1918	74	silica	silica	silica	380 tons	29,585	301,521
	*75	basic	basic	silica	380 tons	37,092	305,505
Record tonnages—No. 2 Open Hearth Shop						141,343	1,500,010
No. 3 O.H.	77	silica	silica	silica	270 tons	22,096	233,809
(11 fces.)	78	silica	basic	silica	270 tons	21,896	220,354
	79	silica	basic	silica	270 tons	22,050	226,338
1937	80	silica	silica	silica	270 tons	22,030	233,589
	81	silica	silica	silica	270 tons	22,018	231,896
	82	silica	silica	silica	270 tons	22,625	236,352
	83	silica	silica	silica	270 tons	21,705	230,267
	84	silica	silica	silica	270 tons	22,668	231,244
	85	silica	silica	silica	270 tons	23,094	228,724
	86	silica	silica	silica	270 tons	23,076	231,431
	87	silica	silica	silica	270 tons	24,064	229,420
Record tonnages—No. 3 Open Hearth Shop						229,982	2,512,373
No. 4 O.H.	**90	silica	silica	silica	390 tons	29,981	230,623
(7 fces.)	**91	basic	basic	basic	390 tons	34,457	247,046
	**92	silica	basic	basic	390 tons	29,464	273,720
1957	**93	silica	silica	silica	390 tons	30,416	289,986
	*94	silica	basic	basic	430 tons	39,735	285,657
	**95	silica	basic	basic	390 tons	29,773	276,144
	*96	basic	basic	basic	430 tons	41,301	273,545
Record tonnages—No. 4 Open Hearth Shop						223,267	1,876,721
35 fces.	Record tonnages—Nos. 1, 2, 3, and 4 O.H. Shops					714,405	5,916,681
Bessemer Production	Three 25 ton vessels	• Last Bessemer blow February 9, 1958				33,554	360,257

*Oxygen furnaces
**To be converted to oxygen furnaces

AVERAGE BURDEN

O.H Shop	Metallics					Non-Metallics (Fluxes)	
	Hot Metal %	Cold Metal %	Stl. Scrap %	Alloys %	Ore %	Burnt Lime Lbs./Ton of Stl.	Limestone Lbs./Ton of Stl.
No. 1	56.84	3.54	31.03	.85	7.74	6.95	132.81
No. 2	51.64	1.41	39.38	.56	7.01	10.15	48.67
No. 3	57.52	3.13	30.09	.99	8.27	3.29	68.74
No. 4	50.88	3.05	38.82	.66	6.59	6.59	64.98

40-inch Blooming Mill

When Bethlehem Steel acquired the Maryland Steel Company in 1916, it inherited all of its equipment. Maryland Steel was primarily a rail-producing mill. The steam driven **36-inch Blooming Mill** was used by Maryland Steel to produce blooms for the **26-inch Rail Mill**. Bethlehem Steel immediately began to modernize the plant and change it from primarily a rail mill to a further diversification of steel products. The 36-inch Mill was upgraded to a 40-inch Mill which was combined with a **24-inch Billet Mill** and an **18-inch Continuous Bar Mill**. The 40-inch Mill is shown here in 1925 with its new line and new pulpit.

At right are the **soaking pits**, which fed both the old 36-inch Blooming Mill and the recently upgraded 40-inch Blooming Mill. The wheeled apparatus shown held the covers for the soaking pits. Under the carriage was a thick layer of brick. The units could be rolled back and forth to either cover the ingots that were placed in the pit for reheating or when an ingot was extracted for rolling in the mill. Shown here, an ingot is being extracted. Note the ingot buggy track parallel to the soaking pit and the ingot buggy at the far end of the track.

The Blooming Mill Process

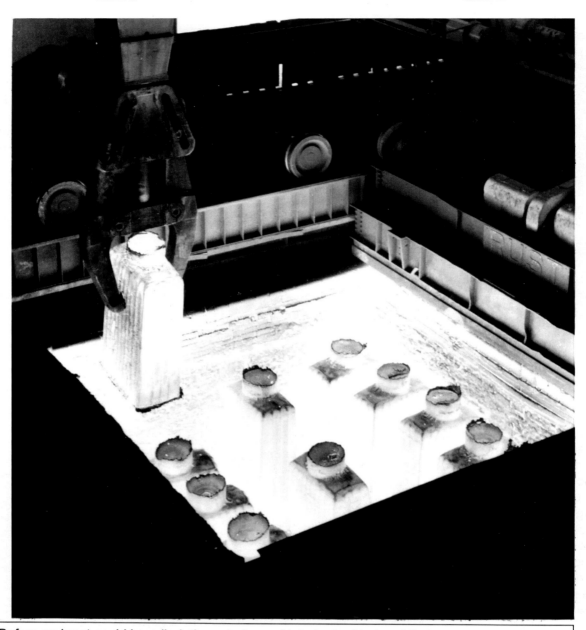

Before an ingot could be rolled, the exterior and interior had to be at the same temperature. Special gas-fired furnaces called soaking pits reheated the ingots to about 2,200 degrees Fahrenheit. They were kept at that temperature from 4 to 8 hours. When removed from the pit, the ingot had been uniformly heated, and was plastic enough to be shaped by the rolling mills. Photo courtesy of Butch Johnson.

"**A pit crane** would take an **ingot** out of the **soaking pit** and place it on an **ingot buggy**. The ingot buggy took the ingots to the **roller line** where it was dumped out onto the **receiving table**. The ingot then proceeded to the **40-Inch Mill**. This same buggy also fed the **54-Inch Slab Mill**. The 54-Inch Mill rolled slabs for the **56- and 68-Inch Hot Strip Mills**. It also rolled blooms to make **skelp blanks**. The 40-Inch Mill was huge. It was a 2-high, 1-stand mill. As the ingot approached the mill, there were two men stationed in a **pulpit.** Their job was to control the ingot. One man was a **roller** and the other was a **manipulator**. He was responsible for turning the ingot. There was a **front table and a back table**. All of the turning took place here. The rollers job was to run the ingot through the mill and back and the manipulator turned the ingot **90 degrees on each pass**. They had a clock to go by. They checked the ingot on each pass and made multiple passes until the ingot was ten inches by ten inches and approximately 40 feet long. At this point, the ingot had become a **bloom**." ~Hillard "Digger" O'Day, Blooming Mill Mechanical Technician A, 1957 - 2001

Glowing Ingots on the Move

A train of glowing ingots make their way to the soaking pits. This was a familiar sight around the Open Hearth.

Steel being "teemed" from a ladle into ingot molds.

45 x 90 Inch Slabbing Mill

The 45-Inch Slabbing Mill was installed in 1957. It was a universal, 2-high reversing mill equipped with 45-inch diameter by 90-inch long horizontal rolls and 37-inch diameter by 96-inch long vertical rolls. Maximum roll lift was 78 inches with a 78 inch maximum opening. Mill power for the horizontal drive was 12,000 horsepower and 4,000 horsepower for the vertical drive. Located between the mill exit and electric-driven slab shear, which was powered by two 1,000 horsepower motors, was an oxygen inline scarfing machine. Photograph courtesy of Bill Goodman. Photo circa 1960.

45 x 90 Inch Universal Slabbing Mill

"I went to the **Blooming Mills** in 1957 as a **Mechanical Helper**. The Mechanical Department was responsible for the maintenance of the mills. There were several levels or positions in the Mechanical Department. They started with **Oiler-Greaser** and moved up to Mechanical Helper, Repairman 'C', then 'B', and 'A', and finished with Millwright. I spent seven years as a **Helper**. We changed bearings, shear blades, and heads on scarfers. One day each week, a mill would shut down for general maintenance. The mills took a beating. There was grit in everything. The maintenance was a constant, never-ending process.

"After several years, I started getting 'C' Repairman pay. This is when you now get a helper. After 1,040 hours, you moved up to 'B' Repairman, and subsequently to 'A' Repairman. At some point, they changed the title from Repairman to 'C', 'B', and 'A' Technicians. Now, in order to move from 'C' to 'A' position, you had to take a test. The test might include making a fitting, or key, using calipers, or cutting pipe threads. Eventually, I became a Mechanical Technician 'A.' Occasionally, I had to fill in as a Millwright. This job required a lot of decision making. If a mill broke down, the Millwright had to devise a plan of action to fix it. We were always putting fires out.

"When the Continuous Caster came on-line, **the Blooming and Slabbing Mills became obsolete and they shut down in 1989**. This displaced the **Bull Gangs and the Repair Gangs**. Many were relocated to the Coke Ovens, steelmaking, and Blast Furnaces. The last ten years, I worked in ore handling where the ships came in. We repaired bucket cranes, gantry cranes, belt lines, and junction houses. I retired in 2001."
~ Hillard "Digger" O'Day, Jr., Mechanical Technician "A", 1957 – 2001.

40-Inch Blooming Mill
In the photograph at left, a **glowing ingot** takes on a new shape as it was worked by the rolls of the 40-Inch Blooming Mill at the Sparrows Point plant. This ingot would eventually be shaped into a **bloom or a billet.** From these semi-finished pieces of steel, finished steel **products such as structural shapes** were rolled. Rolling not only shaped the steel, but also improved its mechanical properties. Photo courtesy of Butch Johnson. Photo circa 1950.

"There was one Blooming Mill when I started in 1957. It was the **40-Inch Mill.** They also had the **54-Inch Mill**, which was primarily a slab mill but could also roll blooms when needed. The 54-Inch Mill was redone from the old 46-Inch Mill. Both of these mills were reciprocating mills. There were no backup rolls like in other mills. Their job was to break down ingots. They also had a 40 x 80 Inch Slab Mill and they had just started up the 45 x 90 Inch Slab Mill. The 45 x 90 was fed by the No. 5 Soaking Pit. The 40-Inch Blooming Mill and the 54-Inch Slab Mill were both fed by the No. 1 Soaking Pit." ~Hillard "Digger" O'Day, Jr., Blooming Mill Mechanical Technician "A", 1957 – 2001

Below is a layout of the primary rolling facilities showing the soaking pits, the 54-Inch Blooming Mill, and the 40-Inch and 45-Inch Slabbing Mills.

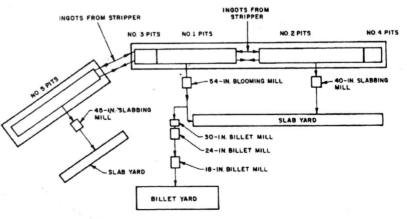

Flow of Material
Blooming – Billet – Slabbing Mills

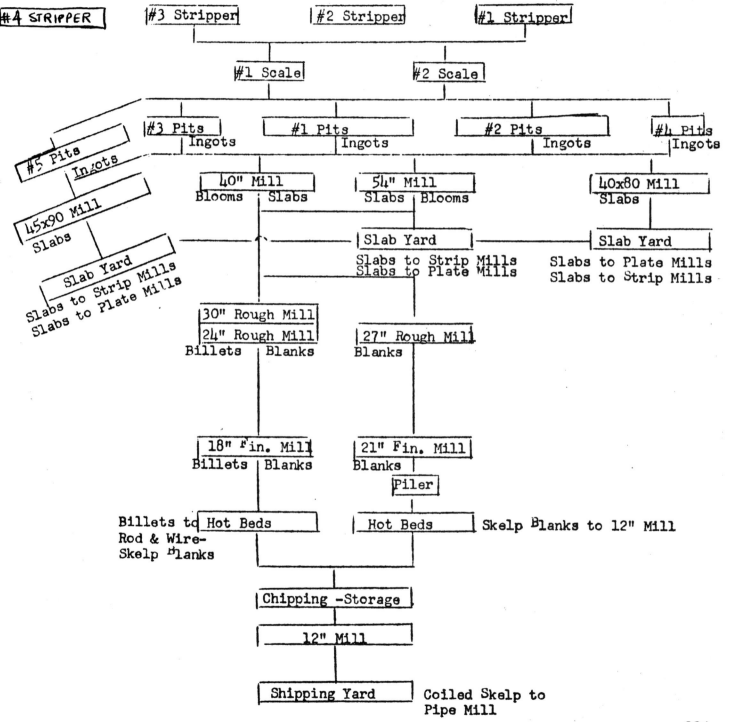

221

No. 2 Soaking Pit Reline

Members of the **406 Department** Labor Crew are shown removing the old ceramic lining from the **No. 2 Soaking Pit**. To start the tearing out process, an overhead crane would use an object like a metal hand. It was lowered into the pit and rotated, tearing out much of the lining. A lot of the work, however, was done manually. Notice the **jackhammer** and **pinch and pry bars** at right. A small hand tool, at the left, that looks like ice tongs were used to pick up the warm to hot bricks. A soaking pit could reach temperatures of **2,400 degrees Fahrenheit** when in use. As the **four chambers** of the soaking pit are dismantled, the bricks are put into hoppers and removed by the overhead crane. Ingots from the No. 2 Soaking Pits went to the Plate Mill. Those from the No. 1 Soaking Pits went to the Billet Mill and the Rod and Wire Mill. Ingots from the No. 5 Soaking Pits were made into slabs and sent to the Hot Strip Mills. The lining of a soaking pit might last six months to a year depending upon use. Photo dated April 4, 1951. Special thanks to Al Hastings.

DON'T gamble with accidents

PLATE AND FLANGING MILL DEPARTMENT

GENERAL

Operating personnel—950

Acreage—43

Annual rated capacity

160″ Plate Mill	840,000 tons per year
60″ Plate Mill	180,000 tons per year
Flanging Mill	24,000 tons per year

(Information compiled as of October 1960)

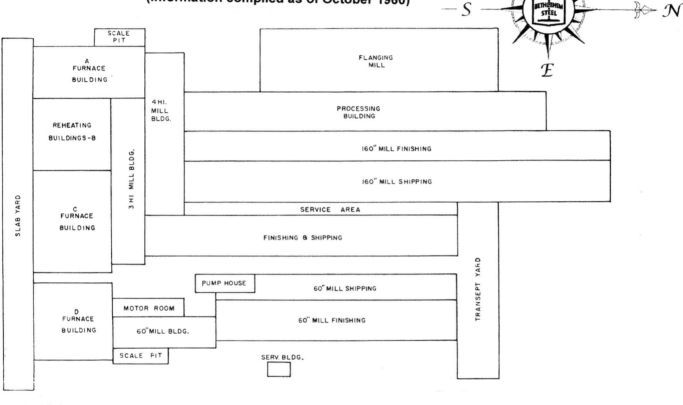

60″ PLATE MILL

Furnaces ("C" and "D" Furnace Room)

8 in and out type regenerative furnaces (4 per furnace room)

Type fuel—Bunker "C" low sulphur oil (149,000 BTU/gal.)

Fuel input—200 to 250 gph per furnace

Individual, steam atomized, water cooled burners

175 lb./sq. ft./hr. hot charge per furnace

100 lb./sq. ft./hr. cold charge per furnace

280 sq. ft. heating area per furnace

240,000 tons annual heating capacity

60″ Mill

First steel rolled in 1920

2 high, single stand, Universal reversing mill

Range of plates rolled

¼″ to 12″ thick

10″ to 60″ wide

150′ maximum length

Horizontal rolls 36″ dia. x 84″ long

Vertical rolls 21″ dia. x 39″ long

Pinions—40″ P.D. x 5′-1″ face, 15 teeth

Rolls changed every six turns

800 ft./min. mill speed

5,000 HP main drive

15,000 tons per month capacity (30,948 record tons including ingot rolling)

Plate Mill, continued

Leveller

Located 166' north of mill
5 top rolls and 4 bottom rolls
Rolls 14" dia. x 96" long
12" maximum opening
140 HP drive

Cooling Beds

2 cooling beds
    Each 150' long x 59' wide
2 straightening blocks
    Each 150' long and 10" to 60" wide capacity
    Two 80 HP motors each

Hydraulic Shear

2¼" x 110" hydraulic shear
Hydraulic pressure from central pumping area
650 lbs. base pressure
800 lbs. to 1600 lbs. to 2400 lbs. intensified pressure
Shears plate up to 2" thick

Miscellaneous

1 — 180" x 1½" hydraulic shear
1 — 125" x ½" electric shear
1 — 110" x ⅜" electric shear
1 Leveller, 3 top rolls and 2 bottom rolls
Approximately 1400' of roller lines (300 feet/min.)

60" Plate Mill Modernization (1961 completion)

New 125' x 350' slab yard
Continuous furnace (relocated from 56" HSM)
    19' wide x 80' long, soaking hearth length 21'
    80 tons/hr. capacity @ 75% hearth coverage
    4 zone, oil fired (1,500 gph)
    Double row slabs 4" x 9" x 48" to 12" x 60" x 100" long
    Single row slabs 8" x 10" to 12" x 60" up to 17'-0" long
    Hazen recuperators (metallic)
New furnace charging equipment
New Falk coupling for mill
New leveller
    Rolls ¼" to 2" thick plate, 10" to 60" wide
    Maximum opening 13"
    400 to 600 fpm
    Roll body 96" long
New plate cooling on mill runout
Rebuild existing cooling beds
Rewind motor on main M.G. Set
Alter existing end shear for 12" opening

160" PLATE MILL

Continuous Furnaces ("A" Furnace Room)

Two triple, oil fired, tile recuperative type furnaces
Type fuel—Bunker "C" oil (149,000 BTU/gal.)
Fuel input—maximum of 1,650 gph.
Steam atomized, nozzle mix burners
3 heating zones, 4 burners each
80' long x 23' wide
12" x 60" x 120" long maximum slab size (24,000 lbs.)
4 skids—2 pair on 4' centers
110 tons/hr./furnace heating capacity at 80% hearth coverage

In and Out Furnaces ("B" Furnace Room)

Four regenerative type furnaces
Type fuel—Bunker "C" oil (149,000 BTU/gal.)
Fuel input—200 to 300 gph.
Heats slabs up to 22" thick
400 sq. ft. hearths
6 tons/hr./ furnace heating capacity

3-Hi Mill

Moved to Sparrows Point from Coatsville, Pa. in 1931
Serves as roughing stand for 4-Hi Mill—since 1957
Top and bottom rolls 44" dia. x 160" long (.020" crown)
Middle roll 27" dia. x 160" long with ⅛" to ¼" grooves
(.030" to .210"   Crown at 125%
4500 HP main drive
490 ft./min. mill speed
Pinion (top and bottom rolls)—44" P.D. x 69" long, 24 teeth
Pinion (middle roll)—39" P.D. x 69" long, 17 teeth
Average 7 passes per slab (65% reduction)
Slabs are spread to maximum of 157" wide
Descaling—600 psi water
Hydraulically operated tables

4-Hi Mill

First steel rolled in 1957
Located 105' north of 3-Hi Mill
Back-up rolls 59" dia. x 156" long (no crown)
Work rolls 38" dia. x 160" long (.010 to .025 crown)
2 — 5000 HP motors—direct connection to work rolls
800 feet/min. mill speed
Average 9 passes per plate (75% reduction)
Rolls plate from $\frac{3}{16}$" to 14" thick, from
48" to 150" wide and up to
90'-0" long depending on width and gauge
Descaling by 1500 psi top and bottom
    hydraulic sprays and steam sprays
    70,000 tons/month average production
    (record 78,380 tons per month)

Leveller

Located 272' from 4-Hi Mill
6 top rolls and 5 bottom rolls
Rolls 13" dia. x 160" long
10" maximum opening
145 to 435 fpm
250 HP drive, 375/900 rpm, total reduction 9.88:1

FLANGING MILL

No. 1 Spinning Machine (1931)

Forms head over solid forms
Maximum blank diameter—66"
Flanged head sizes—9½" minimum
                48" maximum (special sizes up to 59")
Maximum thickness—2½"
Quadrant roll 9" dia. x 11" long
Forming roll carriage drive—5 HP
Forming roll quadrant drive—4½ HP
125 HP main spindle drive

No. 2 Spinning Machine

To be dismantled—(used for rough turning only)

No. 3 Spinning Machine (1931)

Forms heads over form and turndown block
Maximum blank diameter—180"
Flanged head sizes—22" minimum
                144" maximum (limited by size of plate we can roll)
Maximum thickness—4"
Quadrant roll 22" dia. x 22" long
Main spindle drive—twin 125 HP motors
Forming roll quadrant drive—50 HP
Forming roll lift drive—6 HP, maximum travel 8"
Forming roll carriage drive—45 HP
Saddle roll adjustment drive—45 HP
Saddle elevating drive—16 HP, maximum travel 12"
Centering drive—3 HP

Mechanical Press

1400 ton mechanical press
24" stroke
Maximum blank diameter—54"
14" adjustment
1 to 3 strokes per minute
75 HP drive

Hydraulic Presses

1 — 125 ton sectional press
1 — 250 ton sectional press
     Both presses utilize 600 psi central water hydraulic system intensified
         to 2400 psi.

Boring Mills

1 — 84" boring mill
1 — 120" boring mill
1 — 16'-0" boring mill

Furnaces

4 oil fired batch type furnaces
Steam atomized
Furnaces are located as follows
     No. 1 spinning machine
     No. 3 spinning machine—190" x 190" hearth
     1400 ton mechanical press
     Nos. 1 and 2 hydraulic press

DEPARTMENT SCALES

Quantity	Capacity Lbs.	Type
4	60,000 x 20	Industrial
2	60,000 x 10	Built-In
2	30,000 x 5	Built-In
1	20,000 x 10	Built-In
4 Miscellaneous small scales		

60-Inch Plate Mill

The **60-inch Plate Mill** began operation in April 1920. It was located on the east side and immediately joining the **110-inch Sheared Plate Mill**. Both of these mills were served with hot slabs utilizing the same transfer system from the **40-inch Blooming Mill**. This mill had a monthly capacity of 15,000 tons, dependent upon the gauges and sizes rolled.

The 60-inch Sheared Plate Mill, photo dated 4/10/1925.

At right is the storage yard used for the 60-inch Plate Mill. Note the stack of plates ready for shipment to the Andes Copper Mining Company. Also note, at right, the conveyor system for plates traveling into the storage room and at left, the railcars to receive them for shipment. Photo dated 4/10/1925. Both photos courtesy of the Dundalk Patapsco-Neck Historical Society.

The Old 160-Inch Plate Mill

In 1931, Bethlehem Steel dismantled the Flange Mill and the 152-Inch Plate Mill at the Coatesville, PA facility and transferred them to Sparrows Point. The 152-Inch Mill was enlarged and became a single three-high stand. It would become the 160-Inch Plate Mill. This mill produced sheared plate from 145 inches to 150 inches wide and thicknesses ranging from 3/8ths inch to 12 inches. Ingots, from a maximum of 28 inches to 90 inches (50,000 pounds), to slabs of a minimum of 6 inches by 40 inches (2,500 pounds), were heated in three reversing, regenerative roof-fired furnaces. The mill consisted of a single, three-high stand, with top and bottom rolls, 44 ½ inches to 160 inches. The middle rolls were 27 ½ inches to 160 inches. In 1957, a new four-high, 160-inch plate mill was installed 105 feet north of the three-high mill. The three-high mill then became a roughing stand for the new mill.

"Once an **ingot** has been shaped into a **bloom**, it then proceeds to the shears where a steam hydraulic apparatus cuts off the front and back of the bloom. Once the ends have been sheared, the bloom goes to the **hot scarfer**. This procedure worked like a torch. It used a combination of natural gas and oxygen to burn off the surface of the bloom. It cleaned the top, bottom and sides. The bloom then proceeded to the **24-Inch Mill**, where the 10-inch by 10-inch bloom is reduced down to 4 inches by 4 inches. The 24-Inch Mill was a six stand mill and the roller worked from the floor. After the bloom is reduced, it then became a **billet**.

"The billet moves on to the **18-Inch Mill**. This mill was set according to the order that they had. Here, it could be reduced to 2 inches by 2 inches, or 2 ½ inches by 2 ½ inches, or whatever. The 18-Inch Mill was also a **six stand mill**. After leaving the 18-Inch Mill, the billet moved to the **flying shears**. Here, the front end was cut off and the billet was cut into equal lengths. They were then placed outside of the mill to cool. Once cooled, the **straight edge operator** pushed the billets onto a cradle. A **crane operator** then dropped chains down – one long chain and one short. Two men then hooked up a bundle of billets and they were put on a storage rack until ready for use. When they were ready, they were taken out of the storage rack and placed on a railcar and sent to the **Rod Mill**." ~ Hillard "Digger" O'Day, Blooming Mill Mechanical Technician "A", 1957 - 2001

Floor Plan of the 160-Inch Plate Mill

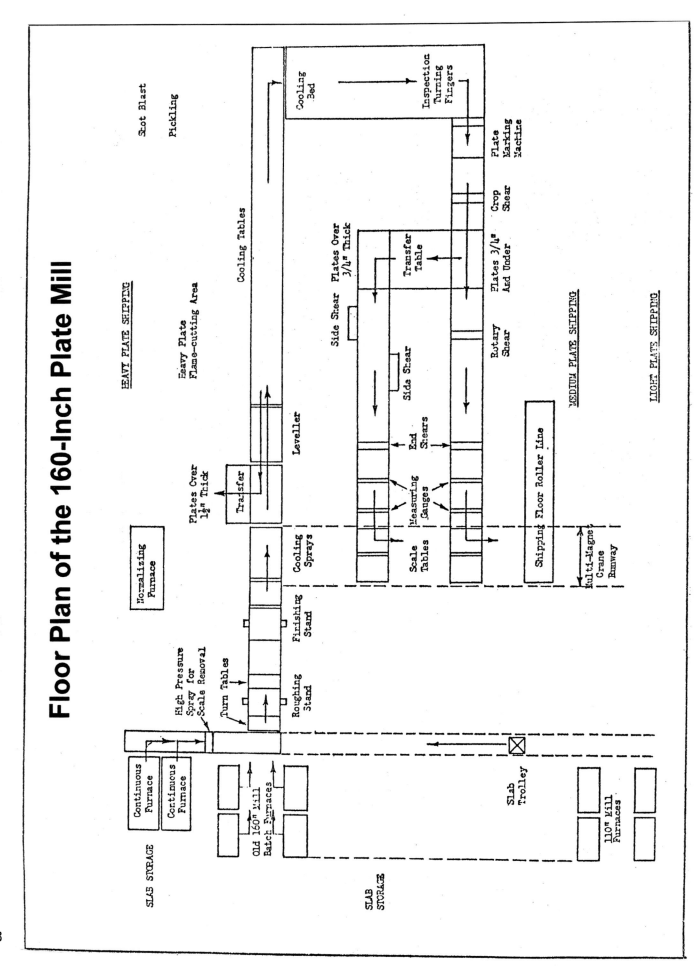

60-Inch Universal Plate Mill

Shown above is the **60-Inch Universal Plate Mill** during an outage. Note the improvised scaffolding. Visible in the photograph are several **grease divider valves**, shown in the diagram at right.

As of 1982, the Plate Mill consisted of a 160-Inch Sheared Plate Facility and a **60-Inch Universal Sheared Plate Facility**. The Sheared Place Facility included a 160-inch 3-high mill, and a 160-inch 4-high mill. The universal plate facility consisted of a 60-inch 2-high mill with vertical edgers. Note: A universal plate mill has both **vertical and horizontal rolls** so that the plate has its width, as well as its thickness, controlled. Photograph and diagram courtesy of Mike Stilwell. Photograph dated 1964.

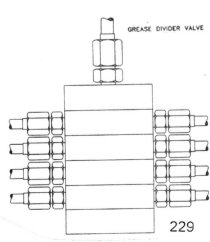

GREASE DIVIDER VALVE

The 110-Inch Plate Mill

The **110-Inch Plate Mill** began operating on September 10, 1917 with two out of six heating furnaces ready. As the **40-Inch Blooming Mill** had not yet been completed, the Plate Mill operated on cold slabs shipped from Bethlehem in Steelton, PA. This mill had a capacity of 12,000 tons per month depending upon gauges and sizes.

The advantage of having a plate mill at Sparrows Point was obvious as it could not only supply the plate demand within its territory, but could also furnish most of the plates used in the Sparrows Point Shipyard. The location of this mill, parallel with and west of the Bloomer, was ideal for the economic delivery of hot slabs to the latter. Sufficient space was left between the two mills for the location of any other mills to be served by the 40-Inch or an additional Slabbing Mill.

A crane runway extended from the 40-Inch Mill to the Plate Mill, beneath which slabs for special steels were accumulated for chipping. This area also served as storage for stocking slabs and blooms. Hot slabs were loaded direct from the shears onto trucks and were delivered to the Plate Mills over a narrow gauge. Photo courtesy of Bill Goodman.   **Footnote 38**

Plate Depot

Loaders Chuck Miller (foreground) and Bob Currier are shown here in 1995 working with a crane operator to guide a steel plate into position. The depot occupied the site that was once the billet conditioning building for the former No. 3 Rod Mill. Photo credited to Rob Smith.

42″ AND 48″ COLD REDUCING MILLS AND TIN MILLS

Finishing capacity 134,000 tons per month
Electrolytic tin plate—105,000 tons per month
Hot dipped tin plate—13,500 tons per month
Black plate—15,500 tons per month

(Information compiled as of October 1960)

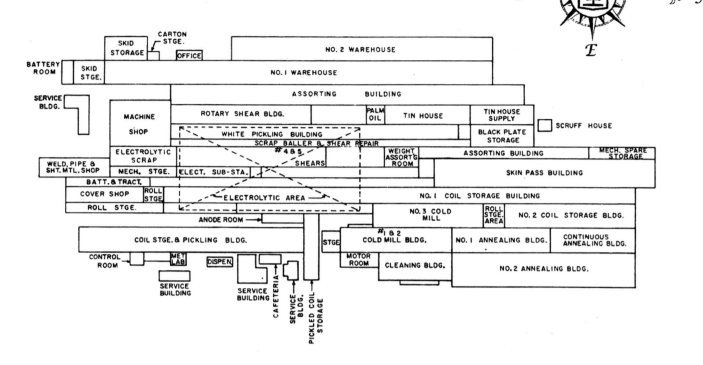

No. 1—42″ Cold Mill (May 1936)

5 stand tandem mill; 4 high

Mill data

Stand No.	HP	Motor RPM	Average Roll Dia.—IN.	Gear Ratio
1	800	600 to 1000	18	12.4:1
2	1500	600 to 900	17.6	7.6:1
3	1500	600 to 900	18.5	4.9:1
4	1500	600 to 900	18.5	3.3:1
5	1500	600 to 900	18.3	2.5:1

No. 2—42″ Cold Mill (July 1937)

5 stand tandem mill; 4 high

Mill data

Stand No.	HP	Motor RPM	Average Roll Dia.—IN.	Gear Ratio
1	500	600 to 800	17.3	11:1
2	1000	600 to 800	18.1	6.9:1
3	1000	600 to 800	17.5	4:1
4	1000	600 to 800	18.1	2.9:1
5	1250	600 to 800	18.3	2.5:1

No. 3—48" Cold Mill (February 1957)

5 stand tandem mill; 4 high

Mill data

Stand No.	HP	Motor RPM	Average Roll Dia.—IN.	Gear Ratio
1	1750	80 to 240	20	1:1
2	3500	150 to 360	20	1:1
3	4000	150 to 325	20	1:1.5
4	5000	225 to 500	20.5	1:1.5
5	5400	275 to 550	19.5	1:2

Batch Annealing

84 bases—8 pedestals each

30 furnaces

Direct fired

Size—24'-10" x 14'-10" each

185 ton capacity per furnace

8,400 cu. ft. per hour fuel consumption initially

1,600 cu. ft. per hour fuel consumption at control heat

Continuous Annealing

Four continuous lines

No. 1 line—April 1956

No. 2 line—September 1956

No. 3 line—January 1957

No. 4 line—March 1957

Production 11,000 tons per month per line

Operating speed—350 feet per minute to 715 feet per minute

Line specifications

Width—18" to 38"

No. 28 gauge and lighter .0147 to .0077

Temper Mills (Skin Pass)

Six mills—total production—140,000 tons per month

Mill data

No.	Type	HP No. 1 Stand	HP No. 2 Stand	Motor RPM No. 1 Stand	Motor RPM No. 2 Stand	Gear Ratio	Avg. Roll Dia.—IN. No. 1 Stand	Avg. Roll Dia.—IN. No. 2 Stand
1	1 stand, 4 high	500		900		2.5:1	18⅜	
2	2 stand, 4 high	300	200	200 to 300	575 to 750	direct drive	17½	18
3	2 stand, 4 high	400	400	500 to 750	500 to 750	direct drive	17½	18⅜
4	2 stand, 4 high	400	400	500 to 750	500 to 750	direct drive	17½	18⅜
5	2 stand, 4 high	500	400	250 to 400	680 to 1050	direct drive	17½	18
6	2 stand, 4 high	500	400	250 to 400	680 to 1050	direct drive	17½	18

Three Continuous Acid Pickling Lines

Line	Upcoiler FT./MIN.	Capacity TON/HR.	Start-up Date
1	390	60	May 1936
2	410	60	October 1937
3	850	90	January 1957

Shearing Equipment

4 Rotary shears (hot dip and black plate)

850 feet per minute
Maximum gauge—0.0317
Maximum width—37 in.
Lengths—14 to 37 in.

12 Rotary shear lines (tin plate)

4 — 850 feet per minute
Maximum gauge—0.0317
Maximum width—37 in.
Lengths—14 to 37 in.

2 — 1000 feet per minute
Maximum gauge 0.0162
Maximum width—37 in.
Lengths—14 to 45 in.

6 — 1250 feet per minute
Maximum gauge 0.0162
Maximum width—37 in.
Lengths—14 to 45 in.

Five Alkaline Cleaning Lines

Line	Line Speed FT./MIN.	Gear Ratio	Max. Coil Size IN. O.D.	I.D.	Start-up Date
1	2150	28:1	51	20.5	May 1936
2	2150	28:1	51	20.5	May 1936
3	2300	28:1	51	20.5	July 1937
4	2300	28:1	51	20.5	July 1937
5	2300	28:1	51	20.5	July 1937

Tinning Lines

Nine electrolytic, alkaline

Line	Ampere Output	Plate Cap'y. Lbs. Tin/Min.	Line Speed FT./MIN.	Start-up Dates
1	120,000	5.1	750	Feb. 1943
2	60,000	2.5	750	Feb. 1943
3	120,000	5.1	750	Feb. 1943
4	144,000	6.2	800	April 1951
6	172,500	7.3	800	Oct. 1955
7	172,500	7.3	800	April 1956
8	172,500	7.3	800	Feb. 1957
9	172,500	7.3	800	Dec. 1957
10	172,500	7.3	800	June 1958

No. 2 42-Inch Tandem Mill

Shown above, the **No. 2 42-Inch Tandem Mill**, which came online in 1937. No. 1 Tandem Mill came online in 1936. Both were 4-high, 5-stand mills. No. 3 Tandem Mill was a 48-inch mill. It came online in February 1957. It was also a 4-high, 5-stand mill. Photo courtesy of Rich Glenn.

"I started work at the Point in December of 1946. I had no marketable job skills other than truck driving experience, from in the army as well as in civilian life. My godfather knew some influential people at the Point, and with his pull, I got a job there in the TMMS (Tin Mill Machine Shop). On the job, I learned to operate grinders and a drill press. For years I worked the night shift, but eventually was scheduled daylight, operating a drill press almost exclusively. I hated coming onto the day shift because the night shift environment was more relaxed, and fewer bosses were around. In 1965, a shop, for repairing hydraulic pumps and valves, was set up in the TMMS. It was set up primarily for repairing and testing 'autopour' valve/cylinder assemblies that controlled the steel ladle stoppers that the Open Hearth Department used for teeming ingots. The valves had to be altered, as they were received from the factory, so that the ladle stopper rods would only be pulled, to open the stoppers. The stoppers fell by gravity to close; pushing them would bend and destroy the stopper rods. Pete 'Butch' Rossi was assigned to that shop. I enjoyed that kind of work and I enjoyed working with Butch, so I sneaked in there to work as often as I could. Occasionally, the shop foreman would be frustrated in looking for me, until he found me there. I eventually became scheduled full time in the hydraulic shop. A few years later, the shop expanded, and moved into larger quarters in another area of the TMMS.

"Over the years, until I retired in January of 1990, I worked in that shop, repairing and testing many kinds of hydraulic pumps, valves, and motors from all of the mills. As the years progressed, these components became more varied and more complex.

"I enjoyed playing pranks. One time I connected a large heavy duty balloon to a plant air line, cracked the valve to inflate the balloon slowly. Eventually, of course, the balloon exploded, and with a loud bang, dust rained down from the rafters. People ran from the shop office to see what had happened.

"Another time, I attached a button near the door of the original hydraulic shop, with a sign 'press for service. The shop foreman actually pressed the button and waited for a response. After a minute or so, he barged into the shop, and Butch asked him what he wanted. The foreman responded 'What the hell's the matter with you? Didn't you hear the bell?'

"Favorite pastimes of the guys in the shop were, on breaks, of course, using aisles in the shop for bowling lanes, and watching the girls (the tin floppers) go to and from their jobs on Assorting Road, which was conveniently adjacent to the shop.

"I had a great time at the Point, and I got along with everybody."
~Bill "Coke" Kotroco, Hydraulic Shop, 1946 to 1990

42-Inch Cold Mill

The Cold Mill building, which was conveniently located with respect to the Pickling building, housed two 42-inch Tandem Mill trains. **Each mill consisted of five 4-high stands.** Each mill had state of the art technology for the time, which included electro-limit gauging equipment to ensure accuracy of gauge. Photo dated 1938. Both photos on this page are courtesy of Rich Glenn.

The Skin Pass Mills **had two 42-inch two-stand 4-high mills**. The rolls of these mills ran at 250 to 375 rpm, giving a surface speed of 1,194 to 1,791 feet per minute. Each mill had a capacity of 8,000 tons per month. **There were also two 42-inch single stand 4-high mills**, each with a monthly capacity of 6,300 gross tons.

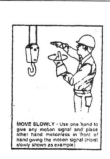

MOVE SLOWLY - Use one hand to give any motion signal and place other hand motionless in front of hand giving the motion signal (Hoist slowly shown as example)

236

48-Inch Tandem Mill

Shown above, the 48-Inch Tandem Mill shortly after it came online in 1957. The view is looking north. This cold reduction mill was a 4-high 5-stand mill with an annual capacity of 583,700 tons. Photo dated February 14, 1957, courtesy of Baltimore Museum of Industry.

"Once I was established on the tinning lines as a Feeder, I would see my grandfather walking to the locker room about 3 p.m. Monday through Friday. At about 3:45 p.m. he would walk back the other direction, heading toward the No. 26 Red Rocket to go to the St. Helena stop."
~Roy E. Shepherd, 56-Inch Cold Mill Crane Operator, 1956 - 1995

No. 3 Duo

"I finished at Sparrows Point High School in 1934. That same year, I went to work in the Tin Mill Restaurant. Mr. Crumlick owned the Beth Mary Inn on "B" Street and he also owned the Tin Mill Restaurant near the Sorting Room where the Tin Floppers worked. I worked at the restaurant for three years. Then, in 1936, I went to work out in the mill. My first job was in the Electrical Department. I was a grunt at first, just helping out wherever I was needed. After a while, I moved up to Tractor Operator in the Tandem Mill and Washers. When the Skin Pass operating expanded, I moved over there as a Tractor Operator, transferring coils from the mill to the shears and from the shears to the Assorting Room. In late 1939, I applied for a transfer to a production job on the Skin Pass Mill and started out as a Feeder.

"My job as a Feeder was to feed the end of a coil into the front of the mill. The Skin Pass Mill positions were **Feeder, Button Man, Catcher, and Roller**. Over the next couple of years, I advanced to Catcher. In 1942, I enlisted in the Navy. When I returned in 1946, I went back to my old job as Catcher. The Catcher's job was to guide the end of the coil out of the mill and onto the coiler.

"When I got back from the service in 1946, they had already built the No. 2 Skin Pass Mill and were in the process of building No. 3 and No. 4 Skin Pass Mills. No. 1 and No. 2 Mill were in a single building. Then they knocked out a wall. They also made the No. 2 Mill a 2-stand mill.

"I eventually moved up from Catcher to Roller. My first rolling job was on No. 4 Skin Pass. I worked there whenever I was needed for about 10 years. In 1973, I moved over as a Roller on the No. 3 Duo Mill. The Roller's job is to supervise the mill. The main job was to work between the stands. You had to monitor the Feeder putting the coil into the front of the mill and the Catcher who put the coil end on the coiler. You had to make sure that everyone was on the same page. Once the mill started up, the Roller's job was to see that the **correct tension** was on the coil as it passed through the work rolls. I remained on the Duo Mill as a Roller until I retired in 1975."
~Dale Kelly, Roller – Duo Mill, 1936 – 1975. Photo courtesy of Dale Kelly.

Note: Of the three men pictured above, Dale Kelly is in the middle.

Skin Pass Crane Operator

42-48 Inch Cold Mill Cranes

Quantity	Capacity	Location
2	5	Warehouse
1	10	No. 2 Warehouse
1	10/10	No. 2 Warehouse
4	5	Assorting Building
1	10	Machine Shop
1	2	Machine Shop
1	15	Machine Shop
1	5	Machine Shop
1	5	Roll Storage
1	10	Tin House
2	5	Tin House
1	15/5	Rotary Shear Building
2	15/5	White Pickling Building
2	15	Coil Storage & Pickling Building
1	15	Black Plate Storage
1	15	Scrap Baller & Shear Repair
1	10	Electrolytic Scrap
1	25/10	No. 4 & No. 5 Shears
1	60/20	Skin Pass Building
1	25	Skin Pass Building
1	75/20	Skin Pass Building
1	25/10	Cover Shop
2	25/10	No. 1 Coil Storage Building
1	25/25	No. 2 Coil Storage Building
1	10	Electric Storage
1	10	Anode Room
1	15	Pickled Coil Storage
1	60/20	No. 1 & No. 2 Cold Mill Building
1	25	No. 1 & No. 2 Cold Mill Building
1	40/10	No. 1 Annealing Building
1	40/10	No. 2 Annealing Building
1	25	No. 2 Annealing Building
1	50/10	Motor Room
1	5	Battery Room
1	5	Battery & Tractor
1	10	Weld Pipe & Sheet Metal Shop
1	3	Mechanical Storage
1	10	Mechanical Spare Storage
1	75/20	No. 3 Cold Mill
1	25	No. 3 Cold Mill
1	5	Continuous Annealing Building
4	5	Continuous Annealing Building

"In 1959, I went to work in the Pipe Mill to learn how to operate a crane. In the summer of 1960, I got laid off. I was off for six to eight months. My father was a foreman in the Pipe Mill and he told me that he heard that they were calling guys back in the Tin Mill and that I should check it out. Somewhere along the line, they lost my records which meant I would have to start my seniority time all over again. Then my old boss, Bill Lentz, called and said that they found my records and the Pipe Mill wanted me to come back. At that time, I was an extra man, and I would fill in wherever a crane operator was needed. Then a job came open in the **Tin Mill Skin Pass** and I bid on it and got the job. I worked the No. 1 Skin Pass crane. The cab was located in the middle. The rest of the cranes in the mill were up against the wall. At one time or another, I worked every crane in the mill. The Skin Pass had four, counting the Duo Mill. The Pickler had two, the Halogen Line, Washer, Shears, Box Anneal, and Scrap all had one crane.

"The job of the Skin Pass crane was to take care of the mill. When they were **changing rolls in the mill**, we took out the **work rolls** first, then we would pull the **backup rolls**. These would go to the Roll Shop for regrinding and surfacing. Once the old rolls were out, we put the new ones in. The bottom backup went in first, then the top backup. Next came the work rolls. After the new rolls were in, we would use the crane to strip the bearings off of the old rolls before they went back to the roll shop. There were roll grinding machines near the mill. When the **grinder operators** were ready, we would lift a freshly ground roll out of the machine and put a dirty roll in its place.

"My last 10 years, I worked a lot of doubles in the 56-Inch Cold Mill, mostly moving coils to and from the Halogen Line, the Washer, the Pickler, and the Warehouse. The boys on the floor used to say, 'Jerry, when you're up in the crane, we are the safest we'll ever be.' I retired in 2000."

~Jerry Lauterbach, Crane Operator, 1959 – 2000

Photo credited to Rob Smith

Tin Mill Pickler

Pickling was the first process in the manufacture of all tin products. It was a chemical cleaning process in which steel was passed through a hot sulfuric acid solution to remove the iron oxide scale on the surface of the strip so that the thickness of the strip could be further reduced in the **Tandem Mill**. The strip was also trimmed and given a coat of palm oil before it was recoiled and sent to the Tandem Mill.

The **No. 3 Pickler** went into production in 1957 and was modernized in 1989. Some of the major features of the modernization included a **new entry end with a walking beam conveyor and a horizontal looping tower.** The new delivery end tension reel was designed to produce a tightly wound coil.

Between start-up in 1957 and 1992, No. 3 Pickler produced over 17 million tons of steel.

↓ Below is a diagram illustrating the pickling process.

Sylvester "Jesse" James (above) worked at the Tin Mill Pickler for 37 years. Photo courtesy of Rob Smith.

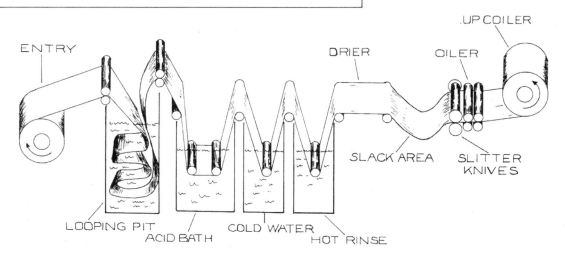

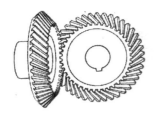

John Henry Hahn, left, →
and Bill "Coke" Kotroco,
just before retirement.
John retired in 1989 and
Bill retired in 1990.

"During the war, I served in the Navy, in the Amphibious Division, in various operations, including the delivering of Marines onto the island of Iwo Jima. In 1946, I was discharged, and became eligible for the "52/20" program (twenty dollars for 52 weeks, twenty dollars being a fair amount of money at the time). I was on that program for only one or two weeks, when I began at Glenn L. Martin, working on converting the military planes C-47's and C-54's to the civilian versions; DC-3's and DC-4's.

"I was laid off from Martin's when that contract expired, and began work at Baltimore Porcelain Steel Co., a real sweat shop operation, and in the summer, at that. I was very happy to get a call back from Martin's to work on the last PBM's (Patrol Bomber flying boats) that they made. Seeing another layoff coming, I applied for, and got, a job at Sparrows Point, in August, 1948, in the 56" Hot Strip Mill shipping department. My first job there was to clean out railcars to prepare them for being loaded with coils of steel. Later, I was a 'sawman' in that department, cutting timbers for chocking the coils in the railcars.

"I got a transfer into the TMMS (Tin Mill Machine Shop) as a learner machine operator, and advanced through the positions of C, B, and finally A rate machine operator. I then took, and passed, the test in # 2 Machine Shop to qualify as a C rate Machinist, and returned to the TMMS. While working in the TMMS, I lived in Dundalk, and rode the Red Rocket to and from work. At the plant, I got off of the trolley at the foot of the viaduct, at Assorting Road, a very short walk to the shop.

"I later returned to # 2 Machine Shop for six weeks where I performed the tasks and passed the tests required to qualify as an A rate Machinist. At this time, I returned to the TMMS, and was finally scheduled for all daylight (7-3) shifts, until I retired. I had worked 18 years on night (11-7) shift.

"At the TMMS then, I worked part-time as a machinist and part-time as a machine repairman. The repairman job involved trouble-shooting and repairing any malfunctioning machine in the following areas: the TMMS proper, the Inner Cover Shop, the Sheet Metal Shop, the Pipe Shop, and the Weld Shop.

"One of my job assignments during this time was very interesting (and unusual, for a machinist). The company wanted to have some machines moved from the Tin Mill area into the TMMS. It involved a crop shear knife grinder, a slitting shear knife grinder, a roll grinder, and two Blanchard surface grinders. The TMMS did not want to be charged with the amount of money required to have the Engineering Department manage and coordinate this project, with millwrights and the Construction Department, so the job was assigned to me. I got the large sheets of paper that are used to wrap coils of steel, and used them to make templates of the machine "footprints", and did the necessary work to successfully move the machines. Those machines were in almost daily use when I retired in 1989, after 41 years at the Point.

"As an 'extra-curricular' activity, I played outfield in a fast-pitch softball TMMS team, in a league that played at Patterson Park."
~ John Henry Hahn, "A" Rate Machine Operator, 1948 to 1989

TIN FLOPPERS

The following are excerpts from Deborah Rudacille's book _Roots of Steel_; used with her permission.

"During the boom, a surprising number of women also worked at Sparrows Point. Most of them were clerks in receiving or purchasing or in one of the mill offices, but three to four hundred worked in the tin mill as 'tin flappers,' inspecting sheets of tin plate used to can soup, soft drinks, fruit, and vegetables. Women had worked as tin sorters on Sparrows Point since the 1920s, but as American women abandoned the thrifty habits of their foremothers and stopped canning their own backyard fruits and vegetables, purchases of canned goods-and thus tin production-boomed." (page 104)

"There was an art to 'flopping' tin, Jessie Schultz, a former tin mill worker, said, demonstrating the fluid motion for me in her living room filled with porcelain angels. Jessie is eighty-five years old but looks closer to seventy, and she is no one's idea of a steelworker. She is five feet tall and must have weighed all of a hundred pounds soaking wet when she was hired to work in the tin sorting room in 1948. 'You had to turn it and flip it real smooth, like this,' she said, showing me how to flip a sheet of tin without 'kinking' it, as she was prone to do at first. 'When you're flipping tin, you have to take it and just gently let it loose.'" (page 104)

"Despite the difficulty of the job, the tin sorters were a bit like a family, and their chief forelady, Elizabeth Alexander, a Hungarian émigré who ran the shop with military discipline for nearly forty years, "was like a mother to all of us-except a lot of the women didn't take it that way." Alexander, the highest-ranking woman on Sparrows Point for many years, was a tough customer, and most of the women who worked under her supervision quaked when they heard her step and smelled her heavy perfume." (page 106)

"Members of Alexander's family who worked on the Point themselves spoke of her fierce protectiveness of 'her girls' and the way she would 'go nose to nose with some of the big bosses down there' to take care of them. 'She took nothing from any of those guys, so they came to respect her,' said her grandson Bill Knoerlein. 'She made that tin mill, and the women in it, a place to be reckoned with.'" (page 106)

"The job was physically grueling. Some of the thick-gauge sheets of tin were quite heavy, but even the thin ones, easier to lift, had sharp edges, so the women wore gloves at all times to avoid deep cuts. Foreladies prowled the room, checking 'to see what you were doing with the defects, what you were putting into waste, which was not salvageable.' Sheets that could be mended were called seconds and were put into a separate pile. If you didn't sort at least a sixty-six-inch stack per shift, you were fired. To meet that quota left little time for socializing, and silence in the tin sorting room was strictly enforced." (page 105)

BETHLEHEM'S WINNING COMBINATION

CHROMIZED: The basic chromizing process dates back to 1923. It was shown to be capable of applying a stainless steel coating to batches of steel parts. Around 1960, an attempt was made to apply the technique to sheet coils, but these attempts were not efficient enough to be economically feasible. It wasn't until 1964 that Bethlehem's **Homer Research Laboratories** developed a technique suited to mass production, which used low cost ferrochrome at 100% efficiency.

GALVALUME: The other half of Bethlehem's winning combination was Galvalume. It was a hot-dipped sheet steel developed in 1972 with a special coating that contained about 55% aluminum, 43% zinc, and 2% silicon. Galvalume proved to have two to four times better corrosion resistance than galvanized steel.

Chromized steel sheets and Galvalume were two new products developed by Bethlehem Steel that enhanced their competitive position for decades to come. Footnote 39

No. 1 Halogen Plating Line

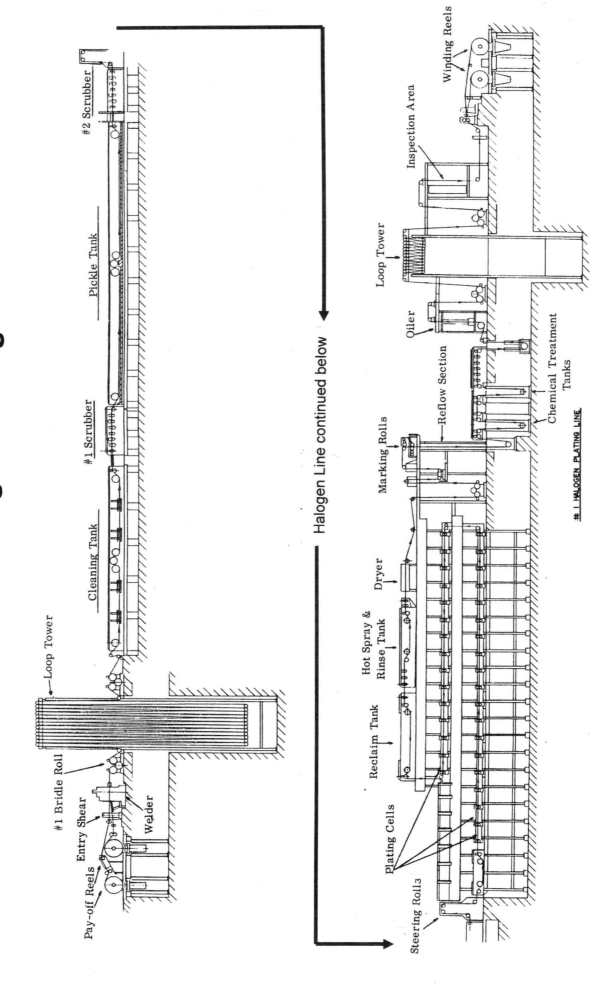

244

No. 4 Electrolytic Plating Line delivery reel. Photo circa 1960.

"When working on the tin lines, we would have about 2,500 feet of metal strip in our line from reel to reel. We plated tin coating onto the strip of steel 36 inches wide with a thickness between 00.51 to .0216 gauge. The line ran at about 800 feet per minute. When the line was running all was okay. But when the strip tore and broke, we had to rethread the rolls. Our tin line had 280 rolls from end to end. We did nine processes on our plating line. The metal strip ran through an acid tank followed by an acid rinse. It continued on through a series of 28 rolls in the plates followed by a plate rinse. It was then pre-cleaned with a soda ash and fluxed. In the next process, the tin was reflowed on the strip in the furnace. It then went to a quench tank to cool the tin so that it wouldn't stick to the rollers. This was followed by a post-cleaning in soda ash and a chemical treatment of chromic acid. The strip then proceeded to its final hot rinse at 198 degrees. The strip was then oiled and went to the front looper to be taken off the line while the line was running at 800 feet per minute.

"We also had to maintain tank levels, tank temperatures, and solution concentrations. Temperatures in the tanks ranged from 185 degrees to 205 degrees. Rolls needed to be cleaned to prevent dents in the strip caused by dirt on the contact rolls. We also had to remove stains on the strip caused by the acid plater, chromic acid, and water quench stains. Sometimes a tear-off would occur, causing a shut down on the line. These shut downs could last from two to eight hours. The tanks on the line would have to be drained and the strip would have to be rethreaded. A weld would have to be made to secure both ends, then the tanks would be refilled and reheated. Once you got the heat up, the line was restarted." ~Benjamin Pritchett, Feed Coiler Assistant Operator/Turn Foreman, 1953 to 1983

No. 1 Halogen Line – October 1964. Photo courtesy of Butch Johnson.

Halogen Tinning Line Equipment: No. 1 Line – two payoff reels, sheer seam welder (narrow lap), bridle rolls, looping tower (24 passes), cleaning tank (hot alkaline solution), scrubber (hot water sprays and rotating brushes), pickle tank, scrubber, steering rolls, plating section (32 cells), reflow unit, chemical treatment tanks, oiler, looping tower, pinhole detector, snip shear, two winding reels with belt wrappers.

The equipment of No. 2 Halogen Tinning Line was essentially the same as No. 1 line, except there was an additional cleaning tank and 12 plating cells.

No. 1 Line started up in 1963; No. 2 Line started up in 1964. Both lines replaced all electrolytic lines.

"My job consisted of pushing anodes with a manual jack. Each anode weighed approximately 80 pounds. Before pushing a new anode, you had to remove the spent anode from the cell. There were several cells. Each individual cell had two beds. Each bed had fourteen anodes. Every cell had a contract roll and a plater solution. This job had two tiers. In the first tier, you coated the bottom of the running. In the second tier, you coated the top of the sheet. The tin was electrified onto the sheet. The responsibility of the Assistant Operator was to make the adjustments on the different coatings. It was very important to wear the proper safety equipment when working with the plater solution and machinery."
~ George Hellems, Assistant Operator, No. 1 Halogen Line, 42 years of service.

HALOGEN LINES

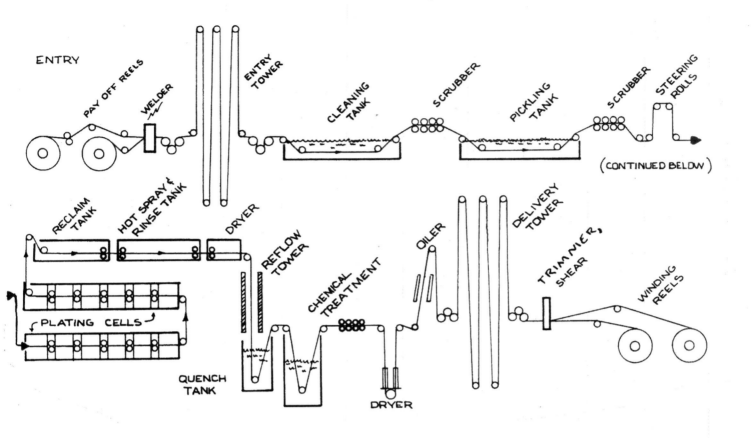

TIN PLATING: In 1992, there were two types of plating lines in the Tin Mill, both of which were continuous processes. They were the **Halogen Lines**, which produced Tin Plate and **No. 8 Chrome Line**, which produced **Tin Free Steel – Chrome Type (TFS-CT)** or Chrome Plate. A third product was **Black Plate**.

"As the Assistant Operator on the Halogen Lines, I was responsible for applying the right amount of tin coating put on the steel strip as it passed through the **plating cells**. It traveled at a speed of 2,000 feet per minute. There were two Halogen Lines. There were many processes between starting at the **entry and ending at the delivery end**. First it traveled through **a cleaning tank and a pickle tank** to prepare the strip for plating. It then traveled through **two tiers of plating cells** where the tin was electrolytically plated on the strip first on the bottom and then on the top. The strip is then rinsed in a series of tanks. The strip then returns to floor level through the **reflow tower**. The strip is then given several post-plating treatments, trimmed, inspected, and recoiled."

~C. Lloyd Hauser, Assistant Operator, Halogen Lines, 35 years of service

No. 5 Continuous Annealing Line

ANNEALING: As a steel strip is cold-reduced in the Tandem Mill, it becomes too "hard" for most uses and must be **annealed** (reheated) to soften it to the correct **temper** for further processing and use by customers. The **No. 5 Continuous Anneal Line** would unwind a coil, and **electrolytically** clean, scrub, rinse, squeeze, dry and heat the strip to 1200 degrees Fahrenheit. The entry tower and delivery tower provided the reservoirs for the excess strip needed for a continuous process.

The picture above shows the No. 5 Continuous Annealing Line when it was new in 1962.

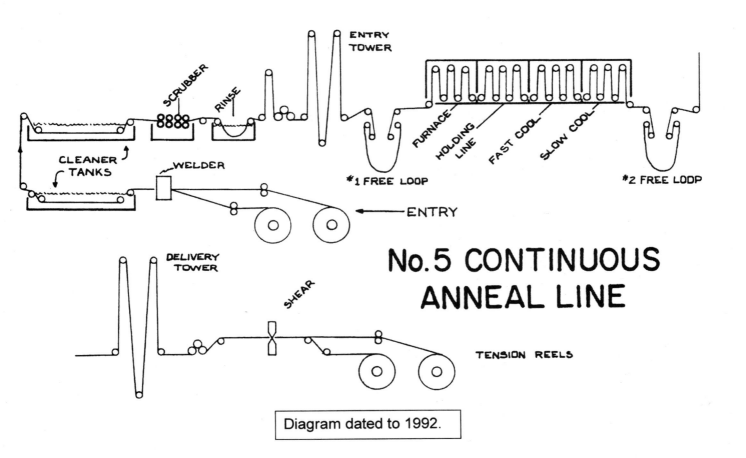

No.5 CONTINUOUS ANNEAL LINE

Diagram dated to 1992.

Tin mill—continuous annealing lines—production and data

Line	No. 4	No. 5
Date installed	1957	1962
Production, tons/yr	132,000	276,000
Nominal tons/month	15,000	33,000
Capacity, tons/hr	25	60
Source	No. 1, 2 & 3 tandem mills	No. 1, 2 & 3 tandem mills
Distribution	No. 5 & 6 temper mills	No. 3 D.R. mill; 5 & 6 temper mills
Strip data:		
Gage, in.	0.0076–0.014	0.0076–0.03
Width, in.	18–40	24–40
Coil weight, lb	7000–38,000	7000–44,000
Coil OD, in., max	72	72
Building dim, ft	284 × 247*	419 × 112.5
Overall dim of line, ft	182 × 19 × 50 high	445 × 28 × 120 high
Line length, ft	182	362
Length strip in line, ft	1450	5422
Strip storage capacity, entry, ft	600	1640
Strip storage capacity, exit, ft	600	900
Method of heating	Direct fired—144 burners	Radiant tubes—176
Fuel	Natural gas	Natural gas (or CO)
Fuel consumption, Btu/ton	821,711 (1980)	919,303 (1980)
Fuel input, Btu/hr max	23,650,000	60,500,000
Atmosphere	4% H_2 in N_2 from prepared gas station	4% H_2 in N_2 from prepared gas station
Annealing practices	TU & T5 practice: strip temp. 1180–1200F; aim Rockwell 60R-30t	Double reduced TU & T5 practice: strip temp. 1140–1160F; aim Rockwell 60R-30T
	T4 practice: strip temp. 1240–1300F; aim Rockwell 56-58R-30t	T4 practice: strip temp. 1140–1160F; aim Rockwell 56-58R-30t
Line speed, fpm	700–1100 max	2000 max

(No. 1 line converted to continuous washer, rewind, and stripper line. No. 2 and 3 lines inactive.)

No. 5 Continuous Annealing Line – 42 Inch Mill

Continuous Annealing Line – No. 5 Equipment: Two payoff reels, scrap reel, shear, seam welder (narrow lap), x-ray thickness gauge, (11 stationary rolls on top; three sets of steering rolls), electrolytic cleaner (two tanks, horizontal pass, eight grids), scrubber (eight brushes, hot water sprays), rinser, furnace (176 radiant tubes), holding zone (10 passes), cooler (slow and jet cool), looping tower (eight stationary rolls on top), double-cut shear, two winding reels with belt wrappers. Water discharged from jet cool blowers was used for makeup water for scrubber and rinse sprays.

Time and Motion

Richard "Wicki" Mouzon operates heavy duty equipment while shuttling coils.

"I graduated from Sparrows Point High School in 1945. After school, I joined the Marine Corps. When I got out of the service, I went to work at the Point. I took an apprenticeship at the No. 2 Machine Shop and became a **tool and die maker**. We did a lot of repair work. The shop did its own maintenance and repair. If a machine broke down, we could make the replacement part and fix it right there. I worked on mill presses, lathes, planers, and other machinery in the shop. At that time in the late 40's and early 50's, our shop employed 600 people and ran three shifts. I worked in the Machine Shop for ten years.

"One day, I was down in a pit working on a lathe. It was really hot and the job was dirty. A guy I knew from **I.E. (Industrial Engineering)** walked by and saw me in the pit. We talked for a while and he said I should come over to I.E. and apply for a position. I told him that I would come over but I couldn't lose money. He said he would make sure that I would get the same money so I went over for an interview and got the job. It was a **time study job**. We went out in the mill and watched a particular piece of machinery and its operations and based on our observations, a rate was set for that job.

"My first job training was at the Duo Mill. I had a **clipboard and a stopwatch**. Sometimes I would watch a job for weeks. You had to really know the whole operation. When we finished, we would take an average and **a rate would be set.** The operator would be paid a piece rate based on our calculations. The bad thing about this job was that I was studying guys that I went to school with and they might not be too happy with the rate when it was set. I worked mainly in the Tin Mill but the job could take you all over the plant. I had a job in the Scarfing Yard where guys would burn the scales off of slabs. We did time studies on the Skin Pass Mills, coil prep lines, and the halogen lines.

"Once a job was done, each step of the process was listed and how much time it took. Once this was completed, a brochure was developed outlining the entire procedure from start to finish and a rate for that job was set. In 1983, things were beginning to change at the Point. I had my 30 years. I took the incentive package and retired."
~John Mason, Industrial Engineering, 1950 – 1983

56″ AND 66″ COLD REDUCING MILLS

Finishing capacity 136,000 tons per month

Cold rolled products—100,000 tons per month

Continuous galvanized sheets (Bethcon)—27,000 tons per month

Conventional hot dipped galvanized sheets—9,000 tons per month

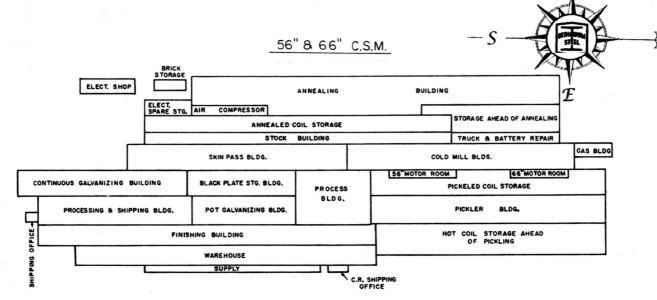

56″ 8 66″ C.S.M.

56″ Cold Mill—(January, 1947—4 stands at time)

5 Stand Tandem Mill; operating speed 2,500 to 3,300 feet per minute

Mill Data

| | Motor | | | |
Stand No.	HP	RPM	Average Roll Dia.-IN.	Gear Ratio
1-4 High	2,000	70 to 175	20	Direct
2-4 High	2,500	130 to 260	20	Direct
3-4 High	1,500	200 to 450	20	1.2:1
4-4 High	1,500	200 to 500	20	1:1.2
5-4 High	1,750	300 to 685	20.7	1:1.2
Tension Reel	400	200 to 800	20.5	Direct

66″ Cold Mill (June, 1951)

4 Stand Tandem Mill; operating speed 1,800 to 2,500 feet per minute

Mill Data

| | Motor | | | |
Stand No.	HP	RPM	Average Roll Dia.-IN.	Gear Ratio
1-4 High	2,500	125 to 275	20	Direct
2-4 High	2,000	150 to 325	20	Direct
3-4 High	2,500	225 to 475	20	1.1:1
4-4 High	2,500	225 to 500	20.7	1.1:1
Tension Reel	500	150 to 600	20.5	Direct

Batch Annealing

2.7 tons per hour

105 bases

62 — 3 pedestals (9 Bethnamel)

9 — 5 pedestals

34 — 8 pedestals

Furnaces—46

Direct fired

32 — 24'-2" x 9'-8"

140 ton capacity

8,500 CFH—coke oven fuel gas

14 — 33'-10" x 16'-1"

400 ton capacity

30,000 CFH—coke oven gas

Open Coil Annealing

40,000 tons per year (anticipated)

3 single stand bases—110" diameter

2 pot annealing furnaces; single stack, gas fired, radiant tube

Coiling and recoiling equipment

330 to 500 feet per minute

Gauges .0135 to .0418

Maximum strip width—66"

Shearing Lines

Six Rotary—flying type

700 feet per minute

18 tons per hour each

No. 14 to No. 32 Gauge—widths 18" to 60"

Lengths 19½" to 240"

Coil Slitting and Trimming Lines

Two—No. 10 to No. 30 Gauge product

ID Coil—24"

Galvanizing Units

Six hot dipped, hand fed

1 — 84" x 90" x 56"; 90,000 lb. zinc

3 — 96" x 102" x 56"; 120,000 lb. zinc

2 — 93" x 136" x 56"; 155,000 lb. zinc

10,000 to 12,000 tons per month capacity

No. 8 to No. 31 gauge

Temperature range—805°F to 870°F

Three continuous lines

No. 1 Line (April 1952)—8,000 tons per month

No. 2 Line (July 1955)—11,000 tons per month

No. 3 Line (January 1956)—8,000 tons per month

Operating speeds—40 feet per minute to 180 feet per minute

Length 60" to 170" (shear range)

Width 20" to 49"

No. 12 to No. 31 gauge

Normal coating weight—0.90 to 1.10 ounces per square foot of sheet

160,000 lb. zinc bath at 860°F

Temper Mills (Skin Pass)

Mill	Motor HP No. 1 Stand	HP No. 2 Stand	Motor RPM No. 1 Stand	RPM No. 2 Stand	Gear Ratio	Avg. Roll Dia. IN. No. 1 Stand	Avg. Roll Dia. IN. No. 2 Stand
1-1 Stand 4 High	400		600 to 750		Direct Drive	20.1	
2-2 Stand 4 High	200	400	800	600 to 750	Direct Drive	16.4	21.0
3-1 Stand 4 High	500		600		Direct Drive	19.2	
4-1 Stand 2 High	300		500 to 1000		7.44:1	27.8	

Pickler Lines (Upcoiler Data)

Line	Speed	Motor HP	Motor RPM	Gear Ratio	Avg. Roll Dia.-IN.
1	400 FPM	50	690 to 1,035	4.2:1	6
2	400 FPM	50	690 to 1,035	4.2:1	6
3	530 FPM	75	850 to 1,275	3.2:1	6
4	530 FPM	75	850 to 1,275	3.2:1	6

56-Inch Cold Mill

The 56-Inch Cold Strip Mill took a roll of steel about ¼ inch thick and ran it through five sets of rolls to reduce it to tin-plate size of about 10- or 12-thousandths of an inch thick and rewound it on a reel at the other end.

"I came out of high school in June 1947 and went into the **Assorting Room** in the Tin Mill. The **Tin Floppers** were nearby. I was in a warehouse weighing the boxes of tin plate just prior to shipment. I only worked there a few months before getting laid off. When I got called back, they wanted me to go to the 56-Inch Cold Mill. When I saw those huge tractors running back and forth, I said 'no way.' They sent me to the 42-Inch Mill. It was the same there. Tractors running everywhere and cranes overhead. I was only 18 years old and not used to the constant motion overhead and on the floor. I didn't think the steel mill was for me, so I quit.

"Several months later, I went back to the employment office and was hired as a laborer in the 56-Inch Cold Strip. They were adding shifts at the time and needed a Scaleman. I broke in as a Scaleman. My job was to weigh the coils as they emerged from the mill. When the shift ended, I would sometimes go over to the Roller and ask him if I could feed the coil through the mill. It was a chance for me to learn a new position so that if an opening came up, I would have some knowledge and experience of the job. Eventually, I moved up to **Feeder Helper, then to Feeder, Catcher, and finally Roller.**

"In 1947, there were two **Skin Pass Mills** in the **56-Inch Cold Strip**. Lifts of steel would come into the back of the No. 3 Skin Pass. Every sheet had to be placed on a conveyor belt. The belt ran continuously. The sheets had to be lifted individually. I wore a cotton glove and had a rubber suction on one finger, which stuck to the sheet and pulled them apart. Me and another guy flipped the sheet onto a conveyor so they could go into the mill. When they came out on the other side, they went through an oiler and then dropped down into a box. The sheets were 48 inches wide and four feet long. The boxes were banded and went by conveyor to another room where a crane picked them up and took them to a **Scaleman** who then weighed them."

~ Dan Yeager, Skin Pass Roller, 1947 – 1988. Photo credited to Rob Smith.

South End of the 56-Inch and 66-Inch Cold Mill; South End of the 56-Inch Hot Strip Mill
South End of the 68-Inch Hot Strip Mill - Blueprint Dated March 17, 1976

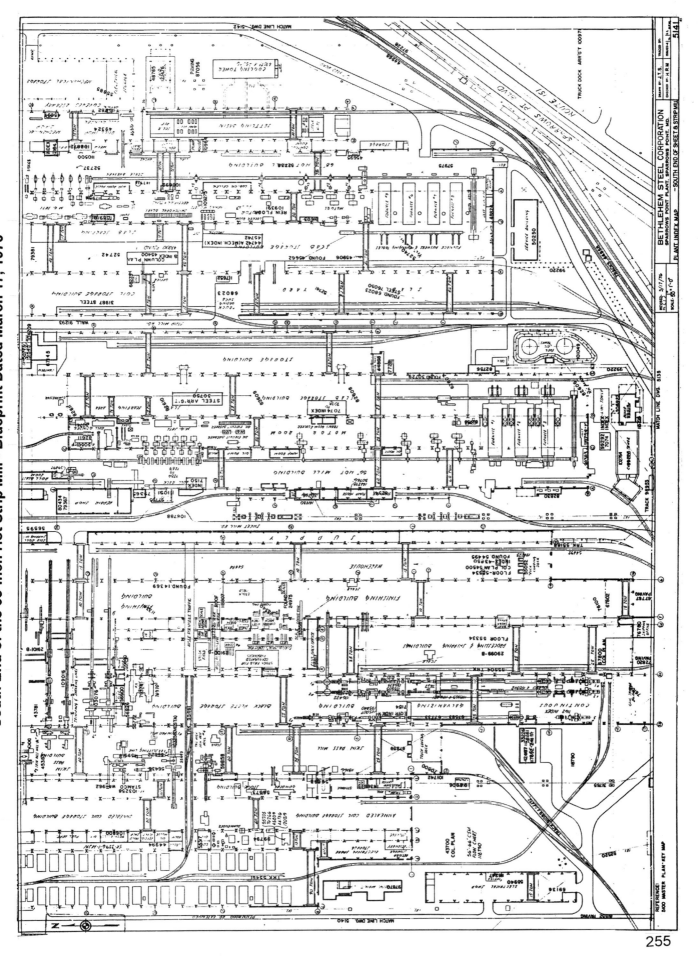

49-Inch Hot Dip Coating Line

The 49-Inch Hot Dip Coating Line started up on December 12, 1992. The 724-foot line ran at 600 feet per minute and was capable of delivering more than 260,000 tons annually. It was officially known as the No. 4 Galvanize/Galvalume line and was located directly south of the 56-Inch and 66-Inch Cold Mills and immediately west of No. 3, No. 2, and No. 1 Coating Lines. Photo dated 1992, credited to Rob Smith.

No. 4 Hot Dip Galvanize/Galvalume Line

"In 1985, I left the Plate Mill Crane Repair and went to the 56-Inch Cold Mill Crane and Tractor Department to become a Crane Operator. What a difference. After a training period of two weeks in the Plate Mill as a Repairman, I was cut loose to become a full-time Crane Operator. I bid on a job in the warehouse loading trucks and railroad cars on the 11 to 7 shift. You mostly put stock away and dug coils out for the next day's shipping. A few years later, I bid on the "A" Man's job. This was originally a salary position. The "A" Man would fill jobs that were added when people called off. You had to walk around the mill and see that things were going as planned. Sometimes you'd call to make a lift or fill in where there was a problem. Shortly after this, I bid on an all-daylight job unloading company trucks. I made less money but worked a double or some overtime to make it up. On April 1, 1995, I ended my career with Bethlehem Steel. I had given them 39 years of my life. They had given me a good living." ~Roy E. Shepherd, 56-Inch Cold Mill Crane Operator, 1956 - 1995

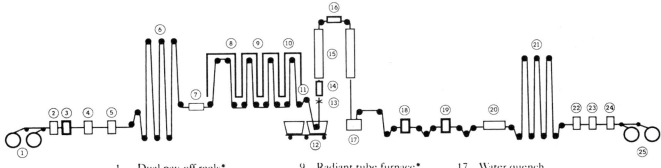

1. Dual pay-off reels*	9. Radiant tube furnace*	17. Water quench
2. Entry thickness gauge; shear*	10. Gas jet cooling	18. 4-high skin pass mill*
3. Narrow seam, prep. lap welder	11. Hot bridle*	19. Tension leveler*
4. Notcher*	12. Dual coating pots*	20. Chemical treatment
5. Side trimmer*	13. Coating air knives	21. Exit looping tower*
6. Entry looping tower*	14. Minimum spangle equip.	22. Shape gauge*
7. Cleaner / scrubber*	15. Forced air cooling	23. Electrostatic oiler*
8. Pre-heat section	16. Coating thickness gauge	24. Terminating shear
		25. Dual tension reels*

No. 4 Coating Line Location At Cold Sheet Mills

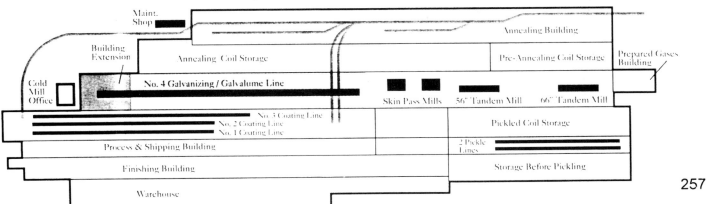

M.I.P. – Methods Improvement Program

M.I.P. Section of the Month – Members of the 56- and 66-Inch Cold Mill receive a plaque in recognition for their ideas and contributions that resulted in improvements in their area of the plant. Second from left, front row: John "Uncle Heinz" Moser, Turn Foreman. Photo circa 1970, courtesy of Dundalk Patapsco-Neck Historical Society.

Methods Improvement Program

Your Boss & MIP...Partners in Progress

Methods Improvement Program

Three steps to improvement

1. Systematically review each job (production or maintenance) for which you are responsible.

2. Look for these signs of trouble:
   - bottlenecks
   - ineffective use of men or equipment
   - idle time—man or machine
   - excessive materials handling
   - low production
   - delays due to production cycle
   - frequent set-ups
   - recurring maintenance
   - operator waiting for movement of material to or from job
   - poor use of material
   - excessive tooling costs
   - high maintenance costs
   - excessive scrap
   - impractical tolerances for end use

3. Use the systematic approach and MIP to correct each problem.

Steel for Strength

Shift Change 1956

The change of shifts before the Steelworkers Union went out on strike in June 1956. Pictured above are workers entering and leaving the Tin Mill Clock House. Below, workers exit the No. 3 Open Hearth. Note the safety message over the entrance to the No. 3 Open Hearth. Photo dated June 30, 1956.

SHEET, TIN AND STRIP DIVISION

GENERAL (Information compiled as of October 1960)

Operating personnel—6,700

Acreage—190

Rated capacity—335,000 tons per month (finished product)

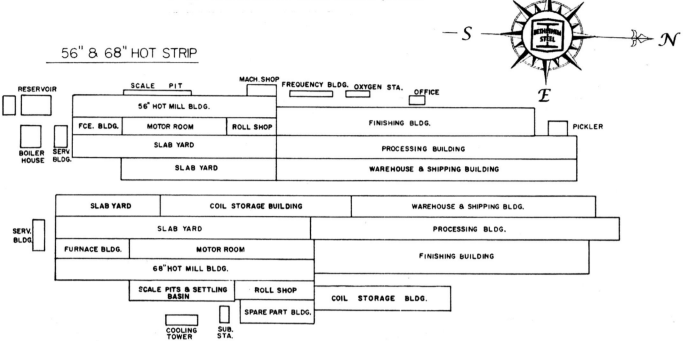

56" & 68" HOT STRIP

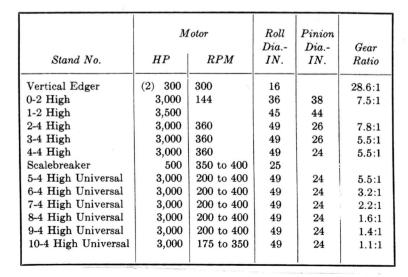

56" AND 68" HOT STRIP MILLS

56" Hot Mill (November 1937)

All data represents status after 1959-1961 modernization program.

Capacity—210,000 tons per month

11 stands—5 roughing, 6 finishing

Maximum slab size 7½" thick, 23' long, 4' wide

Furnaces—3

    Size—26' x 105'

    Gas and oil fired

    200 tons per hour rated capacity each

Mill data

478' runout table

Coilers—3

    Rotary mandrel

    I.D. 26⅞"

    O.D. 58"

    Maximum width—53"

Banding machine

    ¾" x .031 steel strap

    90 psi air pressure for tightening tool

    40,000 coils per month production

    New machine

        ¼" x .031 steel strap

        1 coil every 28 seconds

Stand No.	Motor HP	Motor RPM	Roll Dia.-IN.	Pinion Dia.-IN.	Gear Ratio
Vertical Edger	(2) 300	300	16		28.6:1
0-2 High	3,000	144	36	38	7.5:1
1-2 High	3,500		45	44	
2-4 High	3,000	360	49	26	7.8:1
3-4 High	3,000	360	49	26	5.5:1
4-4 High	3,000	360	49	24	5.5:1
Scalebreaker	500	350 to 400	25		
5-4 High Universal	3,000	200 to 400	49	24	5.5:1
6-4 High Universal	3,000	200 to 400	49	24	3.2:1
7-4 High Universal	3,000	200 to 400	49	24	2.2:1
8-4 High Universal	3,000	200 to 400	49	24	1.6:1
9-4 High Universal	3,000	200 to 400	49	24	1.4:1
10-4 High Universal	3,000	175 to 350	49	24	1.1:1

Hot Strip Mill, continued

68″ Hot Mill (December 1947)

Capacity—268,000 tons per month

11 stands—5 roughing, 6 finishing

Maximum slab size 7½″ thick, 23′ long, 61½″ wide

Furnaces—4

Size—26′ x 105′

Oil and gas fired

200 tons per hour capacity each

Mill data

Stand No.	Motor		Roll Dia.-IN.	Pinion Dia.-IN.	Gear Ratio
	HP	RPM			
Vertical Edger	800	514	16		28:1
1-2 High	2,000	150	36	38	7.5:1
2-4 High	3,500	144	38	38	5.8:1
3-4 High	4,500	267	38	38	7.5:1
4-4 High	4,500	400	34	34	7.5:1
5-4 High	4,500	400	34	34	7.5:1
Scalebreaker	500	150 to 600	25½		23:1
6-4 High	4,000	125 to 250	27½	26	4.2:1
7-4 High	4,000	125 to 250	27½	26	2.6:1
8-4 High	4,000	80 to 160	27½	26	Direct
9-4 High	4,000	100 to 200	27½	26	Direct
10-4 High	4,000	125 to 250	27½	26	Direct
11-4 High	3,500	150 to 300	27½	26	Direct

366′ runout table

Coilers—3

Rotary mandrel

I.D. 26⅞″

O.D. 58″

Maximum width—67″

Banding machine

¾″ x .031 steel strap

90 psi air pressure for tightening tool

40,000 coils per month production

Crane data

Quantity	Capacity	Location
3	15	Coil Storage Building
3	30	Coil Storage Building
3	15	Warehouse & Shipping Building
2	40/15	Slab Yard
1	40	Slab Yard
2	15	Slab Yard
3	50/20	Slab Yard
1	30/15	Processing Building
3	15	Processing Building
1	50/10	Motor Room
2	40/15	Finishing Building
1	7½	Finishing Building
1	30	Finishing Building
3	75/20	68″ Hot Mill Building
1	10	Scale Pit & Settling Basin
1	75/20	Roll Shop
1	15	Spare Parts Building

56-Inch Hot Strip Mill Finishing Train

The **finishing train** of the 56-Inch Continuous Hot Strip Mill was composed of a **scale breaker** and **six finishing stands**. When **new in 1937**, its maximum delivery speed was 1,967 feet per minute. The mill was designed to roll strip in widths of 14 inches to 48 inches down to a minimum of #20 gauge. Sheets up to ¼ inch and **skelp** up to a ½ inch in thickness were also rolled. Slabs ranging 14 inches to 50 inches in widths, 5'-6" to 16'-0" in length, 4 ½" to 5 ½" in thickness and 1,100 to 11,000 pounds in weight were supplied to the mill from the **Slabbing and Blooming Mills**. Photo courtesy of Bill Goodman.

"There was an underground **conveyor line** that went between the 68-Inch Hot Strip Mill to the 56-Inch Cold Mill. Its purpose was to transport coils between the two mills. The coils were spaced at 15 foot intervals. Each coil weighed approximately 30,000 pounds. Every once in a while a coil would 'walk off the chain.' The **Groundhog Crew** would have to get it back onto the conveyor. We would get a crane and a two-inch cable and choke it over and around the coil and get it back on the chain. The Groundhogs had a little office at the north end of the 68-Inch Finishing Mill. The group was made up of guys who were laid off from the other mills. Some were from Electrical, Tin Mill, or Mechanical. I was the Groundhog leader. Much of our work was done under the conveyor line carrying coils to the 56-Inch Cold Mill. We had to clean up the metal bands and any other debris under the line. The line required lubrication and the oil eventually found its way to the floor under the line. We used Speedy Dry on the oil and scooped it up and put it in 55 gallon drums. When they modernized the 68 Hot Strip in 1990, a new conveyor system was installed and they did away with the Groundhog Crew."
~Pietro "Pete" Sorrentino, Warehouse Shipping Foreman, 1955 – 1998

56-Inch Hot Strip Mill Nos. 2, 3, and 4 Roughing Stands

The **56-Inch Hot Strip Mill** came online in **November 1937**. It had **11 stands – 5 roughing stands and 6 finishing stands.** The maximum slab size was 7 ½ inches thick, 23 feet long, and 4 feet wide. It had three furnaces that were gas and oil fired. The furnaces were 26 feet x 105 feet and were capable of producing 200 tons per hour each. The **runout table** was 478 feet long. Shown above are No. 2, No. 3, and No. 4 roughing stands. This view is from the south looking north. The data provided on this mill represents the mill's status after the 1959 to 1961 modernization program. Photo dated March 27, 1961, courtesy of Mike Stilwell.

No. 2 Roughing Stand
56-Inch Hot Strip Mill

The **roughing stand** above was a **4-high stand** with **work rolls 25" x 58" and backup rolls 49" x 54"**. These 4-high stands were in a series of three and were spaced 36'-9", 56'-6" and 82'-6" apart respectively. At right is a chart describing the speed of the strip as it makes its way through each mill of the 56-inch hot strip. Photo courtesy of Rich Glenn, circa 1940. **Footnote 40**

SPEED OF THE STRIP THROUGH EACH MILL

No. 1 Rougher	170.9	ft. per min.
No. 2 Rougher	281.2	ft. per min.
No. 3 Rougher	399.3	ft. per min.
No. 4 Rougher	399.3	ft. per min.
No. 2 Scalebreaker	107/428	ft. per min.
No. 5 Finisher	222.5/445	ft. per min.
No. 6 Finisher	385/769	ft. per min.
No. 7 Finisher	556/1111	ft. per min.
No. 8 Finisher	733.5/1467	ft. per min.
No. 9 Finisher	867/1734	ft per min.
No. 10 Finisher	983.5/1967	ft. per min.

(Data is from 1938 when the mill was new)

56-Inch Hot Strip Mill

Slabs for the 56-Inch Hot Strip Mill were heated in **three continuous triple zone furnaces**, each with a rated capacity of 50 gross tons per hour of cold steel. They were brought to temperatures averaging **2,250 degrees Fahrenheit.** Hearth dimensions were 18 feet in width by 80 feet in length. At right, a heated slab is shown being ejected.

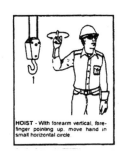

HOIST - With forearm vertical, forefinger pointing up. move hand in small horizontal circle

Once heated to the proper temperature, the slabs entered a 440-foot long roller table. The first unit to receive them was a **vertical edger**. Next, the slab entered the first roughing mill. This was a 2-high stand, 36" x 56". Following this stand, there were three more roughers. All of these were 4-high stands. Both photos dated 1938, courtesy of Rich Glenn.

56-Inch Hot Strip Mill Runout Table and Strip Finishing Department – 1938

At left is a view of a **strip** as it left the finishing stands in the 56-inch Hot Strip Mill and came down the **runout table** where it entered the **coilers**. Both photos dated 1938, courtesy of Rich Glenn.

At right is a general view of the strip finishing and processing department, which was an extension of the 56-Inch Hot Strip Mill.

56-Inch Hot Strip Mill Processing Department and Slab Storage Yard – 1938

56-Inch Hot Strip Mill Processing Department

At the end of the 56-Inch Hot Strip Mill were the strip finishing and processing departments. Two continuous trimming lines, a containing leveler, a fly shear and plier, with necessary conveyors served to bring the product to desired sizes. Sizes ranged up to 50 inches wide and ¼ inch thick.

The Slab Storage Yard

The slab yard had a capacity of about 15,000 tons of slab, which arrived on specially designed standard gauge cars. After **scarfing**, cranes placed the slabs on a magazine feeder for moving to the furnace charging table. Slab scarfing was done in an area located in one corner of the slab yard. It was serviced by a 7 ½ ton gantry crane equipped with a double magnet. Both photographs dated 1938, courtesy of Rich Glenn.

Footnote 41

68-Inch Hot Strip Mill

Above, workers pumped water out of the excavation for the 68-Inch Hot Strip Mill in July 1946 as a steam locomotive chugged along in the background. The **mill came on stream in December 1947**. Ten years earlier, the 56-Inch Hot Mill, at left, was started up. The 56-Inch was taken out of service in 1981 and later dismantled. Below, the 68-Inch Hot Strip Mill nears completion in early December 1947. At left are slab reheating furnaces.

32981 9-3-47
68" Mill. H.S.
FINISHING STANDS

68-Inch Hot Strip Mill

31642 SEND SCALE PIT
6-26-46 LOOK N

↑ The 68-Inch Hot Strip Mill finishing stand under construction on September 3, 1947. Note the wooden scaffolding.

← Excavation is under way for the construction of the Send Scale Pit for the 68-Inch Hot Strip Mill. Note the steam pile driver driving timbered logs into the ground. Both photographs courtesy of Mike Stilwell.

68-Inch Hot Strip Mill - 1947

The exterior of the 68-inch Hot Strip Mill just after completion in 1947.

68-Inch Hot Strip Motor Room – Left foreground: 900 HP flying shear and finishing stand No. 1 (3500 HP), finishing stand No. 5 (4,000 HP). Right foreground: finishing stand No. 3 (8,400 HP), master generator sets for finishing stands. Left center: 1500 KW Mercury Arc Rectifier. Right center: 33 units of 6.9 KV switchgear. Left background: 6 rougher motors.

56-Inch Hot Strip Mill Coiler

Two coilers were placed in the **roundout** table of the 56-inch hot strip mill. They were about 340 feet beyond the last finishing stand. Coils were moved from the coiler by air operated ejectors and were deposited on a coil **transfer car** which moved them to a **conveyor**, shown at right. The conveyor then carried the coils a distance of about 330 feet to the coil storage building. Photo dated 1938, courtesy of Rich Glenn.

The 68-inch Hot Strip Mill also had a similar system for removing coils from the mill. Shown here in July 1953, workers prepare to band coils as they emerge from the **No. 3 Downcoiler**. Photo courtesy of Baltimore Museum of Industry. Photo courtesy of Mike Stilwell.

271

68-Inch Hot Strip Mill Reversing Rougher Specifications

Slab Size
Thickness: 7.5" min. - 10" max.
Length: 162" min. - 396" max.
Width: 24" min. - 62" max.

Hot Band Size
Gauge: .054" min. - .500" max.
Width: 24" min. - 61.5" max.
PIW: 1,100 max.

Two Walking-Beam Furnaces
35' wide x 155' long, each.
300 tons per hour, each
Oil- or gas-fired.
Eight heating zones.
Level two computer heating optimization.
Computerized slab tracking.
Totally automated slab charging/discharging.
300'-high common stack.
Designer: Stein-Heurtey.

Advantages:
Efficient fuel usage.
Minimal skid marks.
Minimal scale formation.
Quality heating.

Descale System
Three pumps: two working, one standby.
Seven descale headers: five at roughers, two at finishing mills.
Working pressure: 2,100 PSI min.

Advantages:
Scale-free surface.

Reversing Rougher
Horizontal mill: four high; 12,000 hp.
Vertical mill: 4,000 hp; heavy edging capability is 6"; hydraulic automatic width control.
Two EES width gauges.
Designer: SMS/GEC.

Advantages:
Power to reduce 10"-thick slabs, resulting in 1,100 PIW coils.
Improved slab width-to-band width flexibility.

Coil Box
Designer: Stelco.
Manufacturer: SMS/GEC.

Advantages:
Reduced temperature loss.
Ability to store 1,100 PIW coil.
Temperature uniformity improves gauge and metallurgical properties.

Crop Shear
Drum type: two knives per drum.
2,000 hp.
Designer: SMS/GEC.

Advantages:
Separate head-end, tail-end cut contours.
Ability to multiple-cut cold strip.

Finishing Mills
Six four-high stands, existing.
33,500 total hp.
Individual main drive power supplies.

Software - automatic gauge control computer.
New set-up computer.
Automatic temperature speed control.
Computerized shape control.

Advantages:
Superior gauge performance.
Improved temperature response, shape.

Two Down Coilers
Retractable type.
Hydraulically-controlled.
Automatic head-end step control.
Designer: SMS/GEC.

Advantages:
Tightly-wound coils.
Minimal coil telescoping.
Minimal head-end marking.

Coil Handling
Three walking-beam conveyors.
Two saddle-type chain conveyors.
Signode automatic banders.
Telesis coil marker.
Toledo weigh scale.
System totally automated.
Designer: SMS/GEC.

Advantages:
Coils handled eye-horizontal for minimal edge damage.
Accurate weighing.
Highly legible marking for improved coil identification.

Footnote 42

Hot Mill Process Flow

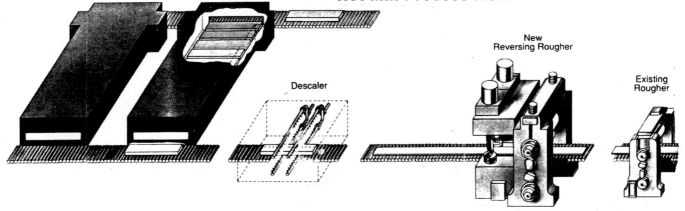

New Slab Reheat Furnaces

Descaler

New Reversing Rougher

Existing Rougher

New Coil Box

Existing Finishing Stands
(with new computerized process control)

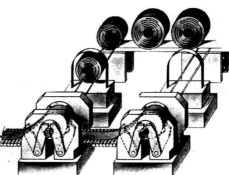

New Downcoilers

68-Inch Hot Strip Mill Modernization

As part of a $200 million dollar **modernization**, the 68-Inch Hot Strip Mill's new **reversing rougher** was powerful enough to roll ten-inch thick slabs, resulting in 1,100 PIW coils. The horizontal mill was 4-high with 12,000 horsepower. The vertical mill had a capacity of 4,000 horsepower with a heavy edging capability of six inches. It also had hydraulic automatic width control. The mill was installed in 1990. Photo credited to Rob Smith.

68-Inch Hot Strip Mill Roughing Stands

Shown above are the **Nos. 3, 4, and 5 roughing stands** of the 68-Inch Hot Strip Mill in 1947. Photo courtesy of Baltimore Museum of Industry.

"I started to work at the Point in 1955. I was 19 years old. My first shift was seven straight midnights. My first job was **Car Cleaner**. I had to clean out debris from gondola cars. When empty cars came back into the mill, they had lumber, paper, and metal bands in them. I had to get the cars ready for a new outbound shipment. I did that job for 8 or 9 months. After that, I became a **Saw Man**. We worked off of a big table saw cutting 2 x 4s and 3 x 4s with tapered ends. These were used in the bottom of the gondola cars to set the packs of steel on. I only did this job for a while before becoming a **Crane Follower**. A **Checker** would tell you what steel had to be shipped. My job was to work with the **Crane Operator** to load the cars. I did this off and on for 20 years.

"I also worked for the **Pack Gang**. We had these long, metal tables 2 feet high, 12 feet long, and 60 inches wide. We would lay out metal straps and put 2 x 4s or 3 x 4s on top of the strapping. Then, the crane would place the steel sheets on the wood and we would tighten up the bands. I was a **Bander** until they did away with sheet steel in 1968."

~Pietro "Pete" Sorrentino, 68-Inch Hot Mill Shipping, 1955 - 1998

274

68-Inch Hot Strip Mill Modernization

Shown above, steel sheet piles were driven into the ground to protect an existing foundation at the 68-Inch Hot Strip Mill. The site was being prepared for an extension of the building and the installation of two new furnaces that will reheat steel slabs. This was an initial step in the **$200 million modernization** of the mill that was announced in July 1988. Completion of the project, intended to improve quality and productivity for sheet steel, occurred in 1991. The company's structural mills at Bethlehem, PA supplied 1,542 tons of sheet and "H" piles for this phase of the project. Photo courtesy of Bill Goodman.

68″ Hot Strip Mill Walking Beam Furnace

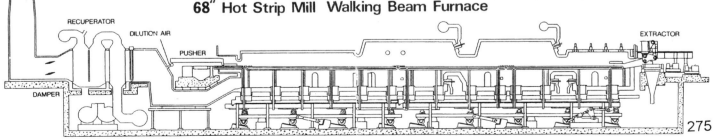

68-Inch Hot Strip Mill Motor Room: Massive electric motors drove the rolls of the 68-Inch Hot Strip Mill. Large shafts turned by these motors extended through the wall to the mill in the adjacent room. The 68-Inch Hot Strip Mill started up in 1947. Photo dated 1953, courtesy of Baltimore Museum of Industry.

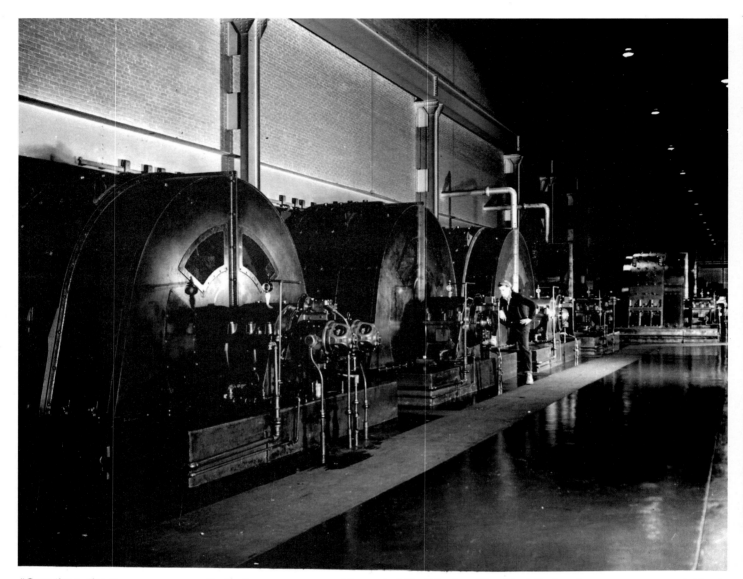

"One time, there were some coils that were supposed to go to Worthington Steel but their edges were warped. The Assistant Superintendent came down and wanted the coils shipped, but it would cost $380 to cut the warped ends of each coil. There were 12 coils altogether. Bill Rawlings was my boss. He was a good man. He wanted to know if we could do the job and I volunteered. I got Wikki Mouzon to bring over a large forklift with a big boom on it. He was able to pick up each coil and we took three or four laps off of the coil and burned that section off. We cleaned up the burrs and recleaned the coil and then rebanded each one. After that, we put new tickets on each coil so that it was ready for shipment by the next morning. All the big bosses were pleased and impressed and we saved the company a lot of money.

"Towards the end of my Bethlehem career, I became a Foreman in Warehouse Shipping. I was still hourly at the time. I supervised the 597. This was a track number at the north end of the 68 Hot Mill. There were three sets of tracks. I had to order cars from PBR. Once they brought in the **empties**, we would load the cars with coils. Each car held 12 coils. When loaded, they would be sent to the 42-Inch Cold Mill for finishing. Once these cars went out, we turned out the **blue light on the doors** and were ready for a new set of empties to come in. It was an ongoing process that required a lot of communication and cooperation between us, Crane Operators, and PBR."
~Pietro "Pete" Sorrentino, Warehouse Shipping Foreman, 1955 – 1998
Photo courtesy of Bill Goodman

New Four-High Reversing Stand

Garland Alston checks the progress of construction on the No. 3 Roughing Mill. The new Reversing Mill was installed as part of the 1990 modernization of the 68-Inch Hot Strip Mill. Slabs being rolled passed through the new rougher untouched. Photo credited to Rob Smith.

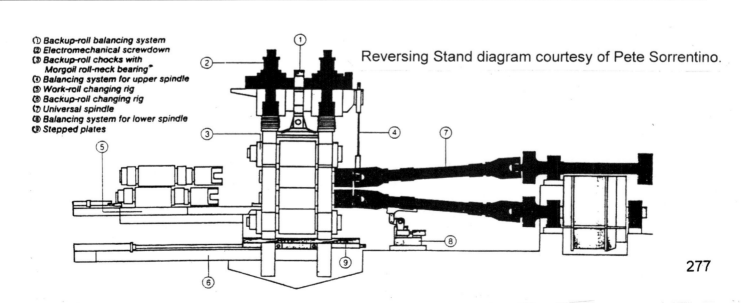

① Backup-roll balancing system
② Electromechanical screwdown
③ Backup-roll chocks with
   Morgoil roll-neck bearing*
④ Balancing system for upper spindle
⑤ Work-roll changing rig
⑥ Backup-roll changing rig
⑦ Universal spindle
⑧ Balancing system for lower spindle
⑨ Stepped plates

Reversing Stand diagram courtesy of Pete Sorrentino.

68-Inch Hot Strip Mill Shipping

Left: Pete Sorrentino
Center: Mare Pickrino
Right: Scotty Japlinski
Photo dated April 13, 1971. All photos this page courtesy of Pete Sorrentino.

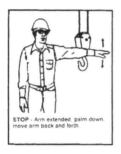

STOP - Arm extended, palm down, move arm back and forth.

Left: Pete "Pietro" Sorrentino
Right: "Razz" Razzniak
Photo dated April 21, 1971

Steel ✦ for Strength
. . . Economy
. . . Versatility

Coil Gang
Left: Pete Sorrentino
Center: "Razz" Razzniak
Right: Frank "the Greek" Stavrakis
Photo dated February 1989

MAINTENANCE 68" HOT STRIP MILL 640 HOURLY SCHEDULES

EMPLOYEES ARE RESPONSIBLE FOR CHECKING SCHEDULES

SHIFT SCHEDULES

2012	JULY		22	23	24	25	26	27	28
640	Employee		S	M	T	W	T	F	S
	TURN A								
81991	BATES	T/CT	1	1	1	1	1		
80577	TRAWINSKI			1	1	1	1	1	
	TURN B								
82687	DAY	T/CT	2			3	3	3	3
80554	HART	EL	2			3	3	3	3
	TURN C								
80465	BONNELL	CT			2	2	2	2	2
81512	KNEZEVICH	EL		V	V	V	V		
82734	CROSBY	EL			2	2	2	2	2
	TURN D								
81728	JONES R.	CT	3	3	3			1	1
81435	KIME	EL	3	3	3			1	1
81430	MARECKI	CT			LO	LO	LO	LO	LO

2012	ELECTRICAL DEPARTMENT		22	23	24	25	26	27	28
81435	KIME	EL		T	U	R	N		
81512	KNEZEVICH	EL		V	V	V	V	V	
80577	TRAWINSKI			T	U	R	N		
82734	CROSBY	EL		T	U	R	N		
80554	HART	EL		T	U	R	N		
82046	DAVIS EL	EL		LO	LO	LO	LO	LO	
82498	EDMONDS	EL		LO	LO	LO	LO	LO	
81828	TRAWINSKI, A.	EL		LO	LO	LO	LO	LO	
81571	SCHRIEFER	EL		LO	LO	LO	LO	LO	
80590	BOOTH	EL		LO	LO	LO	LO	LO	
80799	ELROD	EL		LO	LO	LO	LO	LO	
82427	COBURN	EL		LO	LO	LO	LO	LO	
80322	SHOOP	EL		LO	LO	LO	LO	LO	
82635	HAMMERBACHER	EL		LO	LO	LO	LO	LO	
81143	FRANK	EL		LO	LO	LO	LO	LO	
82271	POLENUR	EL		LO	LO	LO	LO	LO	
82527	RAPPAZZO	EL		V	V	V	V	V	
81622	PREISINGER	EL		LO	LO	LO	LO	LO	
82618	KAMOWSKI	EL		LO	LO	LO	LO	LO	
81198	KNOTTS	EL		LO	LO	LO	LO	LO	
80896	GERDOM	EL		LO	LO	LO	LO	LO	
82033	RAMSEL	EL		LO	LO	LO	LO	LO	
82328	GRISSINGER	EL		LO	LO	LO	LO	LO	
81997	BOSTIC	EL		LO	LO	LO	LO	LO	
80163	NICOSIA	EL		LO	LO	LO	LO	LO	

NO SINGLE VACATION DAYS ALLOWED IF OVERTIME IS REQUIRED TO FILL

TURN WORKERS WILL BE ASSIGNED FIREWATCH AND OTHER WORK

ALL REPORT OFFS USE   EXT-7798
REPORT OFFS WILL NOT BE REPLACED

ALL WORKING EMPLOYEES CAN BE ASSIGNED ANY TASK

YOU MAY CALL 443-286-0481 OR 443-504-9849 IF

YOU DO NOT KNOW YOUR SCHEDULE

DAYLIGHT SCHEDULES (7a-3p)

2012	JULY		22	23	24	25	26	27	28
640	Employee		S	M	T	W	T	F	S
	HSM MECH DEPT SENIORITY LIST								
82687	DAY	T/CT		T	U	R	N		
82721	DILLON	T/CT			SIP				
81991	BATES	T/CT		T	U	R	N		
81728	JONES R.	CT		T	U	R	N		
80465	BONNELL	CT		T	U	R	N		
81430	MARECKI	CT			LO	LO	LO	LO	LO
80675	FREDERICK	T/CT			LO	LO	LO	LO	LO
81508	HEMLING	B/CT			LO	LO	LO	LO	LO
	HUDLER	T/CT			SIP				
81274	McLAUGHLIN	T/CT			COMP				
81034	WICKROWSKI	T/CT			LO	LO	LO	LO	LO
81318	PANICHELLO	T/CT			LO	LO	LO	LO	LO
82100	HERRING	CT			LO	LO	LO	LO	LO
82562	PIROG	B/CT			LO	LO	LO	LO	LO
80526	SCHAUB	A/CT			LO	LO	LO	LO	LO
80762	BROWN				LO	LO	LO	LO	LO
82121	BALDWIN	B/CT	-		COMP				-
82102	ROBINSON	B/CT			LO	LO	LO	LO	LO
81811	ROSE	CT	-	LO	LO	LO	LO	LO	-
82109	FITCH	T/CT	-	LO	LO	LO	LO	LO	-
82090	JONES E.	B/CT		LO	LO	LO	LO	LO	
82152	DYE	B/CT	-	LO	LO	LO	LO	LO	
82560	SPURLOCK	C/CT			COMP				
80267	MISHLER	B/CT		LO	LO	LO	LO	LO	-
81060	AUBERG	B/CT	-	LO	LO	LO	LO	LO	
80363	SAMUELS	B/CT		LO	LO	LO	LO	LO	
81815	**GAJEWSKI**			LO	LO	LO	LO	LO	
81819	KROUSE	B/CT	-	LO	LO	LO	LO	LO	
80791	**KELLUM**			LO	LO	LO	LO	LO	
80870	**KOWALEVICZ**			LO	LO	LO	LO	LO	
80996	KUHN	B/CT	-	LO	LO	LO	LO	LO	-
81843	**HIPP**		-		COMP				
80227	**HORNING**	B/CT	-	LO	LO	LO	LO	LO	-
81182	**COMEGNA**			LO	LO	LO	LO	LO	
80851	KAFER	B/CT	-	V	V	V	V	V	-
82463	WASHINGTON	CT	-	LO	LO	LO	LO	LO	
80899	**PRUCHNIEWSKI**			LO	LO	LO	LO	LO	
80372	WASHKEVICH	CT		LO	LO	LO	LO	LO	
82510	TRUNKA	CT	-		COMP				-
82736	ROUSE	CT	-	V	V	V	V	V	
80043	FORSTER			LO	LO	LO	LO	LO	
80534	BLOCH			LO	LO	LO	LO	LO	

1 = 11p-7a, 2=7a-3p, 3= 3p-11p

CT = Crane Trained   A,B,C or T = Welding Rate

EL= Electrical   FL = FMLA

The above schedule for the 68-Inch Hot Strip Mill Maintenance Personnel was for the week beginning July 12, 2012. This was about five weeks after the last bar went through the mill at 7:21 a.m. on June 15, 2012. Then owner-operator RG Steel was employing a skeleton crew to protect assets of the plant pending a sale of the steel mill as an operating plant. Schedule courtesy of Mike Stilwell.

Mike Stilwell in his office in the 68-inch Hot Strip Mill, 2002.

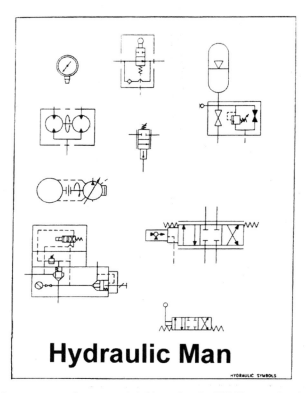

Hydraulic Man

"I was hired at Sparrows Point on June 11, 1962, into the General Mechanical Department, after a very brief interview by Bill Shure, who, I believe, was the Superintendent of the department at that time. As a Technical Trainee, I received orientation, along with the Loopers in that department, in the functions of the various divisions of the Mechanical Department. After about six months of orientation, I was given an actual job assignment, to trace and make sketches of the piping in a Steam Turbo Generator Building. My next job assignment was in the old Sinter Plant - to coordinate the outside crafts (ironworkers, sheet metal workers, etc.) that would supplement the Sinter Plant maintenance forces on Repair Days and during extended outages. The Sinter Plant was a very dirty place. Red dust covered everything in the entire area. Cars parked in the area would be covered with it after eight hours.

One day in 1965, I was told to report to the General Mechanical Office for a new job assignment. I thought I had 'died and gone to heaven.' As a result of some engineers and managers having gone to Burns Harbor to be involved with the construction of that plant, there were some vacancies to be filled. I was given the position of Assistant Lubrication Engineer, but, unlike the name of the position, my actual job was to be the Hydraulics Engineer for the plant. I knew nothing about steel mill hydraulics, but I quickly learned 'on the job,' with assistance from Bill Browning, who had advanced from that position to Lubrication Engineer, and by attending a two-week Vickers Hydraulics course in Detroit. I quickly came to enjoy working with hydraulic equipment and systems, in all of the mill areas, from the Ore Dock and Coke Ovens to the finishing mills, and the facilities that produced strand, cable, and welded wire fabric.

In 1999, the then plant Lubrication Engineer, Chris Fallon, requested and got a job transfer to the New Cold Mill, and I assumed the additional duties of Lubrication Engineer.

In September of 2001, due to down-sizing and reorganization of the plant, my job was eliminated. I accepted an offer from the Hot Strip Mill superintendent, Kerry Gordon, to be a millwright foreman in his mill. This job was not my 'cup of tea,' so after six months in that position, being 62 years old, and having worked at the Point for almost 40 years, I retired from Bethlehem Steel. I was not very effective as a millwright foreman, I was a 'fish out of water,' but nonetheless, it was a very rewarding experience; I had a great deal of help and support from everyone in that mill, and I will always remember and appreciate that.

It came as a complete surprise to me to be called back, almost immediately, as a consultant, by Roger Shackelford, to assist in developing a training program for a new hourly position of Lubrication Technician. Unfortunately, that position never materialized, but fortunately for me, I was permitted to assist the mills in my old capacity as Hydraulics/Lubrication Engineer.

When my retirement was made known, even though, in reality, I never left the plant, a great retirement party was held for me and my wife, Pat, at The Dock of the Bay. The party was produced by co-worker/friends Al Westra, Jose' de Jesus', and Pam Frock.

Since 'retirement,' I was the plant Hydraulics/Lubrication Engineer, as a consultant, for Bethlehem Steel, and through all of the successive plant owners (ISG, Mittal, ArcelorMittal, Severstal, and RG Steel) until being laid off in May of 2012.

Throughout my engineering career at the Point, I have had, as you might suspect, many supervisors. Every one of them has had the confidence in me to allow me to work independently and to assign my own work priorities; for all intents and purposes, I was a 'one-man department.' I have had the opportunity to be involved with the design, installation, and start-up of hydraulic systems on many significant projects, Coke Ovens 'A' Battery, the expansion of the Ore Dock, 'L' Blast Furnace and # 3 Blower House, the Continuous Caster, 1991 Hot Strip Mill modernization, the New Cold Mill, and # 3 Rod Mill, to name only the major ones. Along with this aspect of my work, I also had the opportunity to develop maintenance manuals and provide maintenance training for those systems.

Of my own designs, there are three of which I am most proud: the hydraulic system for the BOF shop Posi-charger, the hydraulic system for the Ladle Turret Lifts at the Caster, and the jacking system for lifting a BOF vessel for maintenance of its trunnion bearings.

My fifty years at the Point have been very satisfying. I have enjoyed the camaraderie of many people over the years, and I hated that the experience came to an end. I never thought that it could end in the way that it did."
~Mike Stilwell, Hydraulics/Lubrication Engineer, 1962 - 2012

Construction of Basic Oxygen Furnace

Iron workers assembled the foundation for one of the 200-ton Basic Oxygen Furnaces on January 10, 1965. Photo courtesy of University of Maryland Hornbake Library.

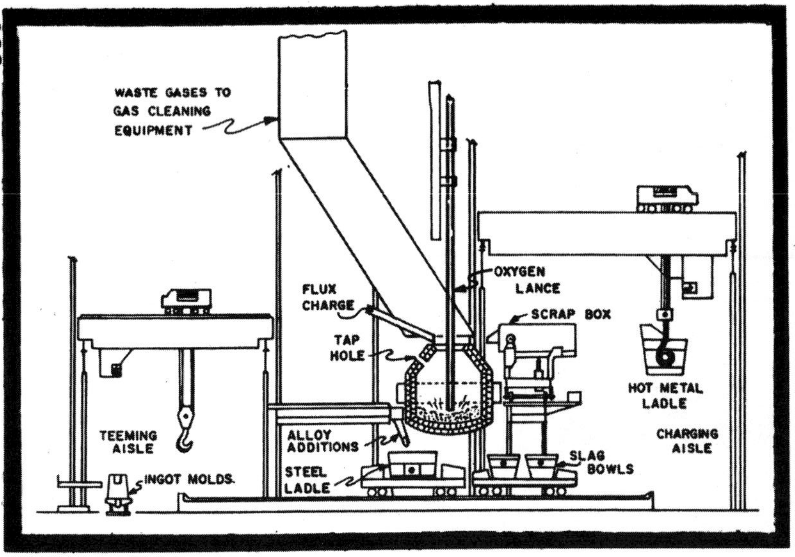

Basic Oxygen Furnace Shop – Cross Section (Looking North)

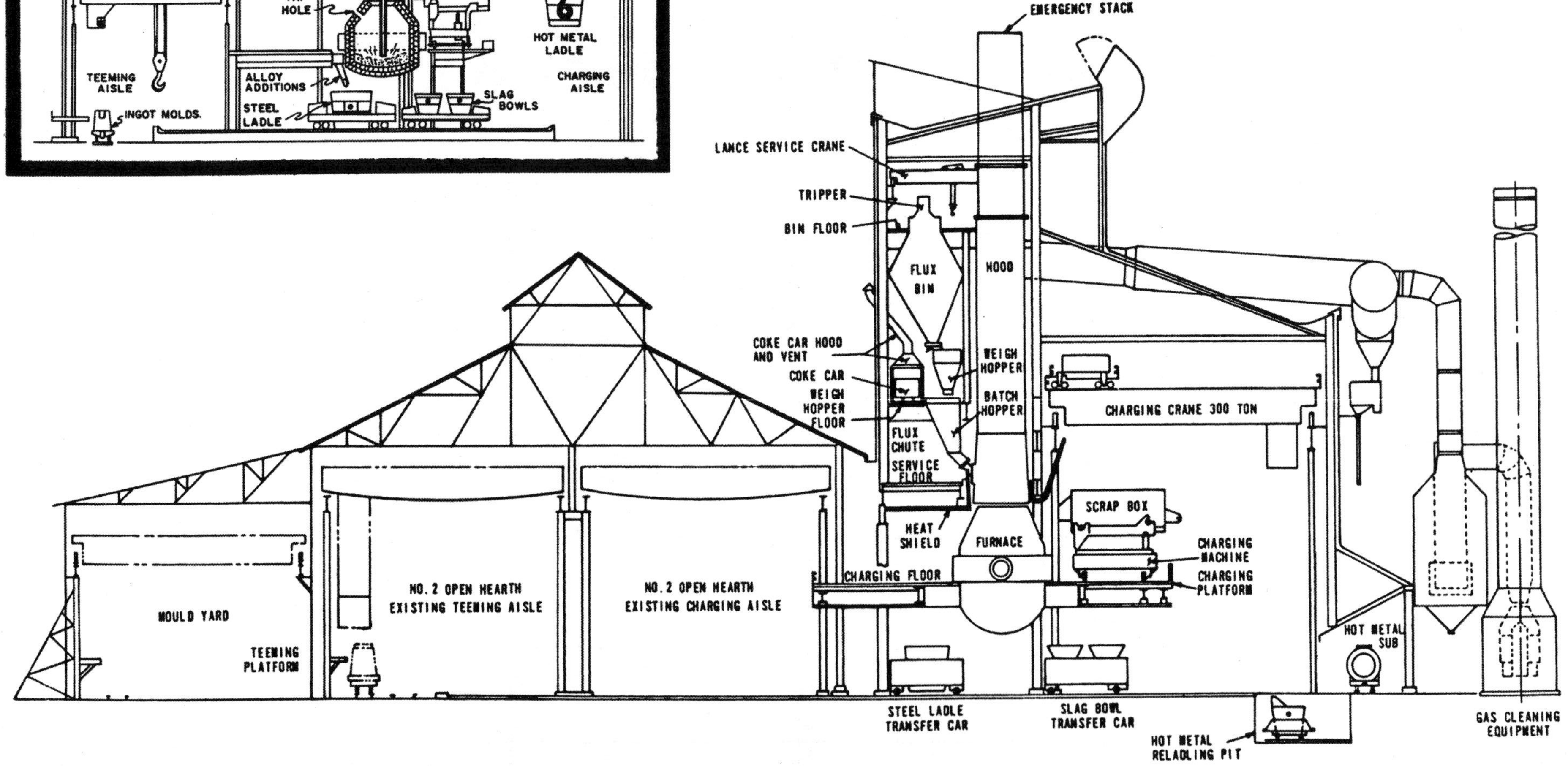

EMERGENCY STACK

HOOD

FLUX BIN

WEIGH HOPPER

BATCH HOPPER

FLUX CHUTE

SERVICE FLOOR

HEAT SHIELD

CHARGING FLOOR

FURNACE

CHARGING CRANE 300 TON

SCRAP BOX

CHARGING MACHINE

CHARGING PLATFORM

GAS CLEANING EQUIPMENT

HOT METAL SUB

HOT METAL RELADLING PIT

SLAG BOWL TRANSFER CAR

STEEL LADLE TRANSFER CAR

NO.2 OPEN HEARTH EXISTING CHARGING AISLE

NO.2 OPEN HEARTH EXISTING TEEMING AISLE

MOULD YARD

TEEMING PLATFORM

LANCE SERVICE CRANE

TRIPPER

BIN FLOOR

COKE CAR HOOD AND VENT

COKE CAR

WEIGH CAR

WEIGH HOPPER FLOOR

WASTE GASES TO GAS CLEANING EQUIPMENT

OXYGEN LANCE

SCRAP BOX

HOT METAL LADLE

CHARGING AISLE

SLAG BOWLS

FLUX CHARGE

TAP HOLE

ALLOY ADDITIONS

STEEL LADLE

TEEMING AISLE

INGOT MOLDS.

Each of Sparrows Point's two BOF vessels was about 38 feet high and had a 25-foot diameter. A typical "heat" required 37 minutes (tap to tap) and yielded approximately 220 tons of steel.

Basic Oxygen Furnace

Shown above, a large overhead crane hoisted the first of two new basic oxygen furnaces at the Sparrows Point plant as workmen prepared to position the recently assembled vessel. Made of steel plate 3 inches thick, and measuring nearly 40 feet in height, the furnace weighed 430 tons. Two of these furnaces were installed in the plant's new Basic Oxygen Shop at a cost of approximately $30 million dollars. The facility, which began operation in 1966, enabled Sparrows Point to produce quality steel by either the open hearth process or this new and faster oxygen method.

The furnaces had a 200 ton capacity. They were designed with an eye toward flexibility in use and toward possible future expansion. The basic oxygen process permitted closer control of metallurgical content than was possible with the open hearths.

Less than an hour was required for production of 200 tons of steel with the new furnaces. In comparison, seven furnaces in the No. 4 Open Hearth shop, built in 1957, the most modern open hearths in the industry each produced about 400 tons in 6 hours. Computers were used to accurately determine the quantities of ingredients that were to be added to the heat and to control time and rate of oxygen blow, to permit quality production of the many types of steel required by modern industry at the time. Photo courtesy of University of Maryland Hornbake Library, dated August 12, 1965.

New Basic Oxygen Furnaces at Sparrows Point

Shown here is one of the two 200-ton Basic Oxygen Furnaces placed in operation in 1966 at the new BOF Shop at Sparrows Point. The new furnaces could produce high quality steel at rates in minutes instead of hours as required for the open hearth process. The annual capacity of the furnaces was anticipated to be 1,900,000 tons. Photo courtesy of University of Maryland Hornbake Library. Photo dated April 14, 1966.

Basic Oxygen Furnace

Shown above, molten iron from the Blast Furnace was poured into **one of the two Basic Oxygen Furnaces** at Sparrows Point. The furnace already contained a **charge of scrap**. The scrap and iron was then subjected to an **intense blast of pure oxygen**, which refined the mixture into pure steel in less than an hour. Photo dated January 2, 1969; courtesy of University of Maryland Hornbake Library.

Basic Oxygen Steelmaking Process

Steelmaking Process Growing in Popularity

Oxygen is invisible and tasteless, and yet is one of the most important ingredients in steelmaking processes.

The basic oxygen steelmaking furnaces, which function by injections of 99.5 per cent pure oxygen, are becoming increasingly important.

The refractory-lined furnaces resemble bessemer converters. However, instead of using bottom blown air, as in the bessemer process, pure oxygen is blown in from the top by means of water-cooled lances. Oxygen combines with carbon and other unwanted elements and starts a high temperature, churning reaction which burns out the impurities from the molten pig iron and converts it to steel.

BESSEMER PROCESS

The famous bessemer steelmaking process, which made most of the steel in the late 19th and early 20th century, is considered by some to be the forerunner of the new oxygen steelmaking process. Both processes produce steel by the pneumatic principle

BLAST FURNACE

Blast furnace makes pig iron which is carried in a molten state via a hot metal car to the steelmaking furnace

HOT METAL CAR

HOT METAL CHARGING

Molten pig iron is added next. Proportion of hot metal may reach 70 per cent. Hot metal is automatically weighed and poured from transport cart to transfer ladle, holding up to 90 tons

SCRAP CHARGING

First Step in making a heat of steel in an oxygen converter is to tilt vessel and charge it with scrap and other metallics. Vessels mounted on trunions can be swung through a wide arc

HOPPER

ADDING FLUX

After scrap and molten metal are entered, and before oxygen injection starts, fluxes are added. Function: to combine with impurities to keep slag fluid

BLOWING WITH OXYGEN

OXYGEN LANCE

WATER COOLED LANCE

WATER COOLED HOOD

TAR BONDED DOLOMITE BRICK

RAMMED DOLOMITE MATERIAL

MAGNESIA BRICK

RAMMED MATERIAL

Oxygen blowing, using thousands of cubic feet of the gas, takes under an hour. Hood conducts gases to cleaning system, which removes most foreign matter

CLEANING SYSTEM

TAPPING THE STEEL

CHEMICAL CONTENT ADJUSTMENT

After steel has been refined, converter is tapped and necessary chemical adjustments are made. Steel is then poured into molds, called teeming the ingot

TEEMING THE INGOT

Footnote 43

286

BOF "Blow"

After completion of a twenty minute oxygen "blow," a Basic Oxygen Furnace vessel is "turned down," or rotated to permit the taking of temperature and samples of steel for analysis. This vessel was one of two 200-ton capacity furnaces at the Sparrows Point plant. Photo courtesy of University of Maryland Hornbake Library.

Blueprint for Replacing Two BOF Furnaces – 1986

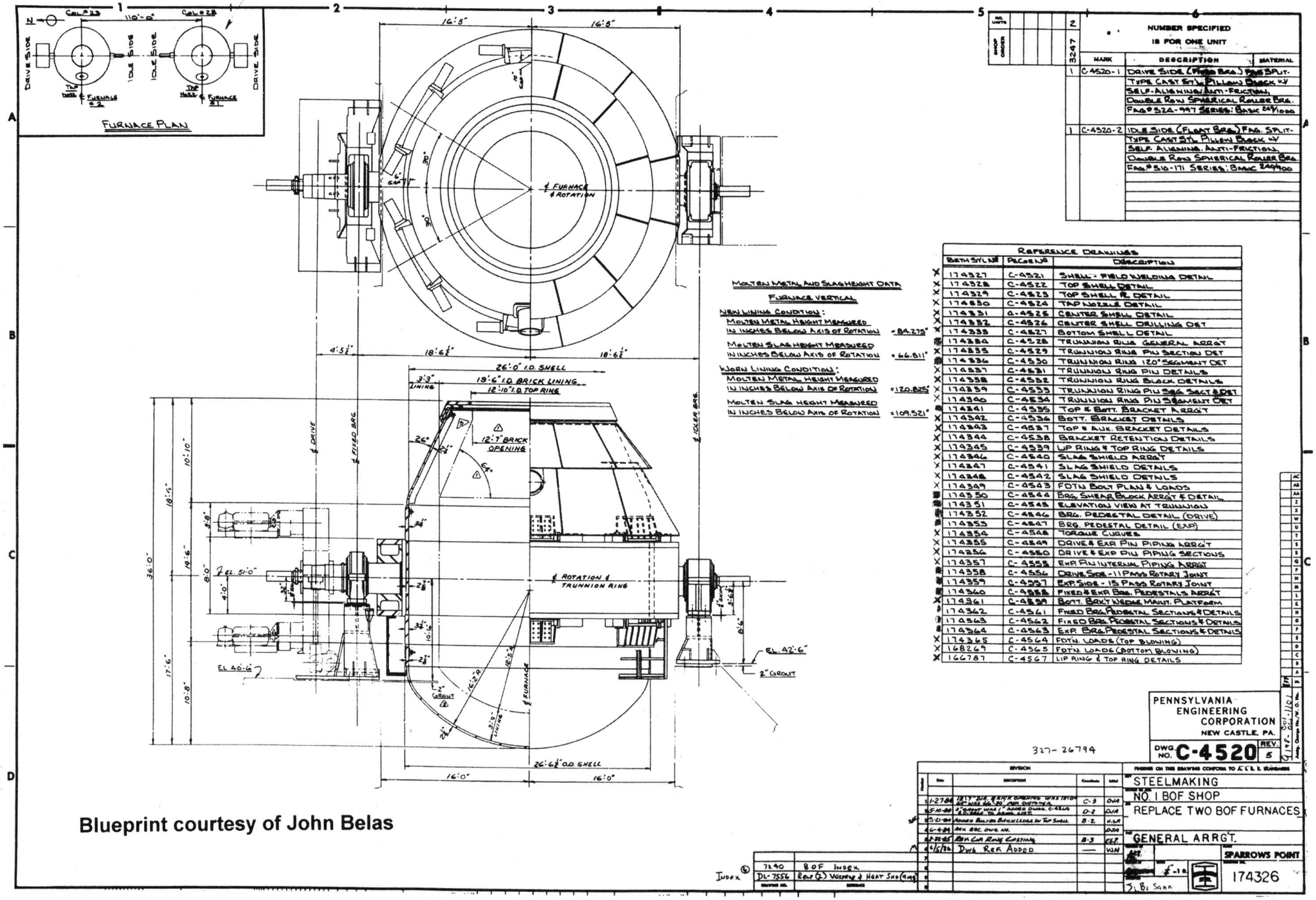

Blueprint courtesy of John Belas

Basic Oxygen Furnace

A huge crane-held ladle weighing 75,000 tons filled ingot molds from its 220-ton cargo of molten steel. Sparrows Point embarked on projects over a two year period to improve the quality of steel at the Basic Oxygen Furnace Shop with an investment of more than $55 million dollars to be spent by the end of 1984. Photo courtesy of University of Maryland Hornbake Library.

Basic Oxygen Furnace Shop (Looking West)

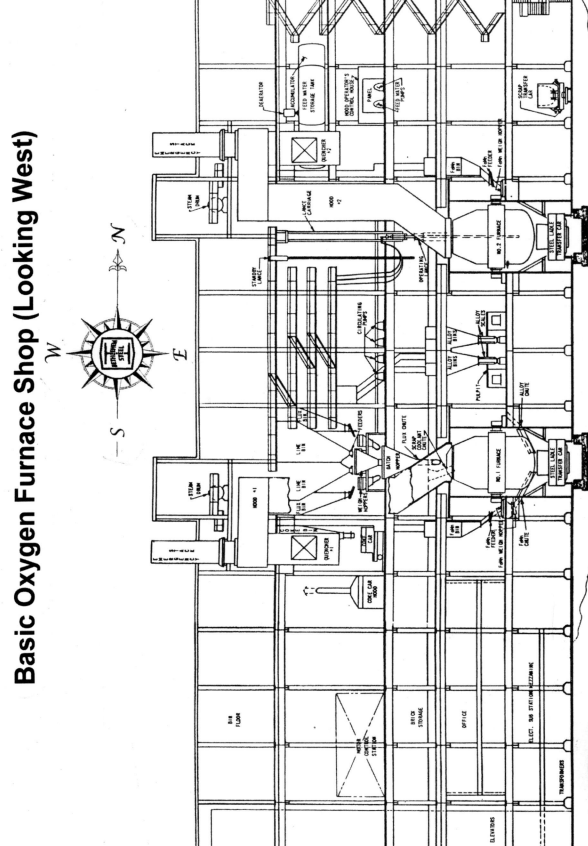

Basic Oxygen Furnace Shop – General Arrangement

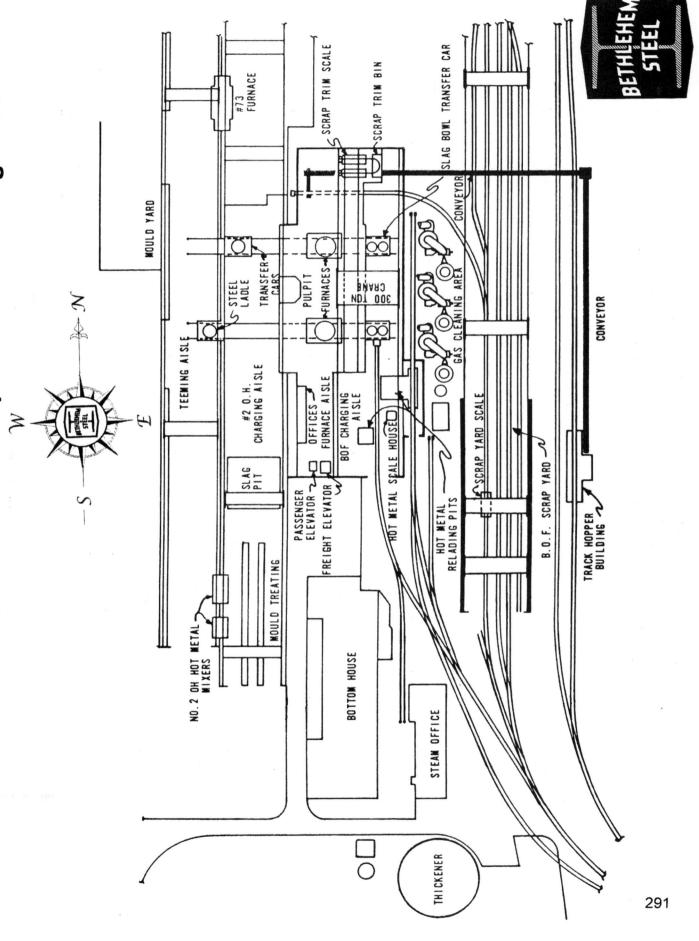

Ladle Liners at the BOF Shop

Photo dated 1991, credited to Rob Smith.

The "L" Furnace

Work to prepare for the "L" Furnace began when the company began razing the turn-of-the-century homes in the company-built town of Sparrows Point. A **new ore pier** and **raw materials handling system** was also designed and built. A new **sintering plant** with a yearly output of 4,250,000 tons of iron-rich sinter was also added. Ground for the "L" Furnace was broken in December 1974. When **completed in 1978**, it reached a height 18 inches short of 300 feet. Aside from its sheer size, "L" Furnace differed widely from Bethlehem's other furnaces. It was fed by belt, controlled by computer, operated at much higher internal pressures, had a bell-less top, had two cast floors, and cast its iron from four notches instead of just one or two. The hot metal cars that carried molten iron to the steelmaking side were the largest ever built in the US at 330 tons capacity. Two computers, one a warm standby, controlled the charging of iron ore pellets, coke, sinter, and limestone. These materials were moved by belt conveyor from the stockhouse to the top of the furnace. They were fed into the furnace through three lock hoppers and a rotating chute. **Sparrows Point's "L" Furnace cast its first iron at 2:22 a.m., Wednesday November 8, 1978**. Photo courtesy of Hillard "Digger" O'Day, Jr.

"L" Furnace Motor Room

"L" Furnace Facts

Height — 298½ feet.

Capacity — Average of 8,000 tons of iron per day at 100% availability.

Ferrous Charge — 40-60% iron ore pellets; 40-60% sinter.

Coke Consumption — 975 pounds per ton of molten iron.

Hearth Diameter — 44½ feet.

Belly Diameter — 49 feet, 2 inches.

Wind Rate — 250,000 cubic feet per minute.

Blast Temperature — 2200°F.

Working Volume — 130,399 cubic feet.

Construction Materials Used — Nearly 60 miles of steel piling; 5,000 tons of heavy plate; 21,000 tons of structural shapes; 24,000 cubic yards of concrete; 23,000 tons of refractories; about 330 miles of electrical conduit and cable.

Two sets of motors and blowers like the ones shown above furnished the hot blast to the "L" Furnace – the **largest furnace in the western hemisphere** at the time. A 30,000 HP electric motor, left, furnished the power to the 150,000 standard cubic foot a minute blower, right, through the speed increaser in between. A third identical set was provided as a standby. In an emergency, the blast could be furnished by other steam-driven blowers in the plant. Photo circa 1978, courtesy of Butch Johnson.

"L" Furnace

A view of the "L" Furnace looking south, circa 1978. The furnace was nearly 300 feet tall and equipped with two casthouses, four tap holes, and fed by a 1,000 foot conveyor. Photo courtesy of Hillard "Digger" O'Day, Jr.

The Star of Bethlehem

Bill Eldridge was a Blast Furnace Welder. Bill worked at the Point for 34 years. He retired in 1984.

"In the 1980s, it was decided to upgrade the star on top of the "L" Furnace. The job of building the star was given to the Tin Mill Weld Shop. They built a five sided pentagon, 10 feet in diameter. They also built five points for the star. Each point was eight feet long. When assembled, the star would be 26 feet in diameter. Once the star was built, the Rigging Department was given the responsibility of putting the star together atop the "L" Furnace, which is nearly 300 feet tall.

"The star was hauled up as far as it could go on an elevator. From there, it had to be hoisted to the top. A hole was cut in the center of the pentagon and a four-inch solid shaft of steel was welded in place to mount the pentagon.

"John Meyer was assigned the job of welding the retaining plates on the four-inch shaft. This required him to go outside and stand on the handrailing to weld the six-inch by six-inch plates on the shaft. Once this was done, the five points of the star were pulled up to the top and bolted in place one at a time. This was tedious work because once a point had been bolted on the pentagon, it had to be rotated on the shaft and secured so that the next point could be bolted on. We continued in this manner until all five points of the star were bolted on.

"Originally the star had green lights but no one liked them. The electricians wouldn't change the lights because they considered it unsafe. They signed off so we put the lights on instead. This required hanging over the handrail and screwing the lights in one at a time."
~Les "Buck" Rabuck, "A" Rate Fitter – Rigging Department, 1974 – 2003

Casthouse Floor Plan for the "L" Furnace

Diagram Courtesy of John Belas

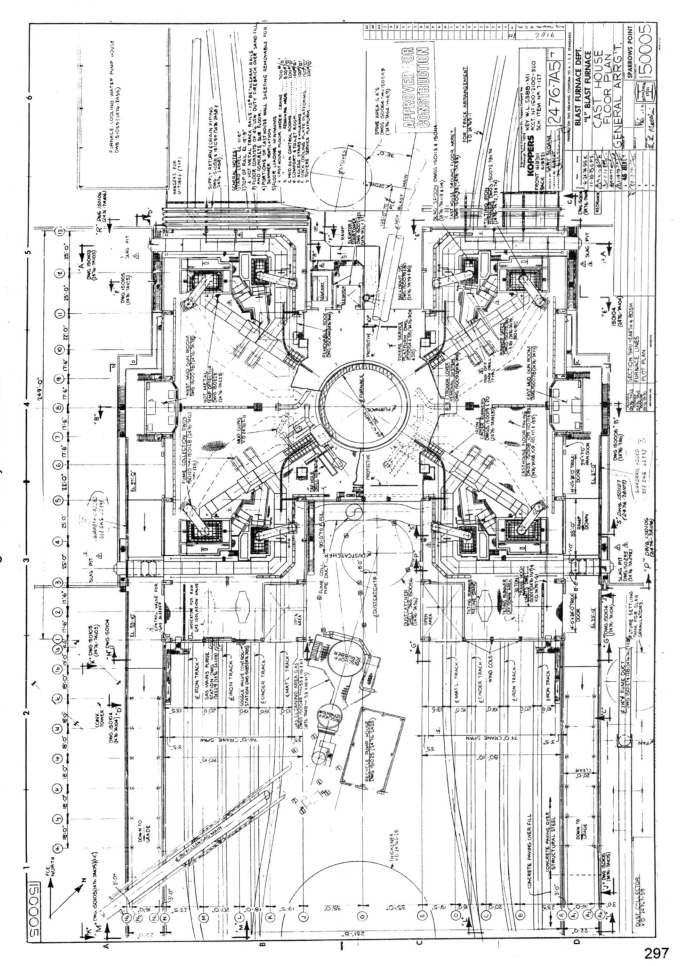

297

Cross Section of the "L" Furnace and Stoves

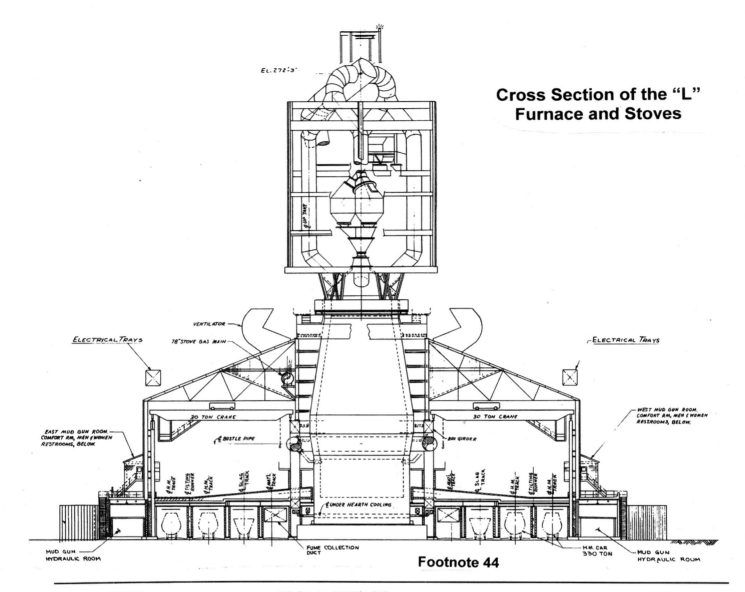

EL. 272'-3"

ELECTRICAL TRAYS

VENTILATOR

78" STOVE GAS MAIN

ELECTRICAL TRAYS

30 TON CRANE

30 TON CRANE

WEST MUD GUN ROOM,
COMFORT RM, MEN & WOMEN
RESTROOMS, BELOW.

EAST MUD GUN ROOM,
COMFORT RM, MEN & WOMEN
RESTROOMS, BELOW.

BUSTLE PIPE

BOX GIRDER

H.M. TRACK — TILTING RUNNER — H.M. TRACK — SLAG TRACK — MAT'L TRACK

MAT'L TRACK — SLAG TRACK — H.M. TRACK — TILTING RUNNER — H.M. TRACK

UNDER HEARTH COOLING

MUD GUN
HYDRAULIC ROOM

FUME COLLECTION
DUCT

H.M. CAR
330 TON

MUD GUN
HYDRAULIC ROOM

Footnote 44

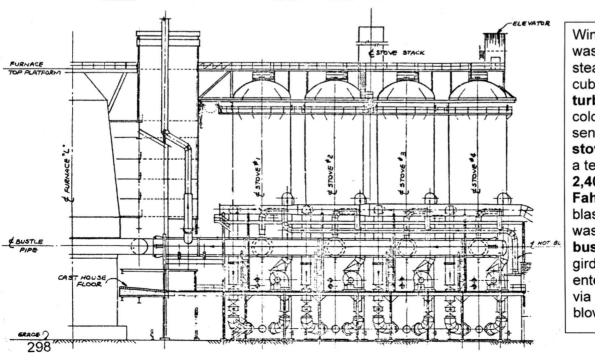

ELEVATOR

STOVE STACK

FURNACE
TOP PLATFORM

FURNACE "L"

STOVE #1   STOVE #2   STOVE #3   STOVE #4

BUSTLE
PIPE

HOT BL

CAST HOUSE
FLOOR

GRADE

298

Wind for combustion was delivered by two steam-driven 25,000 cubic feet per minute **turbo blowers**. This cold blast of air was sent through **four stoves** and raised to a temperature of **2,400 degrees Fahrenheit**. The hot blast from the stoves was routed to the **bustle pipe**, which girdled the **bosh** and entered the furnace via 38 **tuyeres**, or blowpipes.

Footnote 45

End of An Era

"L" Furnace made its first cast on November 8, 1978. Rated at 8,000 tons per day, it was designed to replace the other older furnaces, "A" through "F". "L" Furnace exceeded production estimates and by the end of that year, seven furnaces had been banked. By 1979, only one other furnace was needed on-line to meet the demand for hot metal. Between 1981 and 1983, "A", "B", "C", "D", "E", "F", and "G" were razed. This left "J", "H", and "K" furnaces. "J" and "K" were banked between 1978 and 1980. When "L" Furnace was relined in 1990, "H" and "J" were put back into service to cover the outage. Once the reline was completed, hot metal production became an "L-only" operation. "K" was scrapped that year. "H" and "J" would never run again. Both were razed in 1999 and 100 years of hot metal production ended on Blast Furnace Row. Photo credited to Phil Szczepanski. **Footnote 46**

Sinter Plant

Sintering is a process for fusing into lumps fine iron bearing materials, including ore screenings and furnace dust, so they can be more efficiently smelted in a blast furnace. Sparrows Point in a normal production year consumed about three million tons of sinter produced on six machines that were installed in the 1950s.

In 1976, a new **No. 7 Sinter Strand Plant** was built just east of the old one. It contained a single sintering machine that had an overall capacity around 10% greater than the six old machines combined. It had a rated capacity of four million tons per year.

At left, Bob Hanlin and Dick Foster check sinter as it bakes on the moving grate.

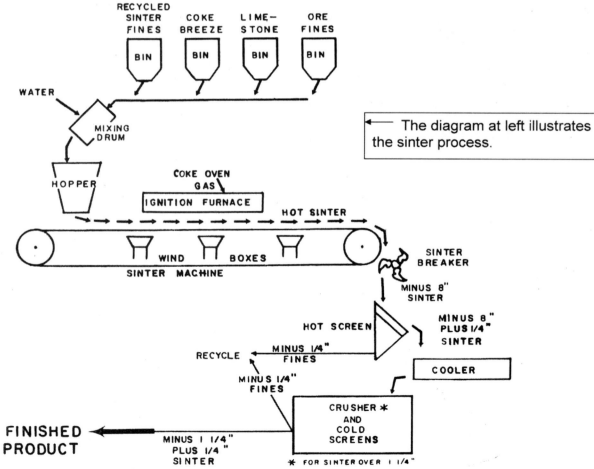

The diagram at left illustrates the sinter process.

300

No. 7 Sinter Strand

At the six-story high **Sinter Plant**, materials such as flue dust, powdery ores, slurry, limestone, scale and coke breeze were carefully blended, pelletized, burned, cooled, crushed, and delivered as finished sinter that was used in the "L" furnace.

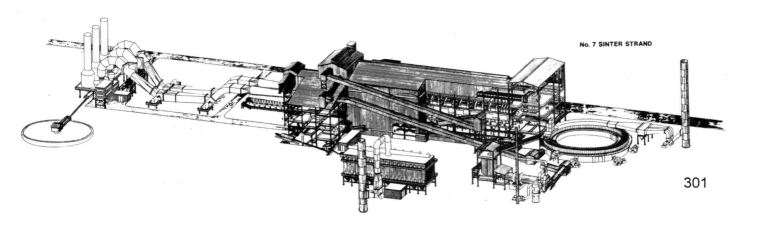

No. 7 SINTER STRAND

Layout of Sparrows Point Plant – 1982

N
W — E
S

BEAR CREEK

ROD MILL

PIPE MILL

COLD STRIP–TINPLATE

COLD STRIP–SHEET

56" HOT STRIP MILL

68" HOT STRIP MILL

ROUTE 151

PLATE MILL

BLOOMING MILL

SLABBING MILL

SOAKING PITS

SOAKING PITS

OPEN HEARTH

MAIN OFFICE

SHIP YARD

BOF

PENNWOOD POWER

GRAVING DOCK

BLAST FURNACES

COAL DOCK

COKE OVENS

ORE YARD

ORE DOCK

STOCK HOUSE

SINTER PLANT

PENNWOOD SHIPPING WHARF

COAL STORAGE

COAL CHEMICAL PLANT

ORE YARDS

BEDDING PLANT

ORE PIER

PATAPSCO RIVER

CHESAPEAKE BAY

Layout of Sparrows Point plant.

BETHLEHEM STEEL

Construction Site of the Continuous Caster

The foundation for the **Continuous Caster** begins to take shape in March 1984. Bethlehem Steel **invested $250 million** in the project to compete with overseas steel industries. The site of the caster overlaps the previous location of the No. 2 Open Hearth. In the background at right is the BOF which came on-line in 1966. At left is the No. 3 Open Hearth. Photo courtesy of Bill Goodman. Photo dated March 1984.

Topping Out of the Continuous Caster

← "Topping Out" nears completion of the **Continuous Slab Bloom Caster**. When completed, the caster would eliminate the ingot mold and rolling processes.

↓ Construction activity peaked in September 1985 with about 500 trades people working on the more than $250 million Continuous Slab Caster at Sparrows Point. The tall structure (left) was the foundation for the casting machine. A crane runway, beginning to jut out from the open end of the two vessel **Basic Oxygen Furnace Shop** (top right), eventually provided the link between the molten steel supply and the new machine. 75,000 cubic yards of material were excavated, 1,438 "H" piles had been driven 186,000 feet and 10,000 of the estimated 32,000 cubic yards of concrete had been poured at the time this photo was taken. The project was scheduled for a January 1986 startup.

Continuous Caster

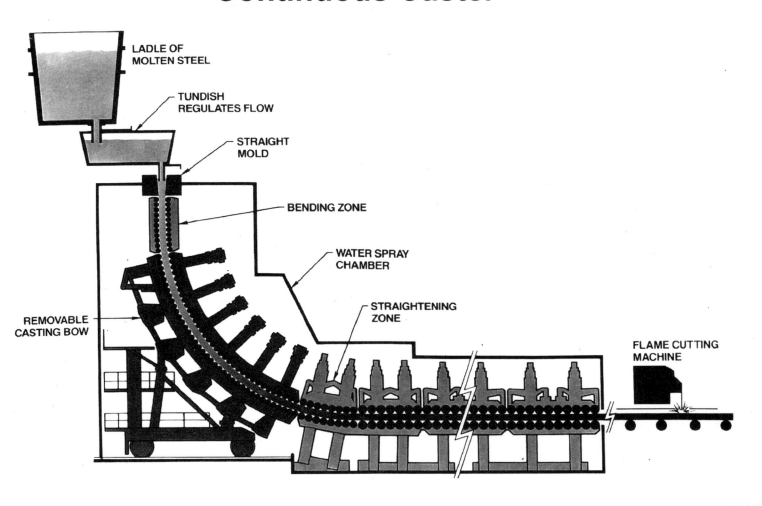

LADLE OF MOLTEN STEEL

TUNDISH REGULATES FLOW

STRAIGHT MOLD

BENDING ZONE

WATER SPRAY CHAMBER

STRAIGHTENING ZONE

REMOVABLE CASTING BOW

FLAME CUTTING MACHINE

(The above diagram illustrates the Continuous Caster process.)

"I was hired Christmas week 1961. My first job was as a **Floor Hand** in the 42-Inch Tin Mill. That was one step above laborer. Then I moved up to **Tin Feeder** on the old electrolytic tinning lines. These lines were numbered 1 through 10. There were also two oiling lines numbered 11 and 14. For the most part between 1961 and 1966, I was a Feeder on the No. 1 Halogen Line. Then I moved to the **Primary Mills**. These are mills where they rolled ingots into slabs. The Primary Mills consisted of the **40-Inch Blooming Mills, the 18-Inch and 21-Inch Bar Mills, the 24-Inch and 27-Inch Bar Mills, the 12-Inch Skelp Mill where they made pipe skelp, and the 54-Inch Slab Mill, and the 40 x 80 Slab Mill, which rolled ingots into slabs.** The 54-Inch Slab Mill was connected to the No. 1 Soaking Pits. The **40 x 80 Slab Mill** was connected to the No. 2 Soaking Pits.

"The **45 x 90 Universal Slabbing Mill** was also part of the Primary Mills. It was the only mill capable of rolling the gigantic **'tiger ingots'** which came from the **No. 4 Open Hearth**. These ingots were so big that the crane had to carry them around the **scarfer.** The scarfer was an apparatus that blew all of the impurities off of the surface of the slab. Between 1966 and 1974, I was a Mechanical Helper. Each mill had a mechanical crew that consisted of a Millwright, **a Mechanical Helper, and an Oiler**. Their job was to perform routine maintenance on any equipment in the Primary Mill that broke down. If there was a problem on the mills, they would blow three whistles for the Millwright and a long and a short for a Foreman. The 45 x 90 Mill was huge. It had a water system that needed constant monitoring. This required an extra Millwright called a **Pump Man.** His job was to prevent an overflow of water into the electrical cellars that would cause the mill to shut down. The Primary Mills had a five man crew on each turn – three Millwrights, a Helper, and an Oiler. This was done for 21 turns a week – essentially 24 hours a day, 7 days a week.

"I went from a Helper to **'C' rate** and eventually to **'A' rate**. Then, I became an **MCBA Turn Foreman**. The MCBA meant that I was not covered for the bargaining agreement. I was in that position between 1975 and 1979. Then, I went to salary as a Planner. My job as a Maintenance Planner was to make sure that specific materials reached a designated job site. I also completely planned an **outage**. Each of the Primary Mills were scheduled for routine maintenance one day each week. During these outages, a General Gang composed of a Millwright and Helpers went in to make repairs and adjustments to the Mill that was down. In 1981, I was promoted to Millwright Foreman. This was an all daylight job. I supervised all of the repair turns and did the scheduling for approximately 200 people in the department. 305

"**In September 1984, the 40 x 80 Slab Mill rolled its last ingot**. At that point, I moved over to the Steelmaking Department to work on the development of the Continuous Caster. I had an office in the old shoe store. Bethlehem sent me to **Burns Harbor** one week a month for several months. The steel plant up there got a Caster in 1970. In 1985, me and 15 others went to Austria. The company there, **Voest-Alpine**, was building our Casters. I took classes there on various components of the Caster, like how to change a casting bow and the operation of a horizontal strand guide. Voest-Alpine made two Continuous Casters for us in 1984. In 2000, we tore out No. 1 Strand and replaced it. This one came from Korea, but was also engineered by Voest-Alpine from Austria.

"The **Continuous Caster** replaced a whole series of operations that previously were used in the process of making a slab. The first of these was **Teeming**. Teeming occurs when molten liquid is poured into a mold. Some of this molten liquid came from the No. 4 Open Hearth and some from the **Basic Oxygen Furnace (BOF).** The molds which were set up on narrow gauge cars were then taken to the **stripper**. There, the ingots were punched out of the mold. There were two kinds of narrow gauge cars. The empty molds were sent back to the Open Hearth or BOF and the ingots went to the Soaking Pits for charging. They went in at approximately 1,400 degrees and the temperature was raised to 2,400 degrees. Once extracted from the Soaking Pits, the ingots were placed on ingot buggies and transferred to the Receiving Table. From there, they went into one of the Primary Mills for the rolling process.

"In December 1999, I went to Finland, and in January 2000, I went to Korea to get training in something called '**Smart Segment.**' It was a computerized method of sensing the cooling and contraction that ultimately would change the thickness of a slab. Once it detected the change, it would automatically adjust the rollers. Prior to this, the old No. 2 Mill had a fixed system.

"The BOF was charged with liquid iron from the blast furnace and scrap metal. The top was tilted to the east. It was heated to approximately 2,750 degrees. It was then tilted in the opposite direction and poured into a **300-ton ladle** that was situated on an east-west track. This car was then transferred west until it was positioned under a crane. The crane then picked up the ladle and put it on a ladle car. It then headed south to the **ladle treatment starter**. There it was doctored up to meet the chemical specification that the customer wanted. Once this process was completed, it left ladle treatment and went to one of two Continuous Casters. There was an automatic slide gate on the bottom of the ladle. When it opened, the hot molten liquid poured into a mold which then oscillated up and down. This oscillation kept it from sticking to the **ladle turret**. When this process was completed, a new ladle came in and the process was repeated.

"When the molten metal comes out of the mold, it is red hot and soft. Its center is still liquid. It then proceeds to the **bender**, where it is sprayed with water. The bender puts a curve in the soft metal. Then it proceeds to the **straightener** and finally to the **horizontal strand guide**. Here, the continuous slab was fine tuned and flattened. It was approximately 10 inches thick and could be any width from 28 to 50 inches wide. It had the potential to cast out to 70 inches wide. At this point, the future slab was still one continuous piece of hot metal. From here, it continued on to the **Run-out Table**, where the torch machine cut it into various lengths that the customer specified. Once cut into slabs, a crane picked up the slab and put it on the ground. Then, giant slab haulers picked up the slabs and took them to the Hot Mill or to the Slab Yard for future use."
~Tom Donet, Lead Mechanical Foreman – Continuous Caster, 1961 - 2001

Torch machine
No. 1 Strand

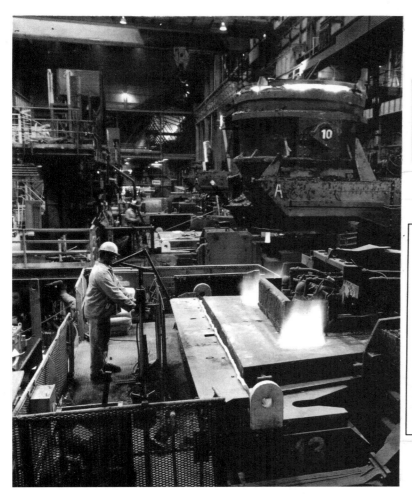

Clarence Bowman works a pre-heater to warm up No. 13 Tundish before it went into service. Photo dated June 1995, credited to Rob Smith.

Brought on-line in 1985 as the savior of the Sparrows Point plant, the Continuous Slab Caster rapidly gained a reputation as one of the outstanding steel production facilities in the United States. The original design capacity was 2.9 million tons annually. Within its first 10 years, it had reached a capacity of 3.6 million tons annually. In December 1995, the caster set a North American monthly record for a two strand vessel, two strand shop of 327,924 tons. **Footnote 47**

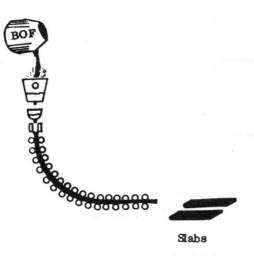

Slabs

At right is an open pour on the Continuous Caster, No. 2 Strand. Photo dated March 18, 2005, courtesy of Bill Goodman.

Continuous Caster Celebrates 10th Anniversary

Brought on-stream in 1985, the Continuous Slab Caster was billed as the savior as the Sparrows Point plant. Shown above in 1995, it was about to celebrate its 10th anniversary. Workers are in the process of charging ladles on the casting floor. Photo credited to Rob Smith.

Sparrows Point

By Henry Harvey Underwood
December 25, 1909 – March 1, 2006

I grew up in a Company town,
Sparrows Point was its name.
The town had streets and roads,
Yes, it even had some fame.

The town had all of human needs,
Of food, clothing and any staple.
Like canned goods, candy, and shoes,
They even had some syrups, like maple.

The town was not without entertainment,
A theater was on the main street.
A Company store served all our needs,
And Caplan's filled the gaps, so neat.

For entertainment, we had the theater,
With bowling alleys down below.
A bathing beach, and baseball diamonds,
Kept us happy, as we all know.

Transportation was not a problem,
Trolley cars ran through the town.
Every 15 or 20 minutes they ran,
The "RED ROCKETS" had considerable renown.

Passenger trains came on their tracks,
For men to come and work and labor.
Three times a day they made their way,
From Baltimore and it was never safer.

And now I have told you about that place,
Where people lived, worked, and survived.
Many things they did, and labored hard.
As for me, I am still alive.

What more can I say about Sparrows Point,
An outstanding Company town.
It is a place that we could come back to,
Unfortunately for us, it has been torn down.

"Henry Underwood lived on 'H' Street in Sparrows Point. He graduated from Sparrows Point High School in 1928. He worked in the steel mill for 40 years. He was a Crane Operator. In August 2004, Henry and his daughter, Mary Ellen, attended the Sparrows Point Bungalow Reunion at North Point State Park. Henry was 94 years old at the time. Henry and Mary Ellen gave me a poem entitled 'Sparrows Point' which Henry had composed. According to Mary Ellen, her father was a prolific writer, composing many poems over his lifetime. One of the lines in Henry's poem states, 'As for me, I am still alive.' Although Henry passed on March 1, 2006 at the age of 96, the words he has penned and his fond memories of Sparrows Point will live on for future generations to enjoy. Above is Henry's poem, Sparrows Point, used with Mary Ellen's permission." ~Elmer Hall, compiler of this publication.

Reckless Rudy and the General Manager's Cadillac

"Albert Rudy was an engineer on the Narrow Gauge Railroad. He operated a steam locomotive. During the late 1930 s, steam locomotives were being replaced by diesel. Albert came over to the **Motor Transport Department** and became a truck driver. He was a tough old man – hard as iron.

"Mr. Charles Clark was General Manager of the plant. He lived in one of the big houses on "C" Street. We kept his Cadillac at the Motor Transport Garage. Each morning, we would take it over to the Main Office Building and park it in his special parking place. Mr. Clark was a nice man – a real gentleman.

"One day, Mr. Clark was traveling down **Blast Furnace Row** in his Cadillac and Albert Rudy was coming the other way in a truck. Without warning, Albert forced the General Manager's car off the road, narrowly missing a collision. Mr. Clark then reported the incident to Rudy's superiors and told them to have him have his eyes checked because of his erratic driving. Rudy was sent to the Dispensary and checked out. The result was that he was nearly blind. We had to take him off the road. This was the start of regular physical exams at the plant.

"Although Rudy couldn't drive anymore, we made a job for him. I got a porthole from the Shipyard and we cut a hole in the side of the building. We got a desk and a high stool for Rudy to sit on. His new job was to keep track of truck numbers and the gallons of gas used. When Rudy retired, he had 50 years of service at Sparrows Point."
~ Jack Yard, General Foreman - Motor Transport Department, 1952 – 1982
Photo courtesy of Jack Yard

"I started to work at Bethlehem Steel in May 1952. I drove a tractor trailer truck over at the Wire Mill. There were 66 drivers at the time. I was the 66th man. In 1953, John Vogler was acting General Foreman and Henry Cumberland was General Manager. I was offered the job to drive the hospital transport vehicle. I did that for one year. In late 1953, they installed radios in the trucks. I became a radio dispatcher and subsequently Chief Dispatcher. I then moved up to Special Foreman and from there to Turn Foreman. In 1964, I became Assistant General Foreman. I was responsible for transportation on three swinging turns. In December 1964, Jim Lynch

left the Point to take a job in Bethlehem, PA and I was promoted to General Foreman of the Motor **Transport Department (MTD).** At that time, I supervised 302 men in the department. We had 272 vehicles in the motor pool and 268 truck drivers. There were also six Radio Dispatchers, six Turn Foreman, a Chief Clerk, three Clerks, and several Mechanics. We drove and maintained a wide assortment of vehicles that included 18-wheel tractor and trailers, 75-ton lowboys, 50-ton highboys, dump trucks capable of carrying 10 cubic yards, vans, cars, and dimster-dumpsters, sweepers, side-a-matic self-unloaders, and vac-cells.

"In 1975, the department name was changed to **Mobile Equipment and Yard Department**. We oversaw the operations of the Crane Department, the Scrap Yards, the Electric Shop, unloaders, and forklifts. My job title was changed from **General Foreman to Maintenance Coordinator**. I was responsible for scheduling safety and maintenance. Our department was responsible for the use of over 1,400 pieces of equipment used at Sparrows Point. These included bulldozers, truck cranes, 1,000 pound lifts, and up to 40,000 pound lifts. We maintained any kind of construction equipment used at Sparrows Point that you could imagine. We even maintained narrow gauge railroad engines. I retired on June 30, 1982 after 30 years of service."
~ Jack Yard, Maintenance Coordinator – Mobile Equipment and Yard Department, 1952 – 1982
Photos courtesy of Jack Yard

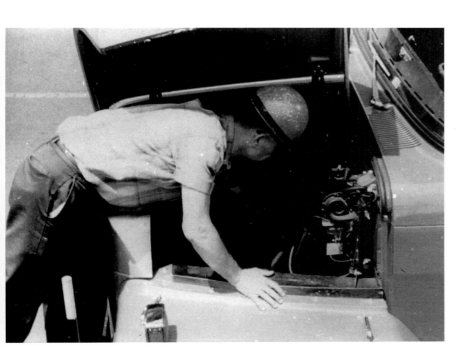

PART OF OUR JOB IS TO TEACH OTHERS TO BE *Careful*

Stratolift

"The old Motor Pool Shop was located at the north end of the No. 3 Open Hearth. It was situated on a triangular shaped piece of land that was located between the running railroad tracks and the narrow gauge line. There was a small building there made of corrugated metal that we used for an office. In 1957, we moved to the **new location** when the No. 4 Open Hearth was built. This was located on **9th Street between "H" Street and "F" Street**. The police and fire departments also moved to this location."
~ Jack Yard, Maintenance Coordinator – Mobile Equipment and Yard Department, 1952 – 1982.
Photos courtesy of Jack Yard.

Transportation Equipment Operated and Maintained by the Sparrows Point Plant Garage in 1960

- 40 dump trucks – 4 yd., 6 yd., and quarry type bodies
- 22 tractors – 2 with 5 ton booms
- 29 trailers – 15 ton to 50 ton capacity, including flatbeds, well beds, and gooseneck
- 19 flatbed trucks – 10 with one ton hydraulic tailgates
- 4 Dempster-Dumpster units operating with 167 Dempster boxes.
- 1 pressure body truck for trash
- 3 pickup trucks
- 2 van-type trucks
- 1 Strato-tower flatbed truck mounted with 75 foot tower
- 3 road sweepers
- 2 water trucks with 1,000 gallon tanks each
- 1 propane dispensing truck with 800 gallon tank

Of the above:
- 50 trucks are equipped with 2-way radio
- 40 trucks are equipped with propane fuel
- 12 large trucks are equipped for snow plows
- 6 large trucks are equipped for slag spreaders
- 4 large trucks are equipped for salt spreaders

Equipment Assigned to Specific Plant Departments and Maintained by the Sparrows Point Plant Garage In 1960

Department	Trucks	Cars
Real Estate & Mail	5	5
Electrical	7	0
Plant Engineering	2	0
Fire	9	1
Locomotive Crane Repair	2	0
Medical	1	2
Fuel (Steam)	1	0
Main Office	0	3
Garage	0	2
Police	0	4
Lubrication	1	0

Other: 2 scooters in Electrical, 2 ambulances in Medical.

The Main Office

Above, the addition to the Main Office under construction in 1956.

The original Main Office of the Pennsylvania Steel Company and later the Maryland Steel Company utilized a portion of the second floor of the old Company Store, which was located on the north side of the 300 block of "C" Street. When Bethlehem Steel purchased the plant in 1916, they built a Main Office across the street from the Company Store. They occupied this building until a new Main Office was built on Sparrows Point Boulevard sometime between 1939 and 1940. An addition was added in 1956 to complete the I-Beam configuration of the building's original design. The Main Office was the central hub of the steel plant. The General Manager's office and staff were located here. The building had three floors, a basement, and its own cafeteria. Photo courtesy of John Belas.

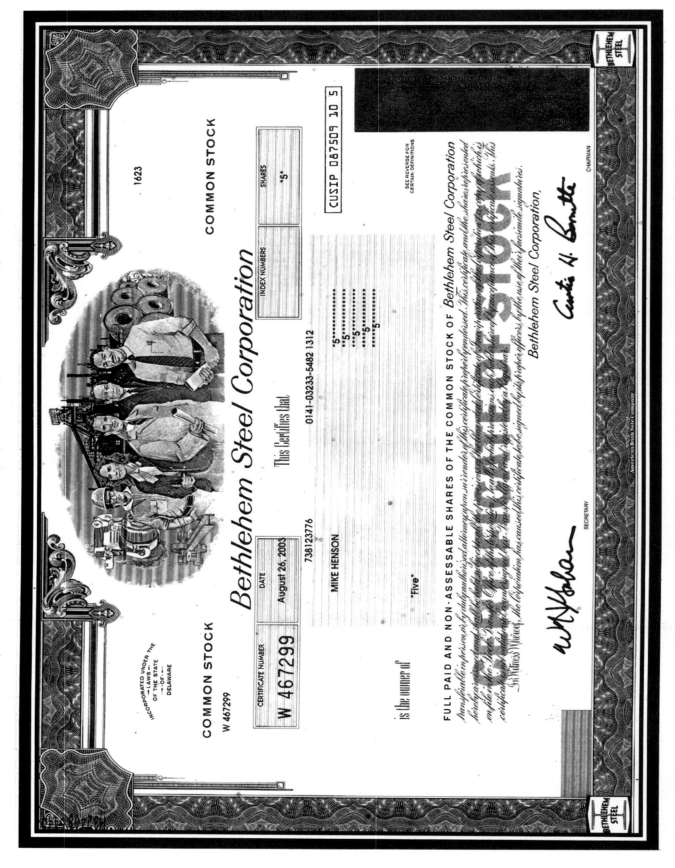

Stock certificate courtesy of Bill Goodman

40-Year Service Award Dinner
April 17, 1991

40-Year Service Award Dinner
Sparrows Point Plant of Bethlehem Steel Corporation
April 17, 1991

Plant Services — Seated, from left: Charles Cooke, Ed Whiting, Robert Fitch, Freeman Williams, Bob Ruby, Jim Knorr, Melvin Graves, Howard Long, Jim Sturdivant, Russ Brocato. Standing, from left: Don Waters, Charlie Weir, Steve Baran, Bob Crampton, Gene Franz, Bill Browning (superintendent), John McEvoy, Fred Warns, Jay Deickman, Bob Nace, Don Walters, Gordon Peters, Ed Fronckowski, Louis Winston, Bill White.

Each year, a dinner was held at the Sparrows Point Country Club to recognize those employees who had accumulated 40 years of service. Photo courtesy of Don Waters.

United Way of Central Maryland

Employees Give $536,000 To United Way

Employees of the Sparrows Point plant pledged $536,000 to this year's United Way campaign.

Per capita giving, the rate of participation and the number of employees who contribute on a continuous basis were all above last year's figures.

When combined with retiree donations and the corporate gift on behalf of plant employees, Sparrows Point's contribution totaled $741,000.

Because of generous contributions from employees, businesses and individuals throughout Central Maryland, United Way was able to reach its goal of raising $29.3 million.

Thanks! As the slogan goes: "Without You There's No Way."

Seventh Street Steam Station Explosion

"I started to work in Bethlehem Steel's Car Repair Shop. We repaired rail cars that were damaged. Many of the cars carried heavy loads of hot coke, coal, and scrap metal. They were constantly being loaded and unloaded by an overhead crane. They took some severe abuse. One time, Bethlehem bought some flat circus cars. They were so long they couldn't make the turns on curves. We cut out a 20-foot section and pieced the car back together. I worked in car repair for about two years. My buddy, George Katrosa, left Car Repair and transferred to the Control Department. He kept bugging me to come over and take the test. He would show me his little pouch of tools on his belt and compare them to the big heavy rivet tools and such that I was using. I finally went over and took the test and passed and transferred to the Control Department. It later became known as the Instrumentation Department.

"My first job was at the Seventh Street Steam Station. My job there was to maintain the four boilers that produced steam that was sent out all over the plant. I also worked at the "B" Street Steam Station. There were two monster boilers there. The main job at the Steam Station was to monitor the boilers and control the level of water. Our office was right next to the Seventh Street Station – right next to the stacks. We were mainly on call but we did a lot of monitoring and preventive maintenance. Most of the work required us to constantly check all instrumentation on machinery and equipment. We monitored temperature, pressure, gas flow, oil flow, water levels, and steam pressure. Our department also took care of all blast furnace instruments. We even checked out the furnaces that were banked.

"As technology changed, we had to keep up with it. When I first started in the department, most instruments were pneumatic (air) pressure. Eventually, everything changed to electronics. A lot of what we learned was on the job, but we did take a college-level electronics course. It was a four year program that we all did in one year. I spent the last 20 years of my employment at the Point in the 42-inch Tin Mill. There I worked on Skin Pass Mills, Tandem Mills, washers, picklers, and annealing lines. Sometimes I would fill in at the Coke Ovens. That was the dirtiest place in the world. It was so hot on the roof of the ovens that the workers had to wear wooden blocks on their boots to keep their soles from melting. Our department worked all over the Point. Wherever there was instrumentation and gauges, we were there to monitor, maintain, and repair them. I retired from the Point in 1995."
~ Frank Cantalupo, Instrumentation Technician, 1965 to 1995

"I remember the Seventh Street explosion like it was yesterday. I was working the 3 to 11 shift in the 160-inch Plate Mill as an NCBA Supervisor filling in for Randy Arnold, the Turn Foreman, who was on vacation. It was about 6 p.m. and I was on the shear end of the mill when the explosion happened. The entire mill shook and turned black as dirt came off the crane runways. We thought the continuous furnaces or the In and Out furnaces exploded. We ran to the furnace area and everything was okay at the mill. We looked around and saw the smoke from the blast at the Steam Station and proceeded there about 30 minutes after the blast. As we got close, we saw sheets of corrugated steel a quarter of a mile away. Windows were blown out of cars as well as significant other damages to the cars. By that time, the emergency workers were there and kept us away from the area. We returned to the mill to check for any damages. The mill was okay."
~ Roger K. Shackelford, Jr., NCBA Supervisor

Note: The Seventh Street Steam Station explosion occurred on May 4, 1968. The blast ripped apart one of the six steam generating plants utilized by the steel mill. The blast blew out windows a quarter of a mile away. Two people were killed and 22 were injured.

Tractor Repair Shop

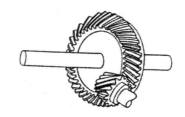

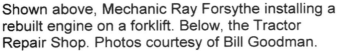

Shown above, Mechanic Ray Forsythe installing a rebuilt engine on a forklift. Below, the Tractor Repair Shop. Photos courtesy of Bill Goodman.

The sign above the entrance of the shop at the south end of the Cold Sheet Mill simply read **"Tractor Repair Shop."** However, it did not give a clue as to the wide variety of repair work done inside.

Mobile equipment mechanics rebuilt and repaired engines, motors, transmissions, gear assemblies, hydraulic systems, and brake systems. They could troubleshoot electrical and electronic problems and make all repairs and adjustments. They could even replace window glass. The words "tractor" was misleading because these were not your garden-variety vehicles. The tractors maintained at the shop ranged from two seat electric scooters, like you see on a golf course, to 100,000 pound boom tractors that move jumbo coils. They were powered by battery, gasoline, diesel, and propane. **Footnote 48**

Your Future depends on Your Safety Today

The Roll Shop: Where Precision was an Art Form

"Jeet". Shifflett is shown above reviewing a profile to make sure the ground roll meets specifications.

Roll Grinder Jim Tenney, shown above, working on a roll that was being prepared for use in the Plate Mills 4-high stand. All photographs credited to Clarence Snyder.

There were **Roll Shops** and **roll grinding machines** all over the plant at Sparrows Point. Each grinding machine was strategically placed in close proximity to the particular mill that it serviced. This was precision work at the highest level. The **Duo Mill** in the Tin Mill, for example, was one of the most demanding mills. There, each roll ground for the mill had to be within one half thousandth, end to end. A pair of rolls had to be within two thousandths. In addition, the surface roughness had to be kept within two micros. That equates to two millionths of an inch. Roll surface was critical because the Duo Mill ran the thinnest material of any rolling mill at Sparrows Point. Quality was critical and precision was an art form. **Footnote 49**

Ward Robbins (left) is shown gauging a roll with an **electronic saddle micrometer**, while Roll Grinder Dave Dreyfus inspects it.

General Physical Laboratory
Metallurgical Department
Plate Mills Division

Row 1, Left to Right: William P. Burdell, Ronald J. Abramowski, Joanne Weir, Joann E. Andersen, Aimee M. Krage, Elnita F. Keener

Row 2, Left to Right: John E. Knepp, John J. Stolba, Dennis W. Terry, Stanley S. Klovensky, Joseph G. Knott, Paul G. Knox, Phillip H. Rhudy, Kenneth P. Schilling, William J. Vollerthum, Jr., Colin W. Stewart, Henry C. Stumpf, Frank L. Johnson, Francis J. Kief, Alfred C. McDonough, Bobby J. Parsons, John A. Speece, William P. Rutledge, Chester G. Schleig, Robert A. Fogle, Charles R. Monn, Sterling E. Shuman

Photo courtesy of Dundalk Patapsco-Neck Historical Society, circa 1962.

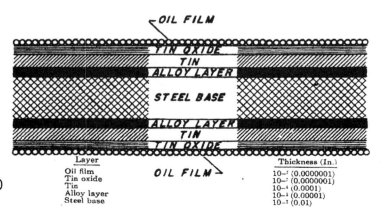

Layer	Thickness (In.)
Oil film	10^{-7} (0.0000001)
Tin oxide	10^{-7} (0.0000001)
Tin	10^{-4} (0.0001)
Alloy layer	10^{-5} (0.00001)
Steel base	10^{-2} (0.01)

← At left is a schematic enlarged cross-section of a sheet of tin-plate showing approximate relative thicknesses of the various "layers." The approximate thickness in inches of the individual layers is shown below the cross-section.

Is America getting trapped by foreign steel as it is by foreign oil?

Last year, foreign steelmakers shipped an all-time record of 21.1 million tons of steel to our shores. And our nation's trade deficit in steel was more than $5 ½ billion. But the worst is yet to come. By 1985, unless we soon start expanding our domestic steelmaking capacity [to meet projected demand by customers for our products], 25 to 30 million tons of steel imports could be entering the US market annually. That would mean an outflow of $12 to 15 billion a year.

Who provides good-paying jobs for 95,000 Americans?

Who paid more than $2 ½ billion in 1978 in wages, salaries, and other employment costs – thus generating a lot of purchasing power that generated a lot of jobs? Who spent more than $2.8 billion in 1978 to buy outside materials and services – thereby creating still more thousands of jobs? Bethlehem Steel. That's who. Jobs – just one of the contributions Bethlehem and steel make to American's national economy.

As Bethlehem Steel approached its 75th anniversary on December 10, 1979, it asked some questions that only government could answer. Their basic question was, "What is needed to supply the growing demand for steel in this country with *domestic* steel?" The answer: government policies that would allow Bethlehem Steel and other domestic steel companies to generate the additional funds needed to modernize and expand steelmaking and related facilities.

On this page are three ads that ran in the Atlantic, Newsweek, Saturday Review, Smithsonian, Sports Illustrated, Time, US News & World Report, the Wall Street Journal and other plant and community newspapers in 1979 and 1980. **Footnote 50**

Can you imagine a strong national defense without an adequate supply of steel?

Just how much should America count on overseas sources for steel? What happens if those sources are suddenly cut off – or if they suddenly decide they need the steel at home? Last year, steel imports reached an all-time record of 21.1 million tons. And unless we soon start expanding our domestic steelmaking capacity, that figure could reach 25 to 30 million tons a year by 1985. And America could find itself as dependent on foreign steel is it is on foreign oil.

Bethlehem
75
1904-1979

The Brass Check

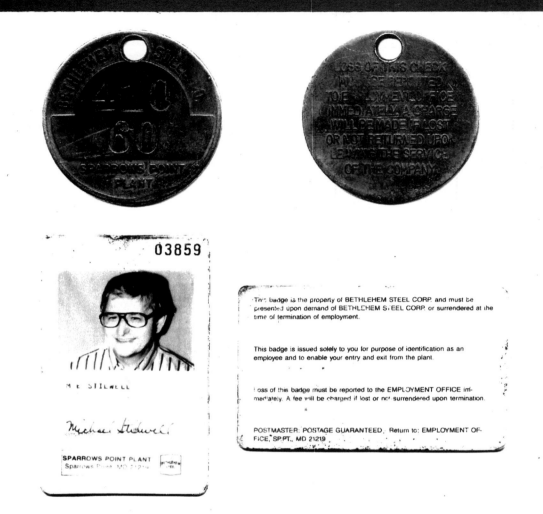

Upon my employment in 1962, as for all employees, I was issued a round brass check, as shown above. My "badge" number was 410 – 60. The number 410 indicated the General Mechanical Department. The text on the back of the check is "LOSS OF THIS CHECK MUST BE REPORTED TO EMPLOYMENT OFFICE IMMEDIATELY. A CHARGE WILL BE MADE IF LOST OR NOT RETURNED UPON LEAVING THE SERVICE OF THE COMPANY."

These checks were used throughout the Bethlehem Steel Corporation, at the steel plants, ore and coal mines, shipyards, etc.

At some time, the brass checks were replaced with plastic identification cards, as shown above. The text, on the back of the card, had a notice similar to wording on the back of the check, about a fee being charged for loss or failure to return it.

~Mike Stilwell, Hydraulic/Lubrication Engineer, 1962 - 2012

Major Accomplishments

48-Inch Tandem Crew Sets Record ⟵

September 15, 1989 was a record day. The 4 p.m. to midnight crew on the 48-inch Tandem Mill rolled 966 tons, or 121 tons per hour. This was the best performance over the previous five years for all gauges. Shown from left are Andy Andrews, Rich Tracy, Carl Gales, Mitch Farmer, Don Rider, Jerry Sands, Don Deacon, Roy Dotson, Jim Sturdivant, Al Mahaffey, and Richard Fox.

No. 1 Skin Pass Crew Rolls a Record at the Cold Mill ⟶

On April 20, 1988, the 3 to 11 turn accomplished a mill record of 112 tons per hour. They are from left: Tom Crusse, Jim Horseman, Mary Rachinskas, Bill Scoggins, Rob Mancinelli, Mark Walters, Wayne Billings, Lee Riesler, and Charlie Johnson.

Steel for Strength . . . Economy . . . Versatility

Tin Mill Maintenance Employees Receive Training Certificates ⟵

Kneeling from left: John Purcell, Bill Bauman, Chick Leikam, Robert Baskette. Standing from left: Joseph Evans, Hoye Breelove, William Patrick, and Dick Moore. Photo credited to Clarence Snyder.

323

Hollywood Comes to Sparrows Point

Shown above is the "Die Hard with a Vengeance" set at Pennwood Wharf. On this location, Sparrows Point became Bridgeport, CT, Jones Creek became Long Island Sound, and Fort Howard became Long Island. **Below** at left are two "Die Hard" extras shown with Mobile Equipment Dispatcher Sherry Sroka and Sergeant Lester Perry of the Sparrows Point Police Department.

Shown above, actor Samuel L. Jackson was going over some last minute details before shooting a scene. The movie opened in May 1995. **Below**: the most popular spot on the backlot was the double van rig of Coast to Coast Catering, whose sign on the side of their truck stated, "A fresh food motion picture catering company."

Footnote 51

The Dispensary

Shown at right is the new Dispensary built in 1958 at the plant's Tin Mill Department.

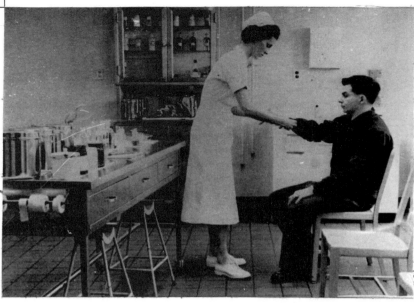

"In 1957, my husband Jan had interviews waiting in Camden, Wilmington, Baltimore, and Chester, PA. Within a week, he received a positive offer from Bethlehem Steel for a position as Industrial Nurse at the Sparrows Point plant. At that time, more than 28,000 employees made a good living there in the steelmaking process. The Dispensary was open night and day. Four shifts worked around the clock staffed by six doctors, about 20 medical people; half of them were RNs, half were Navy Corpsmen. Also, X-ray Technicians, Physical Therapists, Lab Technicians, and Administration.

"Jan was busy learning the rules of his new job at Bethlehem Steel. He drove the ambulance when calls came in late or on night shift, learned to take X-rays and many procedures geared toward the specific needs of this environment. I think of the time when a group of men were overcome by gas and the heat cases in summertime from those working at the furnaces. The serious accidents with chemicals, cranes, hot steel, and because of an unguarded moment with moving machines. Sorry to say, but sometimes accidents happened because of disregard for safety rules. Jan was at the right place here. He always went happy to work and came home satisfied with a job well done. There was a good understanding between the workers, and so what if there were also a few disagreeable characters, no group of people is complete without them. As for me, from the first day on, I was very happy with all that Sparrows Point stood for."   ~ Lettie de Wit, wife of Jan de Wit - Industrial Nurse

Note: On November 1, 1956, Jan and Lettie de Wit and their children immigrated to America from Holland. They came to Sparrows Point in 1957 and lived at 405 "D" Street.

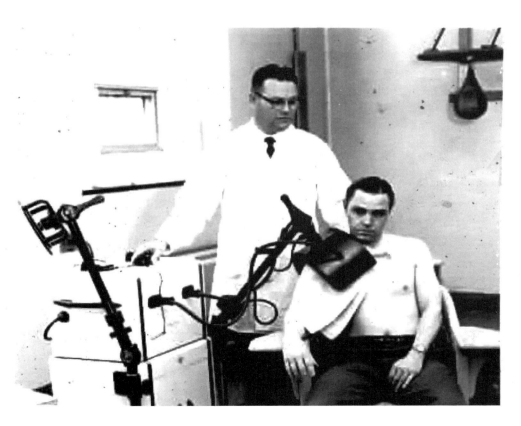

"My grandfather, Harry Ash, worked at the Dispensary at Sparrows Point. He came to the Point in 1938 and worked at the Wire Mill Dispensary for two years. As World War II approached, he enlisted in the Navy and became a Corpsman. He returned home in 1945 and went back to work at the Point. He was a Physician's Assistant at the main Dispensary. He retired after 40 years of service." Harry Ash is the gentleman seated in the chair. Photo courtesy of Bill Goodman, who is also the grandson of Harry Ash. Photo circa 1950.

Bethlehem Steel Family Night at Memorial Stadium
August 11, 1961

↑ Memorial Stadium was located on 33rd Street in Baltimore City. It was built in 1950 and demolished in 2001.

← This tube-like structure was set up across the street from the stadium on family night, August 11, 1961. It was nine feet in diameter, weighed 18 tons, and was 40 feet long. The tube itself was built at Sparrows Point and was to be used for Baltimore City's new water line. Inside the tube were various products made at the Sparrows Point plant. Families were encouraged to walk through the structure and view its contents before the ball game. Photos courtesy of Dundalk Patapsco-Neck Historical Society.

← A packed house of Bethlehem Steel employees and their families get ready for an Orioles game. Note the homemade megaphone hand-painted with "Bethlehem Steel Co."

↓ On August 11, 1961, the Baltimore Orioles played the Boston Red Sox at Memorial Stadium. The Orioles won the game 6 to 3. Players on the lineup card that night were: Brooks Robinson, 3B; Jim Busby, CF; Gus Triandos, C; and Jim Gentile, 1B.

A Backyard Job

Sparrows Point furnished about 5,000 tons of steel for the Baltimore Beltway, I-695 Bridge that crosses Bear Creek between the Francis Scott Key Bridge and the steel plant. The bridge was designed by the Maryland Transportation Authority.

Lighting the Way – A Beacon of Hope

Footnote 52

Ron Belbot, left, and Joe Rosel are shown above introducing the new lighthouse logo in 1996. A large lighthouse replica was fabricated and installed on the front lawn of the main office.

Photo dated 1996, courtesy of Rob Smith.

In 1996, Duane Dunham was Division President of the Sparrows Point plant. Looking to usher Sparrows Point into the new millennium, Mr. Dunham chose a lighthouse as a symbol to guide the way into the future. The beam of light from a lighthouse signified safety and security. It pointed the way night or day and in stormy seas or calm. Mr. Dunham chose the **lighthouse logo** shown above right because he believed it represented what Sparrows Point must faithfully be – **"a steadfast beacon of light and hope, and a safe harbor for our customers, our employees, our communities, and our stockholders."**

The nautical logo also emphasized Sparrows Point's advantageous location. It was surrounded by water and blessed with the commercial advantage of water born transportation for its raw materials and products. The new logo also gave Sparrows Point the distinction and identify as a separate division of Bethlehem Steel.

Shipping to Customers

John Kordek, Warehouse General Foreman, prepares for a large shipment in 1988.

Herb Henson, Tin Mill Coil Pack, prepares to ship out a coil with the ISO 9002 sticker. Customers could recognize Sparrows Point coils from a distance because they are the only ones that had the red, white and blue insignia. Photo dated December 1994.

Bill George, shown above, recording coil information at the Pennwood's Warehouse. Note: Shipment is destined for China. Photo dated 1988.

"BUY AMERICAN"

A warehouse was used to store the packaged coils and sheets of steel before they were shipped to customers. This department also loaded these products onto trucks and railroad cars for shipment. The photograph was dated 1958. Note the absence of hardhats and other safety apparatus that became required a few years later.

Sparrows Point – 1997

Note: This photograph was taken prior to the construction of the New Cold Mill, which began in 1998. In the top center of the photograph, you can see the ground being prepared for the site of the New Cold Mill.

Steel Workers Memorial

USWA Local 2609 constructed a six foot memorial in front of the Union Hall at 550 Dundalk Avenue for those former employees who were killed on the job at the Sparrows Point plant. Shown above is a list of 107 names. Members held an annual ceremony on Worker's Memorial Day to pay tribute to their fallen coworkers. The memorial was dedicated on November 17, 1993. Photo courtesy of Bill Goodman.

Ode to Sparrows Point

Sometimes saying I miss you just isn't enough. You were more than a woman, more than a friend, more than a companion through good times and bad. You were a creature of your own, a life of your own, with more passion inside of you than any man or woman could hope to understand. You were colder than any of God's creatures and hotter than the flames of Hell and I'd like nothing more than to feel your heat on my body again, to feel your cold embrace one last time, to smell you on my flesh and to love you, and to hate you, with all the passion I can muster. One last chance to curse you, one last chance to sit with you, one last chance to spend the night with you, a weekend with you, to tell you how much you meant to me.

The years wore upon you; I can see that now in hindsight. I can see the toll life took on you, on your spirit, your body, your very existence. The years were harder on you than I realized and you weren't loved like you truly deserved. I am beyond sorry for the neglect, the abuse, and the agony you must have felt as you slowly died.

I won't lie. I hated you nearly as much as I loved you. The problem is that I didn't know that I loved you until it was too late. Until you were taken out of my life, stolen from me, and given away to another I didn't realize the passion you created in me. You were loved more than you'll ever know. You provided to me, carried me, and made me the man I am today. You were my family and yet my enemy, the woman that moved me and the woman that inspired me.

I didn't mind that you cheated on me. I didn't mind that there were other men, other women, which you loved like me. A hundred thousand men and women knew your love, your embrace, your unending desire to please and provide. You had needs beyond which I could fulfill. The same needs that so many others had, the same needs that you fulfilled without having your own needs met. You continued to provide while we consumed, to give of yourself while we abused.. Sometimes you lashed out.

Sometimes I saw your dark side, the angry vicious side of a woman scorned. I saw how cruel you could be if I let my guard down. I saw you hurt those you loved, and I saw you hurt those that loved you. I knew you were a murderer yet I trusted you, I trusted you like so many others

trusted you. I trusted you with my life despite knowing how many lives you'd taken in your bloodthirsty rage. I trusted you.............

Your needs were as human as my own. You had the need to feed, to breathe, to consume and to produce. Those same burning desires that we all have as living beings. In the end it was those same needs that doomed you to death. Your continuous need to consume, to produce, meant you weren't going to be with me much longer.......that your time was limited. They didn't tell me how long you had to live, I just woke up and you were gone. A beautiful piece of my life taken from me forever. A beautiful piece of all of our lives, taken from us forever. You were more than a woman to me, you were a piece of the fabric of my life, a part of my very existence, and I can barely breathe at times knowing you're gone.

I still look for you when I drive the long lonely drive past where we used to spend our days and nights. I look to the horizon for your light, for your breath against the sunrise, for some sign that you're alive. I pray one day I'll hear you beckoning to me one last time, calling to me, bidding me to come to your side and to spend one last dark night with you. One last night, one last chance to say goodbye, one last chance to be together. I know it's not to be. The sky will remain clear; the smoke of your soul won't darken the sky any longer. No longer will your silhouette stand tall against the fading of the sun, as if daring the very night sky to darken your flame of life. No longer will the Mighty L produce, no longer will the "Beast of the East" challenge her rivals on the field of battle, and no longer will troops of Steelworkers man the mills and coax liquid metal from your belly. No longer will Steelworkers nurse you through the night, through blizzards and floods, through the brutal summer heat.

You were more than a woman, more than a friend, more than a companion. You were also more than a job, more than a way to make a living, more than a place I went to in order to feed my children. You weren't just a mill or a factory, you were Sparrows Point. I wake up every day and think of you, I go to sleep and I think of you. I know the anguish, the resentment, sadness, despair and rage will fade with time..........but not today.

Today I just want to hate. I want to hate those that took you from me, from us, and condemned you to die. I want to hate those that didn't stand up for you, that didn't throw their bodies into a frenzied self-sacrifice in order that you might survive. I want to hate that you're gone and that we're still here. I want to spend one last night consumed by rage, a rage that burns hotter than the furnaces that poured liquid steel into our very lives.

So when tomorrow comes I'll say goodbye for good. I'll mourn and I'll remember, I'll reminisce and tell stories, but I'll say goodbye. Tomorrow I'll let go.

Poem by Chris MacLarion, USW LU 9447 Vice President

Cheer Up! – Nothing Lasts Forever

The ruins of Ozymandias lay on the desert floor.

Cheer up!

"THERE is no stopping business in this country. It's got to go on. It will go on, in spite of all this gloomy talk, in spite of agitators, in spite of anything any Legislature can do to discourage capital. The reason that it has to go on is because it is bigger than any obstacle in its path. You can't force bad times on this country. We are going ahead, irresistibly, by force of our own resources."

~ Charles M. Schwab
Bethlehem Steel Corporation
Chairman of the Board
(until his death in 1939)

Ozymandias

I met a traveler from an antique land
Who said: `Two vast and trunkless legs of stone
Stand in the desert. Near them, on the sand,
Half sunk, a shattered visage lies, whose frown,
And wrinkled lip, and sneer of cold command,
Tell that its sculptor well those passions read
Which yet survive, stamped on these lifeless things,
The hand that mocked them and the heart that fed.
And on the pedestal these words appear --
"My name is Ozymandias, king of kings:
Look on my works, ye Mighty, and despair!"
Nothing beside remains. Round the decay
Of that colossal wreck, boundless and bare
The lone and level sands stretch far away.'

Percy Bysshe Shelley

Micky's Package Liquors

Micky Narutowicz began his package goods business in 1934 – a year after prohibition ended. The original establishment was located at 2506 North Snyder Avenue near Sparrows Point Road. When North Point Boulevard was built in the late 1930s, traffic bypassed Edgemere. In the late 1940s, Mr. Narutowicz built a new establishment – Micky's Package Liquors – at the intersection of North Snyder Avenue and North Point Boulevard. Thousands upon thousands of steelworkers cashed their checks and purchased the beverage of their choice at Micky's establishment. In 2013, the business was comprised of a package goods store, a bar, a Laundromat, a car wash, a gas station, and a convenience store. In 2013, it was operated by a third generation Narutowicz. Above and below: Micky's Package Liquors as it appeared in 1950. Photo courtesy of Jim Narutowicz, Jr.

MAP OF THE TOWN
OF
SPARROWS POINT, MARYLAND
(NOT INCLUDING THE SHIPYARD PORTION)

AS SPECULATED FROM INFORMATION DERIVED FROM VARIOUS SOURCES

LOGO OF BETHLEHEM STEEL,
OWNER OF SPARROWS POINT PLANT AND TOWN
FROM 1916 UNTIL BETHLEHEM STEEL CEASED TO
EXIST, DECEMBER 31, 2003 (87 YEARS)
LIFETIME OF THE TOWN WAS FROM ABOUT
1890 TO THE EARLY 1970'S (APPROX. 80 YEARS)

Compiled
By
Michael Stilwell
May 28, 2013

MAP OF THE TOWN OF SPARROWS POINT, MARYLAND (SPECULATED)

CONTENTS

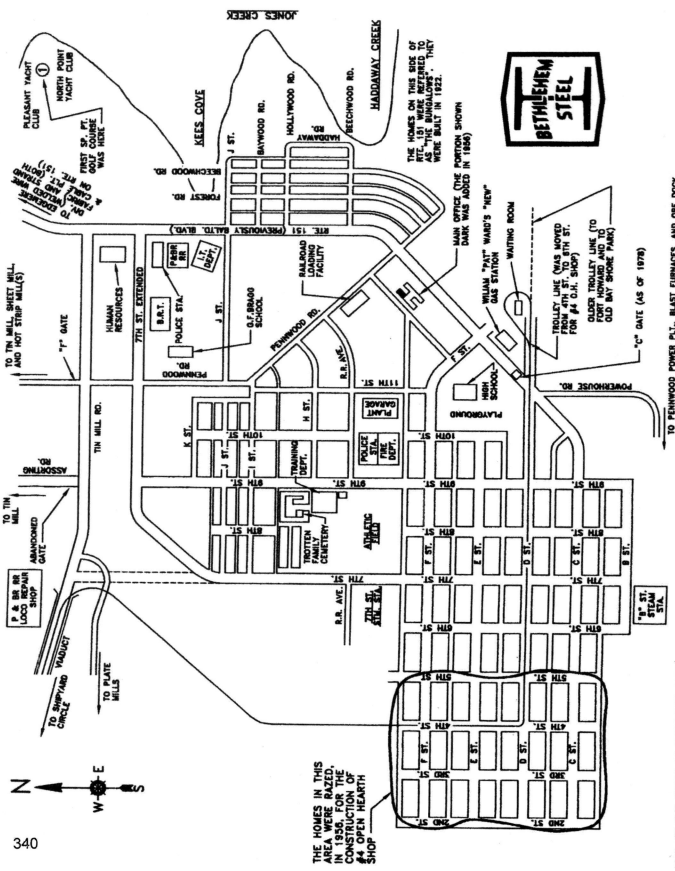

MAP OF THE TOWN OF SPARROWS POINT, AND PART OF THE PLANT, SHOWING THE AREA WHICH WAS RAZED, IN 1956, FOR THE #4 OPEN HEARTH SHOP
SPECULATED; AS OF SOMETIME(S) PRIOR TO "L BL ECE. (1978)
NOT TO SCALE. ALL ITEMS, AS SHOWN, DID NOT EXIST AT ANY ONE SPECIFIC TIME

340

1

5-23-13/MS

REV. 1

SPECULATED—3X

DESCRIPTIONS OF SCHOOLS, CHURCHES, STORES, ETC.
ON MAPS OF THE TOWN OF SPARROWS POINT
GENERAL AREA

REF. #	DESCRIPTION	ADDRESS	REMARKS
1	FIRST SPARROWS POINT COMPANY GOLF COURSE	AS SHOWN IN THE UPPER RIGHT HAND CORNER OF THE MAP	IN 1889, THE MARYLAND STEEL CO. PURCHASED THE TROTTEN FARM, WHICH IN 1918 WAS PURCHASED BY BETHLEHEM STEEL. IN 1925 THE AREA OF THE FARM SHOWN ON THE MAP (AS ITEM 1) WAS OPENED AS A COMPANY GOLF COURSE. THE FARM HAD SUPPLIED PRODUCE TO THE PLANT'S COMPANY STORE. THE FORMER HOUSE OF DR. AND MRS. TROTTEN BECAME THE GOLF COURSE CLUB HOUSE. IN 1814, DURING THE WAR OF 1812, THE TROTTEN HOME WAS TEMPORARILY OCCUPIED BY BRITISH TROOPS. MEMBERS OF THE TROTTEN FAMILY ARE BURIED IN A SMALL OLD CEMETERY PLOT THAT HAS BECOME SURROUNDED BY THE TOWN AND THE STEEL MILL; IT IS NEAR THE INTERSECTION OF 9TH AND H STREETS. ONE GRAVE IS OF DR. JOHN TROTTEN WHO DIED IN 1809, PREDATING MARYLAND STEEL CO. AND THE TOWN. IN 1952, BETHLEHEM'S RAILROAD, THE PATAPSCO AND BACK RIVERS RR, EXPANDED INTO THE GOLF COURSE AREA; CONSTRUCTION THEN BEGAN, ON COMPANY PROPERTY ON WISE AVENUE, OF A NEW GOLF COURSE AND CLUB HOUSE, THE SPARROWS POINT COUNTRY CLUB. IN 1985, BETHLEHEM SOLD THE CLUB TO ITS MEMBERS.

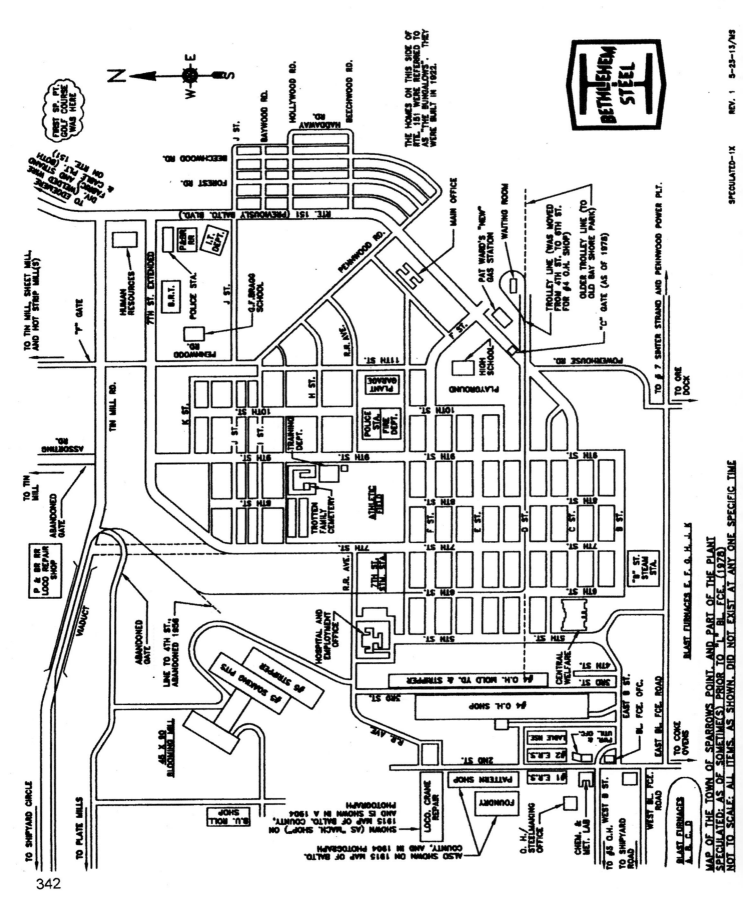

MAP OF THE TOWN OF SPARROWS POINT, AND PART OF THE PLANT
SPECULATED: AS OF SOMETIME(S) PRIOR TO "L" BL. FCE. (1978)
NOT TO SCALE. ALL ITEMS, AS SHOWN, DID NOT EXIST AT ANY ONE SPECIFIC TIME

BETHLEHEM STEEL

SPECULATED-1X   REV. 1 5-23-13/WS

2

342

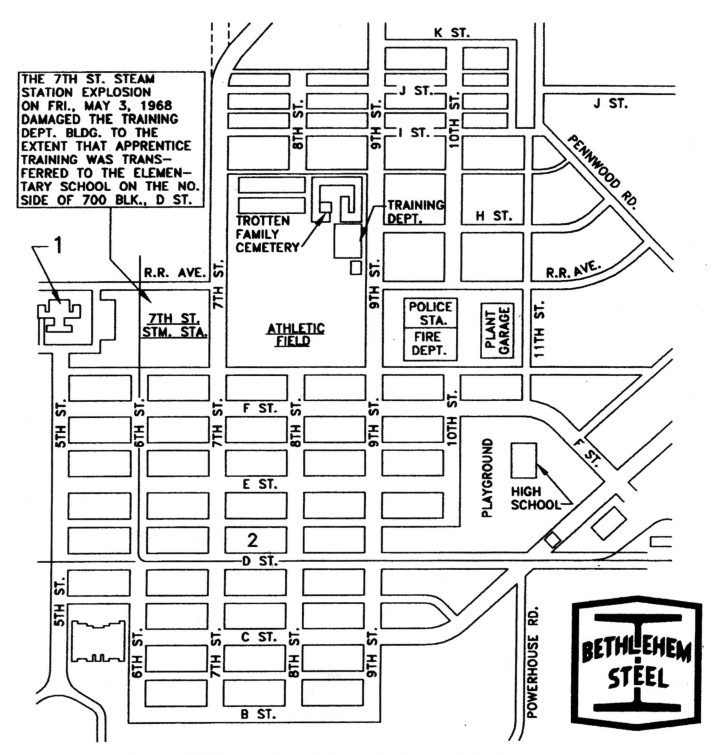

THE 7TH ST. STEAM STATION EXPLOSION ON FRI., MAY 3, 1968 DAMAGED THE TRAINING DEPT. BLDG. TO THE EXTENT THAT APPRENTICE TRAINING WAS TRANSFERRED TO THE ELEMENTARY SCHOOL ON THE NO. SIDE OF 700 BLK., D ST.

MAP OF THE TOWN OF SPARROWS POINT
SPECULATED; AS OF SOMETIME(S) PRIOR TO "L" BL. FCE. (1978)
NOT TO SCALE; ALL ITEMS, AS SHOWN, DID NOT EXIST AT ANY ONE SPECIFIC TIME

SPECULATED—2X   REV. 1 5—23—13/MS

DESCRIPTIONS OF SCHOOLS, CHURCHES, STORES, ETC.
ON MAPS OF THE TOWN OF SPARROWS POINT
NOTES IN REFERENCE TO PAGE 3

REF. #	DESCRIPTION	ADDRESS	REMARKS
1	TOWN HOSPITAL (WITH PLANT EMPLOYMENT DEPT. IN BASEMENT)	SEE MAP	THE BUILDING BECAME TO BE USED AS THE ELECTRONICS DEPT. SHOP. DUE TO LACK OF MAINTENANCE TO THE BUILDING, IT DEGENERATED INTO VERY POOR CONDITION. SUMP PUMPS RAN CONTINUOUSLY TO PUMP GROUND WATER FROM THE BASEMENT. IN 2005, THE ELECTRONICS SHOP MOVED INTO THE ABANDONED HYDRAULIC REPAIR SHOP IN THE TIN MILL MACHINE SHOP. THE HYDRAULIC SHOP HAD EXISTED FROM 1965 UNTIL THEN, WHEN ALL HYDRAULIC PUMP AND VALVE REPAIRS WERE CONTRACTED OUT TO VENDORS' SHOPS.

Sparrows Point Hospital (Dispensary) photo courtesy of Mike Stilwell

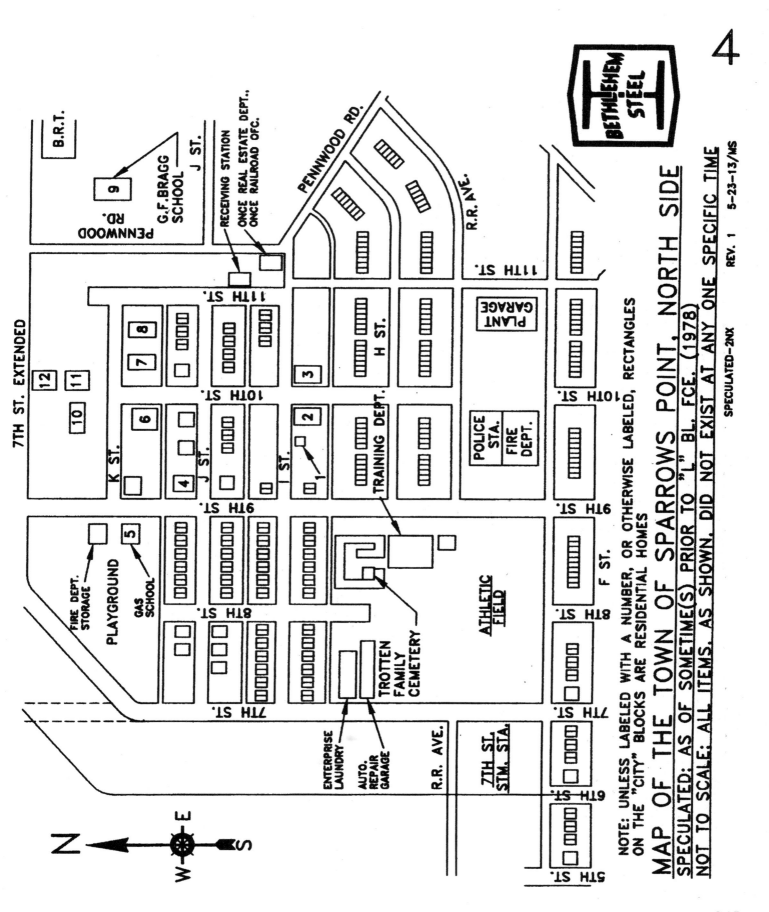

MAP OF THE TOWN OF SPARROWS POINT, NORTH SIDE

SPECULATED: AS OF SOMETIME(S) PRIOR TO "L" BL. FCE. (1978)

NOT TO SCALE; ALL ITEMS, AS SHOWN, DID NOT EXIST AT ANY ONE SPECIFIC TIME

NOTE: UNLESS LABELED WITH A NUMBER, OR OTHERWISE LABELED, RECTANGLES ON THE "CITY" BLOCKS ARE RESIDENTIAL HOMES

REV. 1   5-23-13/MS

SPECULATED-2NX

345

DESCRIPTIONS OF SCHOOLS, CHURCHES, STORES, ETC.
ON MAPS OF THE TOWN OF SPARROWS POINT
NORTH SIDE OF TOWN

REF. #	DESCRIPTION	ADDRESS	REMARKS
1	LIETZEL PRINTING SHOP	AS SHOWN, ON I ST., IN 900 BLOCK	
2	COMMUNITY HALL	913-915 I ST.	AMERICAN LEGION HALL ON 2ND FLOOR
3	EBENEZER METHODIST CHURCH	AS SHOWN, ON I ST., IN 1000 BLOCK	BUILT 1924
4	UNION BAPTIST CHURCH	AS SHOWN, ON J ST., IN 1000 BLOCK	
5	GAS SCHOOL	NEAR INTERSECTION OF 9TH AND K STREETS	FORMERLY THE COMPANY DAIRY
6	NORTH SIDE RESTAURANT	AS SHOOWN, ON K ST., IN 900 BLOCK	
7	BARRACKS BUILDING	AS SHOWN, ON K ST., IN 1000 BLOCK	FOR SINGLE BLACK MEN
8	BARRACKS BUILDING		
9	BRAGG, REV. GEORGE FREEMAN, SCHOOL	EAST OF PENNWOOD RD., NO. OF J STREEET	THIS SCHOOL WAS BUILT IN 1927, AFTER FLOODING, CAUSED BY FILLING IN OF HUMPHRY'S CREEK, DESTROYED THE FIRST PUBLIC ELEMENTARY SCHOOL FOR BLACKS (OPENED IN 1890 AS PUBLIC COLORED SCHOOL # 24), WHICH WAS AT 6TH AND J STREETS (NOT SHOWN IN THIS MAP PROJECT). AT VARIOUS TIMES, THIS BUILDING WAS AN ELEMENTARY, MIDDLE, AND HIGH SCHOOL. THE SCHOOL CLOSED IJN 1964; BETHLEHEM BOUGHT IT AND USED IT FOR OFFICES UNTIL IT WAS RAZED IN 1974.
10	CONTRACTOR'S GARAGE	AS SHOWN, NORTH OF K ST. BETWEEN 9TH AND 11TH STS.	
11	CONTRACTOR'S GARAGE		ALSO SEA SCOUT BOAT REPAIR SHOP
12	CONTRACTOR'S OFFICE		

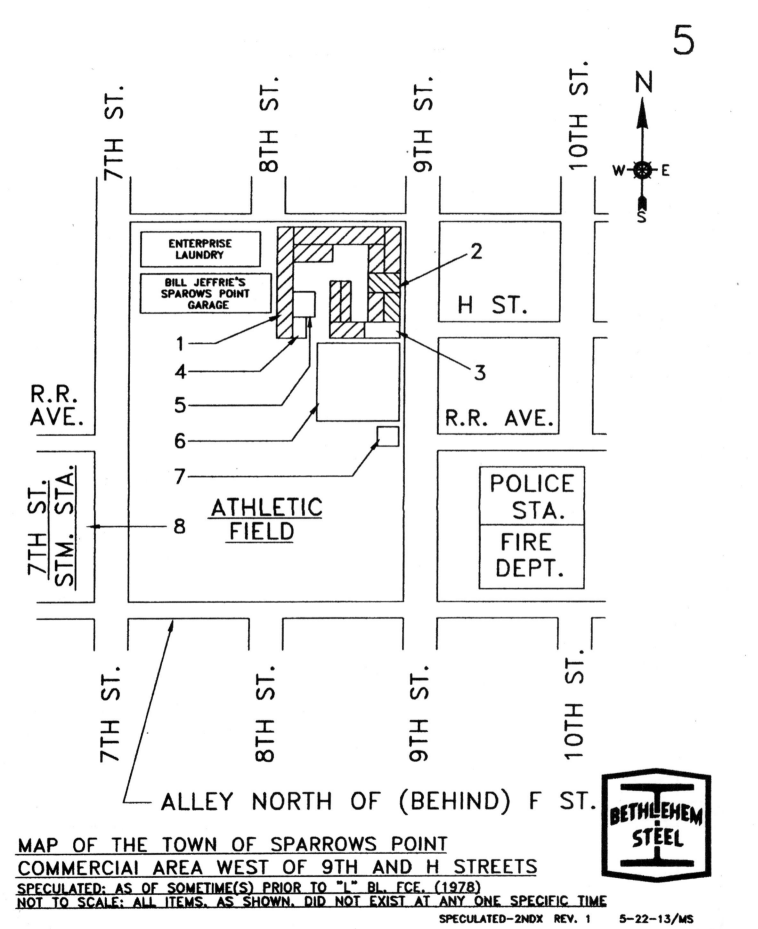

5

N
W E
S

ENTERPRISE LAUNDRY

BILL JEFFRIE'S SPAROWS POINT GARAGE

2

H ST.

1

4

5

3

6

R.R. AVE.

7

ATHLETIC FIELD

POLICE STA.

FIRE DEPT.

8

7TH ST.

8TH ST.

9TH ST.

10TH ST.

R.R. AVE.

7TH ST. STM. STA.

ALLEY NORTH OF (BEHIND) F ST.

BETHLEHEM STEEL

MAP OF THE TOWN OF SPARROWS POINT
COMMERCIAI AREA WEST OF 9TH AND H STREETS
SPECULATED: AS OF SOMETIME(S) PRIOR TO "L" BL. FCE. (1978)
NOT TO SCALE: ALL ITEMS, AS SHOWN, DID NOT EXIST AT ANY ONE SPECIFIC TIME

SPECULATED-2NDX REV. 1   5-22-13/MS

DESCRIPTIONS OF SCHOOLS, CHURCHES, STORES, ETC.
ON MAPS OF THE TOWN OF SPARROWS POINT
COMMERCIAL AREA WEST OF 9TH AND H STREETS

REF. #	DESCRIPTION	ADDRESS	REMARKS
1	AUTOMOBILE GARAGES, FOR TOWN RESIDENTS	SEE MAP	
2	AUTOMOBILE REPAIR SHOP AND GAS STATION	SEE MAP	BILLY WORTMAN'S? DON MASON'S? TWO GAS PUMPS WERE OUT IN FRONT
3	LOBER BROTHERS' GROCERY STORE	SEE MAP	PREVIOUSLY HAD BEEN AN A & P GROCERY STORE
4	DRY CLEANING SHOP	SEE MAP	
5	TROTTEN FAMILY CEMETERY	SEE MAP	THIS CEMETERY PLOT PREDATES THE ACQUISITION OF THE PROPERTY BY PENNSYLVANIA STEEL CO. IN 1886. DR. JOHN TROTTEN'S REMAINS WERE INTERRED HERE IN 1809. THE PLOT ALSO PREDATES THE WAR OF 1812, DURING WHICH BRITISH TROOPS "VISITED" THE TROTTEN HOME ON JONES CREEK IN SEPTEMBER OF 1814. THAT HOUSE LATER BECAME THE CLUB HOUSE OF THE BETHLEHEM STEEL COMPANY'S GOLF COURSE IN 1925.
6	TWO-STORY BUILDING	SEE MAP	THIS BUILDING ORIGINALLY HAD SHOPS ON THE FIRST FLOOR, AND THE SECOND FLOOR SERVED VARIOUS PURPOSES. BETHLEHEM BOUGHT THE BUILDING IN 1945, AND BY 1957, ALL OF THE SHOPS WERE GONE. THE COMPANY'S APPRENTICE TRAINING DEPT. TOOK OVER THE FIRST FLOOR, AND THE SECOND FLOOR BECAME USED FOR A PISTOL RANGE, A RIFLE RANGE FOR A YOUTH CLUB, AND FOR STORAGE. AS A RESULT OF DAMAGE TO THE BUILDING RESULTING FROM THE EXPLOSION OF THE 7TH STREET STEAM STATION (SEE ITEM 8 BELOW) THE BUILDING WAS RAZED, AND APPRENTICE TRAINING WAS MOVED TO THE ELEMENTARY SCHOOL BUILDING ON D STREET.
7	COHILL'S NEWSSTAND	SEE MAP	
8	7TH STREET STEAM STATION	SEE MAP	EARLY IN THE SECOND (3/11) SHIFT ON FRI., MAY 3RD, 1968, AN EXPLOSION IN THE STATION KILLED TWO AND INJURED 22 PERSONS, AND CAUSED DAMAGE TO NEARBY BUILDINGS; THE BUILDING HOUSING APPRENTICE TRAINING WAS EXTENSIVELY DAMAGED.

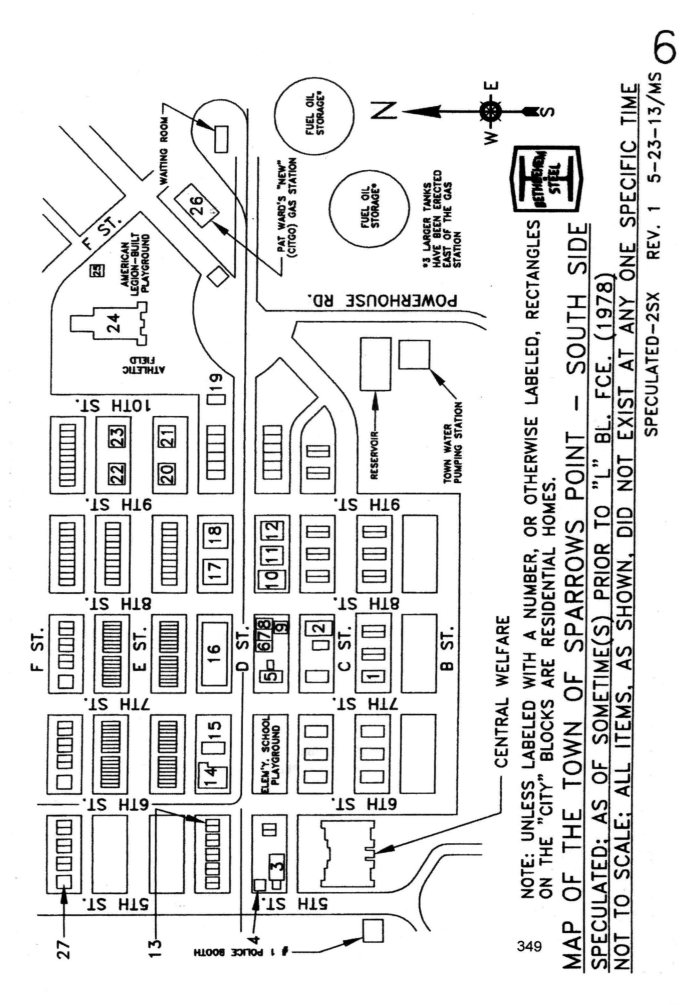

MAP OF THE TOWN OF SPARROWS POINT – SOUTH SIDE

SPECULATED: AS OF SOMETIME(S) PRIOR TO "L" BL. FCE. (1978)
NOT TO SCALE; ALL ITEMS, AS SHOWN, DID NOT EXIST AT ANY ONE SPECIFIC TIME

SPECULATED–2SX   REV. 1   5–23–13/MS

NOTE: UNLESS LABELED WITH A NUMBER, OR OTHERWISE LABELED, RECTANGLES
ON THE "CITY" BLOCKS ARE RESIDENTIAL HOMES.

349

DESCRIPTIONS OF SCHOOLS, CHURCHES, STORES, ETC.
ON MAPS OF THE TOWN OF SPARROWS POINT
SOUTH SIDE OF TOWN

REF. #	DESCRIPTION	ADDRESS	REMARKS
1	SAFETY DEPT.	703 C STREET	
2	FIRST UNITED METHODIST (EPICOPAL) CHURCH AND SUNDAY SCHOOL	AS SHOWN, ON C ST., IN 700 BLOCK	BUILT IN 1888, PARSONAGE IS NEXT TO THE CHURCH
3	FIRST PRESBYTRIAN CHURCH OF SPARROWS POINT	AS SHOWN, ON 5TH ST., SOUTH OF THE BANK	
4	FIRST NATIONAL BANK OF MARYLAND	501 D ST.	WAS ORIGINALLY THE BANK OF SPARROWS POINT, BUILT IN 1918
5	ST. JOHN'S EVANGELICAL LUTHERAN CHURCH	AS SHOWN, ON D ST., IN 700 BLOCK	BUILT 1892, PARSONAGE IS NEXT TO CHURCH; A NEW CHURCH WAS BUILT, IN THE SAME PLACE, IN 1921. WHEN IT WAS RAZED, ALONG WITH THE TOWN, THE ALTAR, PEWS, AND STAINED GLASS WINDOWS WERE SALVAGED, AND INSTALLED IN THE NEW CHURCH IN EDGEMERE.
6	TELEPHONE COMPANY	AS SHOWN, ON D ST., IN 700 BLOCK	
7	A & P GROCERY STORE		
8	GAVER'S DRUG STORE		
9	SUNDAY SCHOOL	AS SHOWN, BACK FROM D ST., IN 700 BLOCK	
10	ST. MATTHEW'S EPISCOPAL CHURCH	AS SHOWN, ON D STREET, IN 800 BLOCK	BUILT 1889
11	ST. MATTHEW'S EPISCOPAL CHURCH PARSONAGE		
12	ST. MATTHEW'S EPISCOPAL CHURCH PARISH HOUSE		
13	DOCTORS' OFFICES	AS SHOWN, ON NW CORNER OF 6TH AND D STS.	1ST FLOOR - DR. WINDSOR 2ND FLOOR - DR. MEANS
14	ST. LUKE'S R. C. CHURCH	AS SHOWN, ON D STREET, IN 600 BLOCK	BUILT 1888
15	ST. LUKE'S PARSONAGE		
16	ELEMENTARY SCHOOL	AS SHOWN, ON D ST., IN 700 BLOCK	BUILT IN 1903, BECAME BETHLEHEM STEEL'S TRAINING DEPT., AFTER 7TH ST. STEAM STATION EXPLOSION ON MAY 3, 1968
17	STORE BUILDING	802 - 808 D STREET	SEE DETAIL SKETCH
18	STORE BUILDING	812 - 820 D STREET	SEE DETAIL SKETCH

DESCRIPTIONS OF SCHOOLS, CHURCHES, STORES, ETC.
ON MAPS OF THE TOWN OF SPARROWS POINT
SOUTH SIDE OF TOWN (CONTINUED)

REF. #	DESCRIPTION	ADDRESS	REMARKS
19	DOCTOR'S OFFICE AND RESIDENCE	914 D STREET	AT VARIOUS TIMES, DR. D. L. FARBER, DR. CONWAY
20	APARTMENT BUILDING	903 E STREET	"THE WHITE ELEPHANTS", BUILT IN 1915, WERE ORIGINALLY BOARDING HOUSES FOR SINGLE MEN; IN 1930 THEY WERE CONVERTED TO APARTMENTS FOR FAMILIES.
21	APARTMENT BUILDING	915 E STREET	
22	APARTMENT BUILDING	904 E STREET	
23	APARTMENT BUILDING	916 E STREET	
24	SPARROWS POINT HIGH SCHOOL	AS SHOWN, ON D ST., EAST OF 10TH ST.	BUILT IN 1921, MOVED TO NEW SCHOOL IN EDGEMERE, IN 1956
25	EQUIPMENT STORAGE BUILDING	AS SHOWN, ON F STREET, EAST OF 10 TH ST.	OLDEST STANDING BUILDING IN TOWN?
26	WILLIAM "PAT" WARD'S "NEW" CITGO SERVICE STATION	ACROSS RTE. 151 FROM THE HIGH SCHOOL	THIS SERVICE STATION TOOK THE PLACE OF PAT WARD'S CITIES SERVICE STATION WHICH WAS LOCATED ON 4TH STREET IN THE SOUTHWEST SECTION OF TOWN.
27	EVA HALL'S BOARDING HOUSE	501 F STREET	

Sparrows Point High School – 1921
Photograph courtesy of Dundalk Patapsco-Neck Historical Society

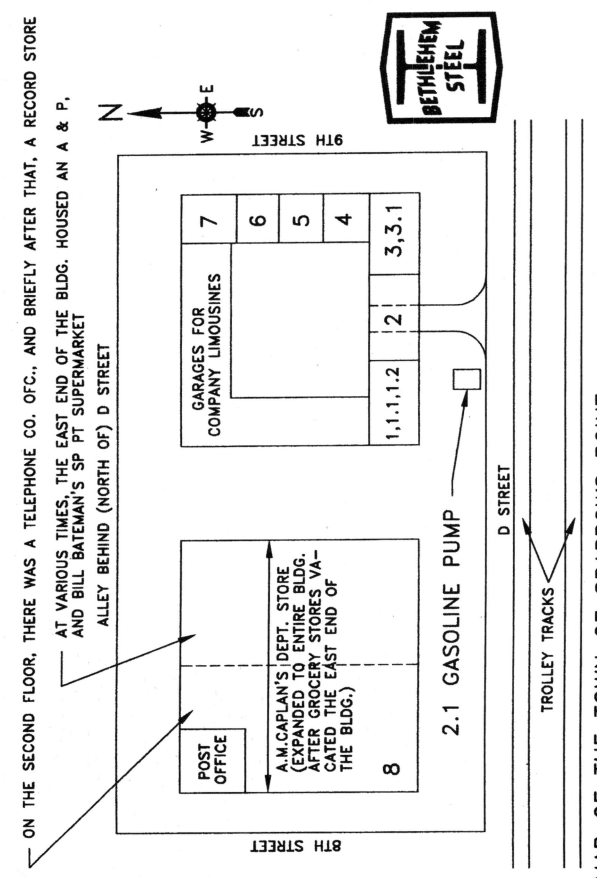

ON THE SECOND FLOOR, THERE WAS A TELEPHONE CO. OFC., AND BRIEFLY AFTER THAT, A RECORD STORE

AT VARIOUS TIMES, THE EAST END OF THE BLDG. HOUSED AN A & P, AND BILL BATEMAN'S SP PT SUPERMARKET

ALLEY BEHIND (NORTH OF) D STREET

N
W E
S

9TH STREET

7
6
5
4
3,3,1

GARAGES FOR COMPANY LIMOUSINES

2

1,1,1,1,2

2.1 GASOLINE PUMP

D STREET

TROLLEY TRACKS

POST OFFICE

A.M.CAPLAN'S DEPT. STORE (EXPANDED TO ENTIRE BLDG. AFTER GROCERY STORES VA-CATED THE EAST END OF THE BLDG.)

8

8TH STREET

BETHLEHEM STEEL

MAP OF THE TOWN OF SPARROWS POINT
COMMERCIAL AREA ON NORTH SIDE OF 800 BLOCK OF D STREET
SPECULATED: AS OF SOMETIME(S) PRIOR TO "L" BL. FCE. (1978)
NOT TO SCALE; ALL ITEMS, AS SHOWN, DID NOT EXIST AT ANY ONE SPECIFIC TIME

SPECULATED-2SDX   3-12-13/MS

7

352

DESCRIPTIONS OF SCHOOLS, CHURCHES, STORES, ETC.
ON MAPS OF THE TOWN OF SPARROWS POINT
COMMERCIAL AREA, NORTH SIDE OF 800 BLOCK OF D STREET

REF. #	DESCRIPTION	ADDRESS	REMARKS
1	PROVIDENT BANK		
1.1	GOLF CLUB AND FALSE TEETH SHOP		BELOW THE BANK
1.2	DENTIST OFC. (DR. VINE)		
2	GARBER'S AUTO REPAIR GARAGE AND CAR SALES		AT SOME TIME, GARBER'S WAS NO LONGER THERE, AND THE PASSAGE WAY FROM THE STREET WAS BLOCKED
2.1	GASOLINE PUMP		THIS PUMP WAS ASSOCIATED WITH GARBER'S GARAGE
3	ORIGINALLY AN A & P GROCERY, THEN EDDIE'S MARKET, THEN NATE'S GROCERY, THEN G & G DRUG STORE, FINALLY NICK'S RESTAURANT		NOTE: "G & G" STANDS FOR GETKA AND GEGENHEIMER
3.1	JOE KUNKOWSKI'S SHOE REPAIR SHOP		IN THE BASEMENT OF THE STORE ABOVE
4	EDDIE DENTZ' BARBER SHOP		AT SOME TIME, ACCESS TO THE SHOP WAS THROUGH THE PASSAGEWAY
5	VACANT SHOP		HAD BEEN A BEAUTY PARLOR
6	CATHRINE ASHTON'S BEAUTY PARLOR		
7	ZUKE'S SWEET SHOP		
8	SEE REMARKS		THE ORIGINAL BUILDING AT THIS LOCATION WAS DESTROYED BY FIRE IN 1945, AND A NEW ONE WAS BUILT IN 1946. OVER THE YEARS, THERE HAVE BEEN MANY CHANGES OF TENANTS, ON THE GROUND FLOOR, ON THE SECOND FLOOR, AND IN THE BASEMENT. THE NOTES ON THE MAP INTEND TO SHOW THE BEST GUESS AS TO THE LATEST TENANTS PRIOR TO THE DEMOLITION OF THE TOWN.

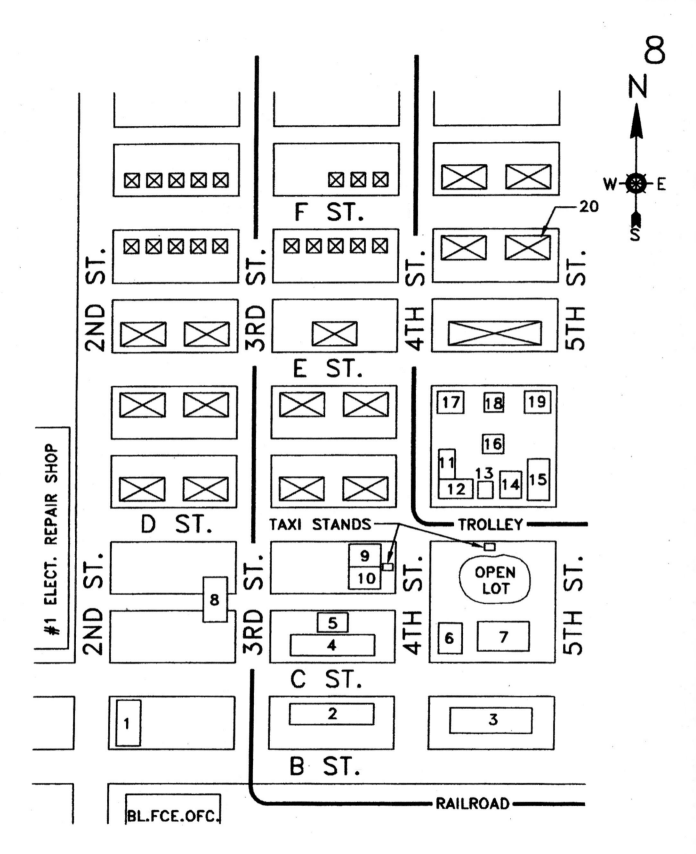

NOTE: ⊠ AND ⊠ INDICATE HOMES AND GROUPS OF HOMES

MAP OF THE TOWN OF SPARROWS POINT — SOUTHWEST SECTION

SPECULATED: AS OF SOMETIME(S) PRIOR TO #4 O.H. SHOP (C.1956)
NOT TO SCALE: ALL ITEMS, AS SHOWN, DID NOT EXIST AT ANY ONE SPECIFIC TIME

SPECULATED—SWX   3-10-13/MS

DESCRIPTIONS OF SCHOOLS, CHURCHES, STORES, ETC.
ON MAPS OF THE TOWN OF SPARROWS POINT
SOUTHWEST SECTION OF TOWN

REF. #	DESCRIPTION	ADDRESS	REMARKS
1	# 1 CLOCK HOUSE		
2	PLANT MAIN OFFICE		
3	B STREET CLUB HOUSE (COMMUNITY CENTER), AND TENNIS COURTS		BUILT CIRCA 1900
4	COMPANY STORE COMPLEX		COMPLETED IN 1888, CONSISTED OF SEVERAL FACILITIES; A TOBACCO SHOP AND SMOKING HALL, STORES FOR FURNITURE, CLOTHING, GROCERIES, MEAT, PRODUCE, WOOD, COAL, ICE, AND BAKERY ITEMS. THE MAIN HALL HAD STAIRS TO THE SECOND FLOOR OFFICES.
5	WILLIAM "PAT" WARD'S GAS STATION	BEHIND THE COMPANY STORE	CITIES SERVICE GAS STATION, WHICH WAS LATER RELOCATED, AS A CITGO STATION, TO ACROSS RTE. 151 FROM THE HIGH SCHOOL
6	COMPANY REAL ESTATE OFFICE		
7	BETH MARY INN RESTAURANT (AND HOTEL)		NAMED THE BETH-MARY INN AFTER 1920'S RENOVATIONS; PRIOR TO ITS DEMOLITION, IT WAS USED FOR THE PLANT'S COMPUTER OPERATIONS. AT ONE TIME IT WAS THE OFFICES OF THE STEAMSHIP SERVICE CORP.
8	RAILROAD STATION		PASSENGER SERVICE STARTED IN 1889
9	FIRE DEPT. (SECOND LOCATION)		SEE ITEM # 16
10	POLICE DEPT.		
11	STORES		
12	DOCTOR'S OFFICE AND COMPANY DRUG STORE		BUILT IN 1888, AS A TWO-ROOM ELEM. SCHOOL HOUSE. BY 1900, THE TOWN HAD EXPANDED TO 1200 HOMES, AND IN 1903, A NEW TWO-STORY, 12 ROOM SCHOOL WAS BUILT.
13	NEWSSTAND		
14	MANUAL TRAINING SCHOOL		FIRST IN THE STATE, HOME ECONOMICS WAS TAUGHT TO GIRLS; WOODWORKING WAS TAUGHT TO BOYS

DESCRIPTIONS OF SCHOOLS, CHURCHES, STORES, ETC.
ON MAPS OF THE TOWN OF SPARROWS POINT

SOUTHWEST SECTION OF TOWN (CONTINUED)

REF. #	DESCRIPTION	ADDRESS	REMARKS
15	LYCEUM MOVIE THEATER		OPENED IN 1912, IT CLOSED AFTER A HEAVY RAIN IN 1947 CAUSED THE ROOF TO COLLAPSE, RESULTING IN NO INJURIES EVEN THOUGH THERE WAS A FULL HOUSE AT THE TIME. SEE ALSO ITEM 15.1
15.1	BOWLING ALLEY (IN BASEMENT BELOW THE MOVIE THEATER)		THE 8-LANE DUCK PIN ALLEY WAS CLOSED, WITH THE THEATER, IN 1947.
16	UNKNOWN		
17	FIRST LOCATION OF FIRE DEPT.		ORIGINALLY A BAKERY
18	NEWSSTAND		
19	KINDERGARTEN		FIRST KINDERGARTEN SCHOOL SOUTH OF THE MASON-DIXON LINE, ESTABLISHED IN 1892, BY RUFUS K. WOOD, GENERAL AGENT, AND BROTHER OF THE PLANT MANAGER WILLIAM FREDERICK WOOD
20	RESIDENCE	APPROXIMATE LOCATION IS SHOWN ON MAP	HOME OF THE PATTON FAMILY WHEN JEFF WAS BORN

Lyceum Theater, located on the northwest corner of 5th and "D" Streets
Photo courtesy of Dundalk Patapsco-Neck Historical Society

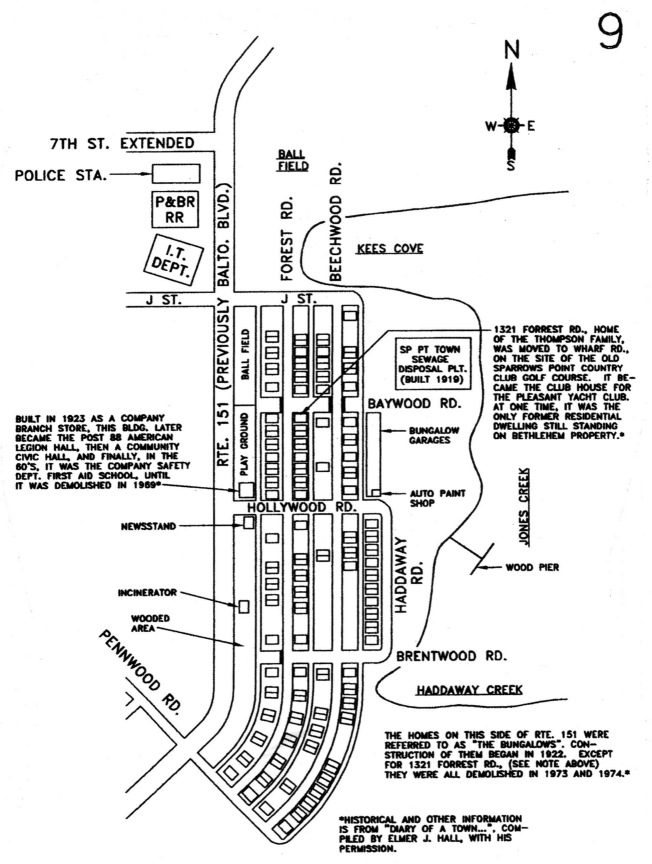

7TH ST. EXTENDED

POLICE STA.

BALL FIELD

P&BR RR

I.T. DEPT.

J ST.

J ST.

BALL FIELD

PLAY GROUND

SP PT TOWN SEWAGE DISPOSAL PLT. (BUILT 1919)

BAYWOOD RD.

Bungalow Garages

Auto Paint Shop

BUILT IN 1923 AS A COMPANY BRANCH STORE, THIS BLDG. LATER BECAME THE POST 88 AMERICAN LEGION HALL, THEN A COMMUNITY CIVIC HALL, AND FINALLY, IN THE 60'S, IT WAS THE COMPANY SAFETY DEPT. FIRST AID SCHOOL, UNTIL IT WAS DEMOLISHED IN 1969*

1321 FORREST RD., HOME OF THE THOMPSON FAMILY, WAS MOVED TO WHARF RD., ON THE SITE OF THE OLD SPARROWS POINT COUNTRY CLUB GOLF COURSE. IT BECAME THE CLUB HOUSE FOR THE PLEASANT YACHT CLUB. AT ONE TIME, IT WAS THE ONLY FORMER RESIDENTIAL DWELLING STILL STANDING ON BETHLEHEM PROPERTY.*

JONES CREEK

WOOD PIER

NEWSSTAND

INCINERATOR

WOODED AREA

HOLLYWOOD RD.

HADDAWAY RD.

BRENTWOOD RD.

HADDAWAY CREEK

PENNWOOD RD.

THE HOMES ON THIS SIDE OF RTE. 151 WERE REFERRED TO AS "THE BUNGALOWS". CONSTRUCTION OF THEM BEGAN IN 1922. EXCEPT FOR 1321 FORREST RD., (SEE NOTE ABOVE) THEY WERE ALL DEMOLISHED IN 1973 AND 1974.*

*HISTORICAL AND OTHER INFORMATION IS FROM "DIARY OF A TOWN...", COMPILED BY ELMER J. HALL, WITH HIS PERMISSION.

NOTE: UNLESS LABELED WITH A NUMBER, OR OTHERWISE LABELED, RECTANGLES ARE RESIDENTIAL HOMES

MAP OF THE TOWN OF SPARROWS POINT — THE BUNGALOWS
SPECULATED: AS OF SOMETIME(S) PRIOR TO "L" BL. FCE. (1978)
NOT TO SCALE: ALL ITEMS, AS SHOWN, DID NOT EXIST AT ANY ONE SPECIFIC TIME

357

SPECULATED-2BX   REV. 2   5-28-13/MS

SPARROWS POINT PLANT - POLICE BOOTHS AS OF 1967
(PER JULY, 1967 PLANT TELEPHONE DIRECTORY)

BOOTH NUMBER	LOCATION
1	5TH ST., OPPOSITE B ST. ALLEY
2	NW OF PENNWOOD POWER STATION
3	RR AVE., OPPOSITE EMPLOYMENT OFFICE
4	MAIN ENTRANCE, SO. END, SHEET, TIN & STRIP MILLS
5	MAIN ENTRANCE, WIRE & ROD MILLS
6	THERE IS NO GATE 6 AT THIS TIME
7	NO. END OF SHIPYARD RD.
8	SO. END, TIN MILL ASSORTING ROOM
9	SO. END, HOT STRIP MILLS
10	NO. END, SHEET, TIN & STRIP MILLS
11	MAIN ENTRANCE, NO. END, SHEET, TIN & STRIP MILLS
12	NORTH END OF WIRE MILL
13	PLATE MILL ROAD EXTENDED
14	BENZOL PLANT GATE
15	WHARF ROAD
16	MAIN GATE, SHIPYARD
17	NO. PARKING LOT GATE, SHIPYARD
18	ORE WHARF
19	RESERVOIR WAREHOUSE
20	TRAFFIC CONTROL BOOTH, TIN MILL & PENNWOOD RDS.
21	EDGEMERE PLANT
22	PENNWOOD WHARF

Works Cited

[1] Lovis, John B. <u>The Blast Furnaces of Sparrows Point: One Hundred Years of Ironmaking on Chesapeake Bay.</u> Canal History and Technology Press, 2005, p. 3.

[2] Ruetter, Mark. <u>Sparrows Point: Making Steel – The Rise and Ruin of American Industrial Might.</u> Summit Books, 1988, p. 34.

[3] Lovis, John B. <u>The Blast Furnaces of Sparrows Point: One Hundred Years of Ironmaking on Chesapeake Bay.</u> Canal History and Technology Press, 2005, p. 90.

[4] Shannahan, J.H.K. *A History of the Maryland Plant of the Bethlehem Steel Company – Its Origin and Development from 1886 to 1925.* Baltimore: Bethlehem Steel, 1925.

[5] Ibid.

[6] "New Blast Furnace of Maryland Steel Company." *The Iron Age.* January 23, 1913, Volume 91, No. 4: 243.

[7] Ibid, p. 244.

[8] Ruetter, Mark. <u>Sparrows Point: Making Steel – The Rise and Ruin of American Industrial Might.</u> Summit Books, 1988, pp. 41-42.

[9] Camp, J.M. and C.B. Francis. *The Making, Shaping, and Treating of Steel.* Pittsburgh: United States Steel Company, 1951, p. 381.

[10] Ibid, p. 390.

[11] Shannahan, J.H.K. *A History of the Maryland Plant of the Bethlehem Steel Company – Its Origin and Development from 1886 to 1925.* Baltimore: Bethlehem Steel, 1925.

[12] Ruetter, Mark. <u>Sparrows Point: Making Steel – The Rise and Ruin of American Industrial Might.</u> Summit Books, 1988, p. 127.

[13] Shannahan, J.H.K. *A History of the Maryland Plant of the Bethlehem Steel Company – Its Origin and Development from 1886 to 1925.* Baltimore: Bethlehem Steel, 1925.

[14] Lovis, John B. <u>The Blast Furnaces of Sparrows Point: One Hundred Years of Ironmaking on Chesapeake Bay.</u> Canal History and Technology Press, 2005, p. 25.

[15] Shannahan, J.H.K. *A History of the Maryland Plant of the Bethlehem Steel Company – Its Origin and Development from 1886 to 1925.* Baltimore: Bethlehem Steel, 1925.

[16] Ruetter, Mark. <u>Sparrows Point: Making Steel – The Rise and Ruin of American Industrial Might.</u> Summit Books, 1988, pp. 41-42.

[17] *From Ore to Ships – The Maryland Plant of the Bethlehem Steel Company.* Baltimore: Bethlehem Steel, 1938, pp. 8-9.

[18] "Barge Conveyor." *Tow Line Magazine.* Winter 1973-74, p. 7.

[19] "The Golden Days Had a Little Tarnish – 1953 & 1954." *The Sparrows Point Spirit, Issue 14.* Baltimore: Bethlehem Steel, 1994, p. 10.

[20] Camp, J.M. and C.B. Francis. *The Making, Shaping, and Treating of Steel.* Pittsburgh: United States Steel Company, 1951, p. 450.

[21] *First Helper's Manual.* Baltimore: Bethlehem Steel Company, 1957, p. 1.

[22] Camp, J.M. and C.B. Francis. *The Making, Shaping, and Treating of Steel.* Pittsburgh: United States Steel Company, 1951, p. 435.

[23] "Skull Cracker Vs. Tuff Steel." *The Sparrows Point Spirit, Issue 7.* Baltimore: Bethlehem Steel, 1990/1, pp. 5-6.

[24] "Good Times – Bad Omen." *Forging America – the Story of Bethlehem Steel.* Tribune Publishing Company, 2003, pp. 84-85.

[25] Lovis, John B. <u>The Blast Furnaces of Sparrows Point: One Hundred Years of Ironmaking on Chesapeake Bay.</u> Canal History and Technology Press, 2005, p. 45.

[26] Camp, J.M. and C.B. Francis. *The Making, Shaping, and Treating of Steel.* Pittsburgh: United States Steel Company, 1951, p. 307.

[27] *Iron & Brass Foundry and Pattern Shop – General Mechanical Department Manual.* Baltimore: Bethlehem Steel Company, 1969, p. 10.

[28] Ibid, p. 16.

[29] "Hard Work Makes Steel's Centennial." *The Sparrows Point Spirit, Issue 11.* Baltimore: Bethlehem Steel, 1991, pp. 25-26.

[30] Lovis, John B. The Blast Furnaces of Sparrows Point: One Hundred Years of Ironmaking on Chesapeake Bay. Canal History and Technology Press, 2005, p. 89.

[31] "The Sparrows Point Police Department Pistol Club." *American Rifleman* August 1951: 30-31, 43.

[32] Peden, Jr. Henry C. Historical Register of the Sparrows Point Police Department: 1901 -1986. Bel Air Copy Center, 1986, pp. 1-5.

[33] Hall, Elmer J. Shipbuilding at the Sparrows Point Yard: A Century of Pride and Tradition. Gazette Printers, 2007, p. 5.

[34] *Bethlehem Steel Company Sparrows Point Plant Booklet.* Walk Press, 1990, pp. 4-5.

[35] *Modern Steel and Their Properties.* Bethlehem Steel, 1961, 6th edition, pp. 146-147.

[36] "Everyone Ready and Waiting – A Long Time – For Modernization." *The Sparrows Point Spirit, Number 200.* Baltimore: Bethlehem Steel, 1988/3, p. 10.

[37] Hall, Elmer J. The Patapsco and Back Rivers Railroad: Chronicles of the Push, Bump & Ram. Gazette Printers, 2010, pp. 6-7.

[38] Shannahan, J.H.K. *A History of the Maryland Plant of the Bethlehem Steel Company – Its Origin and Development from 1886 to 1925.* Baltimore: Bethlehem Steel, 1925.

[39] *Bethlehem's Winning Combo.* Bethlehem Steel, 1972, pp. 3-5.

[40] *From Ore to Ships – The Maryland Plant of the Bethlehem Steel Company.* Baltimore: Bethlehem Steel, 1938, pp. 17-18.

[41] Ibid, pp. 19-25.

[42] "Hot Mill – Hot Future." *The Sparrows Point Spirit, Issue 11.* Baltimore: Bethlehem Steel, 1991, pp. 5-12.

[43] *Introducing Sparrows Point's BOF Shop.* Bethlehem Steel, 1964, p. 11.

[44] *From A to L: Management Conference Agenda Feature.* Bethlehem Steel, February 1974, p. 10.

[45] Ibid, p. 5.

[46] Lovis, John B. The Blast Furnaces of Sparrows Point: One Hundred Years of Ironmaking on Chesapeake Bay. Canal History and Technology Press, 2005, p. 26.

[47] "Pinch Point – Caster is Still King." *The Sparrows Point Spirit, Issue 15.* Baltimore: Bethlehem Steel, June 1995, pp. 9-10.

[48] "Lean Mean Tractor Shop Keeps Steel Moving." *The Sparrows Point Spirit, Issue 7.* Baltimore: Bethlehem Steel, 1990/1, p.18.

[49] "Turning Out Quality Rolls to Roll Quality." *The Sparrows Point Spirit, Issue 2.* Baltimore: Bethlehem Steel, 1988/1, pp. 18-20.

[50] "Bethlehem Asks Some Questions that Only the Government Can Answer." *Bethlehem Review, Issue 164.* Bethlehem: Bethlehem Steel, 1979/2, pp. 8-9.

[51] "Pennwood Wharf is Connecticut and the Bay is Long Island Sound." *The Sparrows Point Spirit, Issue 15.* Baltimore: Bethlehem Steel, June 1995, pp. 14-16.

[52] "Introducing the New and Improved Sparrows Point." *The Sparrows Point Spirit, Issue 16.* Baltimore: Bethlehem Steel, March 1996, pp. 2-3.